The First Beverly Hillbilly

Ruth Henning

The First Beverly HILLBILLY

The Untold Story of the Creator of Rural TV Comedy

Ruth Henning

WOODNEATH PRESS

Kansas City

Published by Woodneath Press
8900 NE Flintlock Rd.
Kansas City, MO 64157

Cover design and typography: David Reynolds

Publisher's Cataloguing-in-Publication
(Provided by Woodneath Press: A Program of Mid-Continent Public Library)

Henning, Ruth
    The First Beverly Hillbilly: The Untold Story of the Creator of Rural TV Comedy / by Ruth Henning
    p. cm.
    LCCN
ISBN-10: 1-942337-03-5
ISBN-13: 978-1-942337-03-4

    I.   Television writers – United States – Biography,
    II. Henning, Paul (1911-2005)

To Paul, the First Beverly Hillbilly, for the love and laughter he gave to millions of people… and especially to me.

Table of Contents

Foreword
Jackson County Historical Society

This is the story behind this story – short in the telling, but held together by a common theme: people who care about preserving, sharing and remembering.

Sue Gentry, a longtime Independence, Missouri. journalist and local historian, was much beloved by many; myself included.

She loved people, her community, stories and shared much of what she found out and learned in her regular newspaper column - appropriately name "The Local Gentry" – that appeared in <u>The Independence Examiner</u> .

It was a 70-year career during which she shared the news from Main Street, marriages, famous visitors, small-town gossip, presidential scoops and recounting the history of a community that grew from 12,000 to 115,000 during her lifetime.

Her knowledge of the community was encyclopedic.

She was a rare combination of vitality, curiosity, gentility, humility, good humor and industry.

Good fortune, mine, allowed us to be close.

We were friends, neighbors and journalistic colleagues who had an abiding deeply interest in local history. She was a capable teacher; I was an attentive student.

Late in her life, Sue gave me a humbling assignment: give her eulogy at memorial services – date, as yet, undetermined – but with proviso: "Make it sound good, but not too good, so people will believe it."

Sue was wonderful in so many ways.

This wonderful memoir about Paul Henning, written by his loving wife, is but one example. Frankly the exact details are a little murky, but the memory is clear.

One day, or perhaps evening, I had wandered over to Sue's house where she ultimately lived for 75 years. At some point during the visit, I remember her pulling out a photocopied manuscript with the fetching title *The First Beverly Hillbilly*.

I recognized the Henning name – the hometown boy who as the creator of the Beverly Hillbillies. I glanced at the manuscript but paid no mind.

Gentry knew the Henning family. In fact, Henning's mother Sophia (then a widow) lived in a house two doors south of Gentry's home during the 1940s and they undoubtedly knew each other well.

When first married, my wife and I actually lived in the very house but only realized the Henning connection years later. There were lots of stories in the neighborhood – many of them involving someone named Truman.

Years passed and on some unclear impulse I became curious as to the whereabouts of the Henning manuscript. My hope was it could be found somewhere amongst the endless boxes of Gentry materials which came to the historical society following her death in 2004 at age 99.

Diligence and assistance from others discovered the manuscript which proved to be a loving memoir by Ruth Henning about her enormously talented by self-reserved husband Paul.

Found tucked inside the manuscript was a November 1994 letter from Ruth Henning to Gentry which shared some personal news and an update on a project discussed during an earlier visit to Independence.

"The copy of the manuscript I'm sending has had some revisions since I wrote this, but most of it is the same," Ruth wrote. She had written a new first chapter and an extra chapter about Hollywood in the 1940s and more names from the industry.

She closed her letter on a hopeful note for her project: "Thank you for being on my side about this book. I really believe one day it will find a publisher."

And two decades later it has.

For that many deserve of our thanks and gratitude: Ruth who it wrote it, Sue who it saved it, the Jackson County Historical Society for preserving it and countless others, particularly the Mid-Continent Public Library, who have made this book a reality.

In working on this project, we have discovered additional information about Henning: oral histories, photographs and other details which we are sharing online at www.beverlyhillbilly.org.

Paul Henning used his love of the Ozarks and rural America as an endless storehouse for comedy. The premise was simple: cultural conflicts. Rural folks were transported to the big city (Beverly Hillbillies) or the city folks moved to rural life (Green Acres). The juxtaposition provided fodder for misunderstanding and figuring out how to fit in and be part of the new community. These cross-cultural challenges continue to challenge contemporary American.

Henning started out in early radio – he wanted to sing – but found his true gifts as a writer and pioneer in early television and movies.

We are happy for our small part in this project and extend our heartfelt thanks for the immeasurable efforts of others to finally share this story about a particular time and a shy, but special man of enormous creative talent that shaped the collective memory of a generation.

Thanks abound.

Brent Schondelmeyer
Jackson County Historical Society
August 2017

1
What Time Is Dinner?

Once upon a time, a new television show made its debut on CBS in prime time. Everybody hated it: the sophisticates, the industry insiders, the intellectuals, and most of all, the critics. Some of the things they wrote or said were:

"If television is a vast wasteland, this show is Death Valley."

"Too absurd to be even slightly amusing."

"Pure corn."

"A one joke show."

"Fifth grade mentality."

"It won't last the season."

Pretty mean, huh? Pretty hard to take. The amazing thing though, was that the third week it was on, it was rated number one by Nielsen, which everyone knows is the show business Bible. The talk escalated.

"It's the hicks!" said the smart guys, eating lunch on the Sunset Strip and trying not to drop bean sprouts on their imported jeans. "The hicks! Between the east coast and the west coast, there are millions of them."

"It's the novelty," others said, twining pasta on their forks and wiping virgin olive oil from their chins. "As soon as they realize how bad it is, they'll change the channel."

But they didn't. The modest little show stayed on for the whole season, and what's more, it stayed number one. It even beat out such surefire winners as Perry Como and Bob Hope. How could anyone predict that? CBS had slotted it on Wednesday nights just before *The Dick Van Dyke Show*, which was in trouble because its ratings had slipped. Soon everyone could see that another strange

13

thing was happening. Now that Dick Van Dyke had the lead-in of the number one show, his ratings went up, and even Mary Tyler Moore admitted, "Our show would have died after the second season if it had not been for that show."

The critics (most of them) were stubborn, however. They still heaped it with scorn and got some really funny reviews out of it. It's always easier to be clever when you're being cruel. Even one of the CBS executives was heard to remark, "I always hated it. I never watched it."

The man responsible for the whole thing – a rather quiet, modest, unassuming writer – was hurt by all the barbs aimed at him. How could he not be? But he just kept on working hard: creating amusing situations and funny lines while keeping his characters true, the humor clean, and his fellow workers happy. Two things puzzled him: he never expected everyone to be so hateful, and he never expected the show to be so popular. You might say the two things canceled each other out. Everyone at General Service Studios was ecstatic. Life in show business is precarious at best, but if you're on a hit show, you can expect a long run. Maybe you can pay off the mortgage or even buy a new car.

They all loved the writer. They lit candles for him in church.

One CBS executive, a kinder one, sent him a telegram on his birthday: "We all thank the good Lord for you each night before we go to sleep."

Of course, the show I'm talking about is *The Beverly Hillbillies*, and the writer is my husband, Paul Henning. He always claimed he didn't care what the critics said, but I cared. I wrote several nasty letters to Cecil Smith, who was then the TV critic for the *Los Angeles Times*. I didn't send them. After a day or two to cool off, I tore them up and consigned them to the wastebasket. At the Emmy

Awards that year, the show *The Beverly Hillbillies* had saved from cancellation, *The Dick Van Dyke Show*, got the Emmy. I cried.

"Smile!" my husband whispered. "The cameras are on us." But I couldn't. I was too hurt. It was too unfair. Many awards later, I've learned that fairness has nothing to do with it.

Much later, in 1987, a study was published which proved that *The Beverly Hillbillies* was the most popular situation comedy of nearly two decades, perhaps of all time. The data was compiled from the Nielsen Ratings from July 1960 to January 1987, showing the all-time top 50 programs. In the honored list, seven separate episodes of *The Beverly Hillbillies* appeared appear – and wouldn't you believe it? – NO OTHER SITCOMS. *The Hillbillies*' Nielsen rating was 44. Today, programs are lucky to get half that.

The Beverly Hillbillies stayed on for nine years, highly-rated the entire time. It had a global appeal in 17 countries, including England, Japan, The Netherlands, Australia, Mexico, Africa – you name it – and wherever it played, it was popular. Ever since that time, you could always find a rerun somewhere on the schedule. Paul still gets fan mail, sometimes from young people who weren't even born when the show went on the air.

Of course, in time, some of the critics ate their words and some others who wrote for really classy publications found that the show had value as social commentary. My French professor at Cal State Northridge likened my husband to Moliere, who often wrote about simple, honest people whose values allowed them to come out on top.

Still, Paul Henning never won an Emmy or an Oscar, but he was nominated for both. He never got a star on Hollywood Boulevard. He never had a book written about him. People have been telling him for years that he ought to write a book. One whole wall of our living room, floor to ceiling, is covered with shelves containing nothing but books by and about show business personalities, but none about the creator, writer, and producer of the most popular, most watched TV sitcom of all time.

So why didn't Paul write one? It took me a while to realize that he never would and why: he is shy, modest, and unassuming, and maybe the key word is private. It is literally impossible for him to talk or write about himself. He's been called the writer nobody knows.

We were all resigned to the fact that there would not be a book about Paul Henning in the grand tradition of show writers before him.

Then came September 1992, the 30th anniversary of the debut of *The Beverly Hillbillies*. Interest in the show heated up; there were celebrations, publicity, interviews, photographs, and now, after all this time, the show was no longer deemed a disaster. It had gained the respectability of a legend.

One night as I lie in bed thinking about the lack of a biography highlighting Paul's life and accomplishments, I received an unmistakable message. "You know him. You write the book. Do it now before it's too late!" I hope you won't think I'm pretentious if I say I believe the message was from God. How could I refuse?

Surprisingly, I got Paul's permission and went to work. Now my question was this: Is the world ready for a story about a Hollywood writer with no scandal in his life? No kinky sex? No criminal record? No drugs? No connections with the mob? No divorces? Not even any dirty tricks?

During the course of my writing, I read the biographies of Marlene Dietrich, Kirk Douglas, Howard Hughes, and Walt Disney. Ye Gods!

I startled Paul out of a football game on TV. "Good grief! Didn't you ever do any of this stuff?" I cried. "How do you expect me to sell a book without any dirt to dish?"

Paul looked at his watch. "I think if I start now I've just got time to go out and do something," he said. "What time is dinner?"

16

2

A Song, a Soda, a Sweetheart

I believe that certain key people play a role in shaping the life of every person. These four, albeit a strange combination, formed the major influences in Paul Henning's life: Sophia Henning, Ted Malone, Ruth Barth, and Harry Truman.

Paul was born on a farm in Missouri, but his family moved to a town called Independence while he was still a baby. Paul's dad, William, was given some land by his father; however, he was a square peg in a round hole. Artistic by nature, he wasn't a good farmer and just couldn't make it pay. His mother, Sophia, was something else, too. She took her ten children (of which Paul was the youngest) to town, bought a big rambling frame house, took in boarders, worked hard, and somehow managed. She was a tiny woman, less than five feet tall, with a head of blonde hair always perfectly coifed, and she was always immaculately groomed and dressed. It was a story the kids liked to tell that she wouldn't even answer the telephone without being fully clothed.

The older boys all got jobs and brought their pay home to mother. The girls all had assigned tasks in the running of the house. Sophia was a strong woman and a good manager. Father Henning stayed in the country and worked on the fine cabinet making that he loved. It was beautiful but not profitable. This background was radically different from that of most comedy writers who tend to come from New York and learn their trade from the famous old comedians they saw in the clubs of Manhattan and the Catskills.

Paul always wanted to sing. When he was five, he stood up bravely in church in a black velvet Little Lord Fauntleroy suit made for him by his sister, Florence, from somebody's old coat or portières (curtains) or something, and sang a solo. The Hennings were German, a stoic breed who didn't believe in showing their emotions. When the lady next to her in church asked Sophie, "Who is that darling boy?" Sophie answered, "I don't know him." She was proud, of course, but she didn't want to give the appearance of bragging. You can see how much encouragement he had for a singing career.

On other occasions, Paul would stop on the way home from Sunday school and visit a lady who lived in the neighborhood and received the Sunday paper (the Hennings didn't). In exchange for singing a song, she would give Paul the funny papers. Singing opportunities didn't come around too often, so he did other jobs like standing on a box behind the grocery counter to work off part of the family bill, working for a cleaning establishment (I still consult Paul about stubborn spots), and jerking sodas at Brown's Drug Store on the town square.

In high school, Paul was editor of *Gleam*, the school annual, and won a gold medal in Extemporaneous Speaking. The former seems quite natural, but if you know Paul, the latter is hard to picture because he's so shy. Paul didn't get much credit from his family for honors won. His mother thought that praising a child would make him conceited.

In 1929, another chance for Paul to sing came along. On the NBC radio station, WDAF in Kansas City, they had a regular program called *Nighthawk Frolics*. It was on late at night and almost anyone could be on it. So Paul and his best friend, Mel Pratt, who played the piano, went down to WDAF and Paul sang. Nothing came of it, but it kept the dream alive.

Enter Harry Truman. Already deeply involved in state politics, Truman and some of his co-workers would stop after work in Brown's Drug Store for a Coke before going home. Paul remembers how they matched nickels to see who would pay. A rapport grew up between the friendly county official and the engaging young man behind the soda fountain. Sometimes Paul talked about his future, still undecided what direction he should take.

"Study law," Harry advised him. "It opens the door to many possibilities, including politics."

So Paul enrolled in night classes at Kansas City School of Law. During the day, he had to have a paying job and was soon taken on at a local law firm, Stone and Taylor. At that time in Missouri, civil cases that involved less than five hundred dollars could be tried in a court by a student who wasn't a member of the bar. One case had an important influence on Paul. Two farmers had a dispute regarding a fence. If the fence was deemed necessary and one party refused to help build and pay for it, the other party could go ahead with the construction and bill his neighbor. Paul, who represented the plaintiff, kept filing and the lawyer for the defense kept sending postponements. In frustration, Paul visited the lawyer in his office to ask why he kept postponing the case.

"Kid," the lawyer said, "this ain't never comin' to trial."

"Why not?" asked Paul.

"Cause I can't win, that's why."

With that, he spit a large gob of tobacco at one of the many cuspidors in the office. This and other similar experiences made Paul feel disillusioned about the law, and after two years, he dropped out of law school in favor of show business.

The real turning point in Paul's life came through a frequent date of his sister's. Drusilla was a tiny platinum blonde with big brown eyes who attracted the attention of Independence man-about-town, Ted Malone. Ted was, at that time, just getting started in radio, but everybody in town knew he was in solid at Radio Station KMBC, the Kansas City CBS outlet owned by the Latter Day Saints. Paul used to waylay Ted and talk about his desire to sing on the radio, and when

19

Ted was made Program Director of KMBC, he made Paul a standard offer.

"Come on down, offer to work for nothing, and see what happens," Ted said.

This was during the Great Depression, and if you aren't old enough to have gone through that, I'll just say that nothing since then has been so depressed. Nobody had any money and very few had jobs. Paul readily accepted Ted's challenge and before long, he was singing on KMBC. However, he soon realized that you had to have a sponsor or no money changed hands… and to get a sponsor, you had to have some kind of program to offer. Never at a loss for ideas, Paul soon went to Ted just overflowing with program ideas, all of which featured Paul Henning, a tenor. Then Ted asked the sixty-four dollar question.

"Who's going to write the program?"

"Write?!" Paul replied, dumbstruck. It had never occurred to him to write a program, but it seemed he'd have to try at least.

Thus began a whole series of radio programs, all of them combining music, story, humor, and usually a little something extra. One of the most popular was "The Musical Grocers" sponsored by the Associated Grocers or the AG Grocers as they were called. He and fellow staff member, Gomer Cool, were Al and George, the musical grocers. They waited on customers, did food commercials, wove a story line in with the music, and had the catchiest theme song on radio at the time. It went like this:

If you want string beans or tomatoes
Spinach, carrots, or potatoes
Well, honey, if you wanna save money
Just shop at the AG stores.

20

If you have a family budget
Keep in line, don't try to fudge it
And honey, if you wanna save money
Just trade at the AG stores.

A little later on, Paul sang occasionally with a girls' trio, Those McCarty Girls, sisters who sounded not unlike the Boswell Sisters. Paul added the fourth voice for sweet, close, four-part harmony. They became a part of a program called "The Tattler and His Four Little Gossips." The Tattler was a Kansas City gossip columnist and the program was so good they got a week's engagement at the Mainstreet Theatre, which had a vaudeville show along with the feature film.

Paul also loved to do what they called "remotes." Big bands were popular then and quite a few played the area. The radio station would broadcast dance music usually late at night and, of course, they'd send an announcer and an engineer to handle the details. It was during that time that Paul got a chance to sing with Ted Weems and his band who were playing at the Mayfair Supper Club.

Then Paul got a really big idea. He would be the Movie Editor of KMBC. Nobody objected, so he began to meet, greet, and interview every big-time star who came to town. His crowning achievement as the Movie Editor was a trip to Hollywood. He flew to California on a due bill – which meant you got tickets in exchange for advertising on the air. He stayed in a fine hotel in Los Angeles (also on a due bill) and as a result of letters sent ahead by Ted Malone, he enjoyed the hospitality of the major studios whose representatives picked him up in company cars, wined and dined him, and introduced him to really big stars. There was Gary Cooper and Lupe Velez, who were currently an item. There was Olivia De Havilland and Errol Flynn, who were filming *Captain Blood*. He also met Rochelle

Hudson, Jack Oakie, Roger Pryor, and Ginger Rogers. He was actually invited to Ginger's house because, after all, she was an Independence girl. He came back with stars in his eyes and vowed someday to make it to Hollywood on his own.

By this time, Ted Malone had become a really big radio star. He had a program, "Between the Bookends," in which he read poetry and told stories in his own inimitable style, with a sweet, romantic pipe organ playing in the background. It was beamed from Kansas City to the CBS western network, and he talked his way into the hearts of millions of women. He was loaded with charisma and really good at what he did. He was Paul's idol and inspiration.

There was somebody else at the radio station who had a certain influence – a young lady named Ruth Barth who worked in the Continuity Department, but like everyone else on staff, she also acted, sang, announced, wrote, took dictation, and occasionally swept out the studio. One of the main things she did, however, was to fall in love with Paul Henning.

Ruth had noticed Paul the first time she ever went to KMBC. He was in the Artists' Lounge clowning around with the McCarty Sisters, and she was struck by his bubbling enthusiasm; though, in his white linen knickers, he looked about twelve years old. And he hadn't noticed her at all.

Now, a lot of Paul's programs involved parodies and rhymes at which he was very skilled, but it seemed he always had to work far into the night writing a program for the next day. Miss Barth, who also had a certain knack at rhymes, often offered to stay and help. That was me, of course, and if Paul didn't get encouragement at home, I more than made up for it. We became a regular couple at the studio and as a result were cast as the young lovers on a daytime serial, *Happy Hollow*, originated by – who else? – Ted Malone. Paul often told me he loved me but that he never wanted to marry. He had seen

22

too many failures, beginning with his own mother and father. Blithely, and with fingers crossed, I said, "Oh neither do I! I want a career!" That was half-true.

We often give Ted Malone credit for our romance and marriage. He got tired of various couples kidding around in the lounge and not tending to business, so he sent around a memo stating there would be no more interdepartmental dating on pain of dismissal of one or both parties. What a dreamer he was! After that, Paul and I, who hadn't been really serious, were determined to date. We left the studio separately and met a block away.

Paul made several more trips to California flying on passes and sometimes got "bumped" for a paying passenger. Stranded in Amarillo or Albuquerque, he always made desperate phone calls and I sent him the money to come home.

Once, we both got raises at the same time. I was now making thirty-five dollars a week and Paul fifty dollars. When we added it up, the total seemed heady in that depressed time. We thought we were on top of the world.

3

The Writer, the Actress, the Blonde

Radio was exciting in the '30s. There wasn't much theater in our neck of the woods – who could afford it? Movies were fantasy, too rich to aspire to, and television was still a gleam in somebody's eye. Not mine. I hadn't even heard of it.

But radio – that was here and now – and so exciting. There were no unions, no high salaries, and no holds barred. Creative young people swarmed the studios at KMBC, and it was a three-ring circus. As far as I was concerned, it was the answer to everything. Radio gave me a way to be an actress without surrendering to the pitfalls of the profession. Everyone knew that actresses were fast. They painted their faces, played love scenes with any number of actors who were often scoundrels and cads, showed their legs in scanty costumes, and possibly even smoked. Radio was sage enough to get my parents' approval.

Kansas City was a wide-open town at that time. I didn't know it, of course. I didn't know there was a restaurant just a block or two from our studio that featured a "Businessman's Lunch," served by pretty waitresses in the altogether. I didn't know that when Paul drove alone along Tenth Street, prostitutes would jump on his running board soliciting trade. Some wise man eliminated running boards. I didn't know we were full of gangsters. Then one day there was a shootout at Union Station. The train announcer made the announcement and marked the time on his log. Later, he was subpoenaed as a witness. Drama! You could go down there and actually see the bullet holes. They called it The Union Station Massacre.

MGM came to town with a traveling unit and offered a screen test to likely candidates, supposedly looking for a star. KMBC gave them publicity and in exchange, MGM took two days and did screen tests of all our staff. Boy, was that ever exciting! Never mind that the lighting and camera work were inferior, and we all looked like we'd spent the night in a damp cellar. Ted Malone then made a deal with a phrenologist, a guy who reads your character by the bumps on your head. We were all sent to his office, supposedly to see if we were suited to the jobs we held. My bumps, among other things, said I had a remarkable memory. Then I walked away and left my pocketbook, my hat, my gloves, and my umbrella... and also my faith in phrenology.

Country music was very popular in our area. It's popular everywhere now, but it wasn't then. We had a group of singers and musicians called The Texas Rangers who were a smash; so much so that Gomer Cool, one of the Musical Grocers, wrote a script called "Red Horse Ranch" for Socony Vacuum Oil Company whose symbol was a flying red horse. The Texas Rangers were the cowboys in the bunkhouse. One of our announcers with a southern accent was Alabam, the foreman. And guess who played Rose, the rancher's daughter, who was in love with Alabam? That's right – yours truly.

The program was sold, Gomer wrote thirteen scripts, which we rehearsed in our studios and then went to Chicago to record on electrical transcriptions. We didn't have the facilities for that in Kansas City. We did all 13 episodes in less than a week, but I was never the same again. This was glamour time. The big city. Working with Chicago actors who played the incidental roles. Yet, those actors got paid fifteen dollars an episode. I only made all thirteen episodes for my weekly salary of thirty-five dollars. That didn't seem right somehow.

After a while, we went up to Chicago again and made another batch of episodes. Besides the lure of the money, one of the big producers at World Broadcasting kept telling me how talented I was

25

and how he was sure I could be a hit in Chicago as a freelance actress. In hindsight, I think he had lascivious motives, but at the time, I was too naïve to recognize it.

Meanwhile, back in Kansas City, Paul was still creating and performing in his own shows. I kept talking to him about Chicago and the opportunities there, but Paul wasn't much interested. He didn't see how he could leave his, by then, very successful career and take a chance in a strange city. Moreover, all his siblings had grown up and left home and Paul was the sole support of his mother. Only fair, they all thought. Hadn't his parents supported him as he was growing up? Now it was his turn.

A program I still get the shivers thinking about was called "The Midnight Muse." Every Monday night at 11:30 p.m., lovely pipe organ music wafted into the airwaves and with no announcer, no commercials. Ted Malone read beautiful, sentimental poetry, and Paul sang songs that fit the poems' mood. Every Monday night I pretended to go to bed, and after my family had retired, I sneaked downstairs to listen to "The Midnight Muse" and what followed.

What followed was Paul coming up our driveway with his car lights out so as not to disturb the household occupants and the neighbors. You can't get any more romantic than that. However, moreover, and nevertheless, there was no commitment coming out of the silver throat of Paul Henning, tenor.

I made a decision. It was about time. I had been saving my money, so I headed for Chicago. I had a contract with KMBC. We all had contracts. I asked for a two-month leave of absence from KMBC – about the length of time I figured my money would hold out. Nobody begged me to stay. Nobody mentioned the contract. They all smiled at each other and said, "She'll be back." Of course, I was sorry to leave Paul, but that seemed to be going nowhere. I was sorrier to leave my happy home and my much-loved mother and father. Mother knew that this was for good (and she was probably the only one who did). I would not be back.

And I didn't go back. I never went back except for an occasional visit.

In my travels around Chicago's world of radio, I heard that Don Quinn who wrote *Fibber McGee and Molly* was overworked and in need of a co-writer. I wrote to Paul immediately and suggested this just might be his big chance. He sat down and wrote an entire radio script for *Fibber McGee and Molly* and sent it to Don Quinn who hired him on the spot.

In due time, Paul arrived. He moved into the posh Lake Shore Athletic Club just a couple of blocks away from the DeWitt Hotel where I lived and a strange interlude began. Paul and I had been engaged, sort of – for a long time, much too long a time. He had even given me a ring, but when I left town, we had agreed that we'd each be free to see other people. I'd been gone about six months; it was my first taste of freedom, a career girl out on my own, and I was having a ball. I didn't really know what Paul had been doing, but I soon found out when she followed him to Chicago.

She was a cute, little blonde, the type Paul usually went for, and she had a lot more than blonde hair in her little head. She had chutzpah! I was a cute, little brunette, but I ranked very low in the chutzpah department. The blonde had met Paul at a party, they'd been dating, so when he went to Chicago, she divorced her husband, quit her job, and hotfooted it to the Windy City. She got an apartment nearby and a real drab job in the office of a garage and there we were.

Paul said he didn't feel like getting married right away, but he didn't say what he did feel like doing. He still took me out regularly, but it was soon evident that the blonde was ahead on points. I offered to give Paul back his ring. He wouldn't take it, so I transferred it to my other hand. I had a really great Christmas that year. I did most of

27

my Christmas shopping at Marshall Fields, wandering around to the tunes of recorded Christmas carols, tears running down my face and dripping off my chin. Every time I got a glimpse of myself in a mirror, I cried harder.

"I'm old!" I sobbed. "I'm past my prime! I'll never marry!" I was all of twenty-two.

A year passed. Paul was successful in writing for Fibber and Molly. They were not like most comedians or comedy actors. When they were not on the air, they were just plain, midwestern folks who happened to be very talented at what they did. When Paul first got to Chicago, he attended a meeting at the ad agency, Needham, Louis, and Brorby. All during the meeting, a little fellow, casually dressed kept going around emptying and cleaning out the ashtrays. Afterwards, Don Quinn asked Paul what he thought of the group.

"They were all very nice, but I'd really like to meet Fibber McGee," Paul said.

"Oh – didn't you know? That was Jim Jordan, the little guy in the plaid shirt," Don replied.

It was hard to believe. Paul had thought that casually-dressed man was some kind of junior member of the agency, sort of a gofer. He'd not imagined it was Fibber.

Marian Jordan, the actress who played Molly McGee, was a delightful lady with an Irish sense of humor and an infectious laugh, but she was ill almost the whole time Paul worked on the show. Jim loved her a lot and worried constantly that if any of the fans saw him out with the group, they might think he was with one of the women.

The man who really impressed Paul was Jack Louis, one of the agency men. He was a handsome man, a hero of World War I who'd been injured flying a mission which later resulted in a slight limp. Paul admired him so much he soon began walking with a limp. He didn't even realize it until someone pointed it out to him. Paul was

28

like that. When he liked someone, it was never halfway. He genuinely liked them.

Meanwhile, I had gotten a regular part on *Don Winslow of the Navy*. We did the show at NBC as did Fibber McGee. Paul and I saw each other often. When we met, we were always jolly, but at least one of us was laughing on the outside while crying on the inside.

Directly in front of my apartment were some tennis courts where Paul played in his leisure hours. He was a very good player, took a stunning tan, and had shapely legs in his little white shorts. Sometimes I watched him out my window. Then I'd sigh, and with stubborn resolve, I'd march back to my bedroom, fluff up my hair, put on some lipstick, and make the rounds to the studios and agencies once more in search of work.

NBC had a program called The Story of the Month. Five episodes a week, a new story every month. I counted the weekdays in a month and cleverly submitted an outline of a murder mystery called Twenty-Two Days to Live. They bought it. It always began with a series of gongs to show how many more days the hero had to live. Of course, the hero couldn't die. Afterall, the person who portrayed the hero was MacDonald Carey, and though nobody knew it then, there was an important career waiting for him in Hollywood films and as the star of *Days of Our Lives*.

I loved to write dialogue, but plots were not my specialty. Always helpful, Paul, bless his heart, came over to my apartment, and together we plotted the whole twenty-two episodes. That way I was able to write my daily episode before breakfast (radio was a piece of cake) and still have time to make my rounds.

About a year to the day of his coming to Chicago, Paul decided on his own to leave and go to Hollywood. He took me out to dinner and told me that he could see he'd never advance his career working for Don Quinn. He said Don had been doing it all on his own for so long that it was hard to share with another writer, no matter how competent. Paul paused. That wasn't the only reason he was leaving. He'd known almost from the beginning that he didn't want the blonde. I was the one and always had been.

"You could have fooled me," I said.

"She gave up so much for me. Her husband, her job – all that. I didn't know how to get out of it."

"Stop. You're going to make me cry," I said sarcastically.

"Well, I'm a coward, I guess. But this was the only way I knew to end it – to leave town," he confessed sheepishly. Then he continued, "I want you to wear your ring again and as soon as I get a job in Hollywood, I want you to come out and marry me."

"We'll see," I said. A girl has some pride.

He asked me not to come to the plane with him.

"Oh, naturally," I said. I didn't go to the plane. My life went on as usual. I got some new clothes on Michigan Boulevard, I made a date for New Year's Eve and went home for Christmas. While I was there, Paul called.

"I've got a job!" Paul said triumphantly, "Writing for *The Joe E. Brown Show*."

This isn't something Paul usually mentions in his résumé. It wasn't a very good show, but it was a job. He also had an agent, George Gruskin, at the William Morris Agency. You couldn't do better than that. What he said then is ALWAYS in my résumé.

"How soon could you come out and marry me?" he asked.

I'm not the coy type. Anyway, it was much too late to be coy. He knew exactly how I felt. "Would tomorrow be too soon?" I asked.

Of course, I didn't go the next day. I finished my holiday celebration in Kansas City, went back to Chicago, tearfully told my beloved roommate, Dolores, told NBC with whom I had a writing contract, and then I started packing. Dolores cried, but she was happy for me. Nobody at NBC cried, and I never knew if any of them were happy or not. I kept my New Year's Eve date. We were double dating with Dolores and her steady, Ed Allen, and it seemed too cruel to break an important date like that at the last minute. At midnight, I even kissed him for "Auld Lang Syne," but I felt like a dog.

My actor friends threw me a party and gave me a pair of silver candelabra. I took the train to Kansas City and had a round of showers and parties by KMBC folks and high school girlfriends. I took another train at midnight on January 12th and arrived in Yuma, Arizona in the early afternoon of the 14th. All the stars got married in Yuma in those days because it wasn't required to take a blood test and wait three days.

Paul met me along with a writer he'd become friends with, Johnny Greene, and his wife, Helen. We checked into the hotel. I had always wanted to get married at sunset. That was several hours off, though, and we didn't know what to do to fill in the time, so we went to the courthouse, which smelled of old cigars, and got a Justice of the Peace. I asked him if we could go outside and stand under a palm tree; he acquiesced, slightly bored, and it wasn't till I saw the snapshots later that I realized it wasn't a palm tree at all but a large cactus. Then we drove out to the desert – the real desert, just sand dunes like in the Rudolph Valentino pictures – and watched the sunset.

The next day Paul and I drove back to Hollywood with the Greenes, as man and wife. In spite of previous reluctance, I want to say in all fairness, that Paul was just as gaga as most new grooms.

4

I Can't Give You Anything but Love, Baby

Paul had rented a single apartment, one room with a Murphy bed, on Whitley Street above Hollywood Boulevard.

"I walked up the hill as far as I could till the air got thin, I fainted; the landlady came out, gathered me in her arms, carried me in and rented me an apartment," he wrote to me, singing in the tune of "Your Good Yuma Man."

We arrived Sunday night to find that all the tenants were waiting for us with a party – spaghetti, red wine, and a big crowd. Everybody who lived there was trying to get into the movies. Our neighbor across the hall had only one qualifying factor: he looked like John Carradine. There was one working actor living there, Lyle Talbot. Everyone was in awe of him. We never got to meet him until later.

That night when we left the party and retired to our own apartment, Paul hung our marriage license on the door. That's the kind of time it was. You didn't spend the night with a girl without a license.

So, to backtrack a bit – on the first day of Paul's job with *The Joe E. Brown Show*, the head writers had given him an assignment. "Pull all the fortune teller jokes out of your file and bring them in tomorrow," they said.

"My what?" Paul asked.

"Your file – your gag file!" they explained.

"I don't have a gag file," Paul admitted.

"You call yourself a comedy writer and you don't have a gag file?"

"Well, no – I usually just make up the jokes."

The writers all rolled their eyes and shook their heads. Who was this kid from the boondocks who didn't even know what it was all about?

The first morning after we returned from Yuma, Paul had to report for work. He got up at the crack of dawn and started to write a scene. He waited as long as he could – 6:00 a.m. – then sat on the side of the bed and shook me gently.

"Honey, is this funny?" he asked and started to read me what he'd written. I wasn't even awake yet, and I didn't laugh. Paul soon learned that he wouldn't get much of a reaction from me that early in the morning. When Paul met with the writers that day, he apologized for not having more written but explained he'd gotten married Saturday. "But I have an idea," he said.

"Yeah, we know what it is," they all laughed. "Go on home!"

While Paul got started on his Hollywood writing career, I explored Hollywood. On foot, of course. It was so different then. No smog. Very little traffic. No pornography along the boulevard, no weirdos in strange costumes. It looked like any other small town except for the palm trees. They practically took the sidewalks in by nine o'clock. I was perfectly, blissfully happy in our little apartment, but in my walks I stumbled on a place that blew my mind: the St. George Apartments on Vine Street, right across from the Hollywood Ranch Market. In front there was just a brick wall, but once inside, it was a paradise; a court ringed by town houses, each with its own little garden, all Spanish architecture. That really appealed to me because there was nothing like that in Kansas City. The one I looked at had a big living room with a two story high ceiling, and a wrought iron, curvy stairway with a balcony that led to a bedroom and bath. Besides that, there was a large dining room and kitchen. It was only sixty dollars a month. I couldn't wait to show it to Paul. He loved it too, and we moved there two weeks after we were married. We drove with friends down to Tijuana to buy some tapestries, serapes, Spanish shawls, and pottery vases to decorate our little hacienda.

By that time we had made one really good friend, another writer, Charlie Isaacs, who is still one of our best friends today. He lived in the apartment house just up the street on Whitley with only a courtyard separating us. The weather was balmy, the windows were open, and we could talk back and forth, Paul and Charlie often trading quips.

Charlie liked to sing but was no singer. He often got the words to the wrong tune and sang, "There's honey on the moon tonight" when it should have been "There's silver on the sage."

"You've got it wrong again!" I'd call out to him.

Once there was a long pause and then he sang, "There's honey and silver on the moon and sage tonight."

Charlie was writing for Tizzie Lish at the time. Remember Tizzie? He was a man who played a gossipy woman and was very funny. I think he was on *The Horace Heidt Show*.

. Loyally, when we moved to the St. George, so did Charlie. The new place was just like our first apartment – everybody there was trying to get into the movies. The Hollywood Ranch Market across the street was unbelievable by today's standards. For twenty-five cents you could bring home almost more than you could carry. I learned to cook Mulligan stew in a dishpan and in the late afternoon when the cooking smells began to waft into the courtyard, the St. George hopefuls began to waft into our apartment. Everybody tried to contribute something. Charlie's special was grated carrot and raisin salad. He was very strong and could grate a vat of it. One fellow lived on a small trust fund. When his check came, he paid his rent and then headed for Santa Anita to the races. When he won, he came back with wine, flowers, candy, and all kinds of gifts for us. And when he lost, he shared our Mulligan stew.

The Joe E. Brown Show wasn't thriving. Paul was fired and a week later hired back at half the salary – seventy-five dollars a week – to write just the tag, which was between Joe and his girl, played by Paula Winslow, a very sweet little spot that was right up Paul's alley. He didn't have to work very hard or long to do it, so we did a lot of walking. Paul and Charlie often hiked up to the Hollywoodland sign – that's what it was then. Later, after a fire, they cut it to just Hollywood. I wasn't much of a climber, but one time they talked me into it. Oh wow! I didn't think I'd make it and coming down was even harder. I slid most of the way on the seat of my pants.

We went to the movies at least once a week – always on Cash Club night when they gave away real money. Everybody, including us, certainly needed cash and we all went feeling hopeful.

Speaking of cash… I'd like to give you an example of the kind of guy Paul is. One day he was walking down Hollywood Boulevard and met Gomer Cool. Remember him? One of the Musical Grocers?

"Oh gosh, I'm glad I ran into you, Paul," Gomer said. "I want to buy Margaret a valentine, but I'm broke."

So Paul gave him his last two dollars and came home without a valentine for me.

"I knew you'd understand," he said and gave me a big hug. I did, of course. We were a month into our honeymoon. But that's my generous Paul. Sometimes it wasn't so easy.

To make some extra money, Paul sold a script to Eddie Cantor who had his own radio show. Meanwhile, Fibber and Molly had moved to California, and occasionally, Paul sold a story line to Don Quinn. But in June, the axe fell. Joe E. Brown was canceled, and of course, so was Paul. It seemed, though, that God was looking after us. One day, walking along Vine Street, Paul and I ran into Don Quinn.

"Oh, Paul! Thank goodness!" Don said.

"What for?" Paul asked.

"Thank goodness you married the right girl!"

We didn't know it, but everybody had been making bets about whether it would be me or the blonde.

Don continued by telling us he wanted to give us a wedding present, and we could have our choice of anything we wanted OR two months at his beautiful apartment just off the Sunset Strip.

Don, who was a widower, was getting married again. He had bought a house and planned to move in with his bride, but he still had two months to go on his lease. Don said that we could have it if we wanted it. Did we want it?! It was beautiful – two floors with a living room, dining room, and kitchen downstairs, two bedrooms and two baths upstairs. It was all furnished with turquoise carpets, white and gold furniture, and a beautiful balcony just off the master bedroom. The kitchen contained a lot of good Scotch, bourbon, and champagne, plus caviar, pate, cheese, and all those expensive snacks an affluent bachelor would stock.

We invited Charlie to move in with us and occupy the second bedroom. I made a deal with the boys. I would do the cooking, dusting, and vacuuming if they'd scrub the bathrooms and the kitchen floor. They readily agreed, and we lived like kings on unemployment insurance. Ours was seven dollars a week, and I think Charlie's was about the same.

Just before Paul became "at liberty" as everyone used to call it politely when you lost your job, we had added a new member to our family, a brand new deluxe Plymouth sedan. Paul got it through his brother, Cotton, an automotive genius who lived in Indianapolis and entered cars in the Indy 500 – which, by the way, he won several times. Of course, he had all the connections with automobile manufacturers, and we got our deluxe car for six hundred dollars. Other times!

36

Paul and Charlie kept seeing George Gruskin, their agent, and hoping for employment, but it was 1939 and times were tough. About that time, an executive from KMBC in Kansas City, where Paul and I had started out, wrote that he was coming to Hollywood and certainly wanted to see us. We panicked. When Paul had left the station, unlike me, they had tried to hold him to his contract. He showed it to one of his former law school professors who'd showed it to his colleagues, and they all had a good laugh. He told Paul not to worry, that it was the craziest contract he'd ever seen, certainly not legally binding, and that Paul could leave any time he wanted to. He wasn't sure whether there were any hard feelings or not, but he certainly didn't want any of the home folks to know that he was out of work.

Well, we got our heads together, invited the executive, Mr. Fox, to dinner, and it went like this. Don Quinn had had a manservant who'd left a starched white coat in the pantry. Charlie donned the coat, served champagne, caviar, and other upscale hors d'oeuvres. I had cooked a leg of lamb, which Charlie served, and the evening was a rip-roaring success. Les Fox went back to KMBC and reported that "Paul Henning is knocking 'em dead in Hollywood!"

At the end of the summer, the lease on the apartment was up and we had to face reality. So we moved to the Alto Nido at Franklin and Ivar. It meant "high nest" in Spanish, and that it was. The hill up Ivar Street was so steep Paul had to push me the last few steps.

Our apartment was another single, one room, Murphy bed, half underground on account of the hill. Remember the movie, Sunset Boulevard? William Holden, playing a struggling writer in the film, lived at the Alto Nido. Very appropriate. What was above ground was level with the sidewalk, so there were bars on the windows. Interesting.

Our cat Golden Boy had long since gone to live with my mother in Kansas City since most apartments didn't welcome pets. However, one night we left our windows open and a little street cat came in through the bars. We named her Gertrude and she was a regular guest.

We were happy there.

So we weren't on the Sunset Strip anymore! So we weren't high class anymore! No more gold and white furniture, good Scotch, and caviar! It really didn't bother us. We were still in our honeymoon year and just as happy as rich people, happier probably. We often invited guests for dinner – sometimes important people like Don Quinn or Fibber and Molly. I always cooked my standard meal – spaghetti salad, store-bought pie – all accompanied by cheap, red wine. The wine was a problem. They wouldn't sell it to Paul at the corner liquor store, he looked too young. In disgust, I'd walk down there and they never questioned me. Villains!

We played a lot of rummy together (not gin rummy, that hadn't been invented yet) just plain, old-fashioned rummy. Often our day would go like this:

"I'll play you a game of rummy to see who chops the onions!" Paul said. And of course, Paul won.

"I'll play you a game of rummy to see who grates the cheese!" Paul won again.

"I'll play you a game of rummy to see who washes the lettuce!" Again, Paul.

And so it went until close to the time of our guests' scheduled arrival. Then he'd have to pitch in and help me anyway. Ah – youth! Today, if I had stellar guests coming to dinner, I'd work two days getting everything just so. And we probably wouldn't enjoy it as much.

We were carefree kids, but we did have a couple of worries. Our slender savings was about used up and rent was always looming. Paul sold more ideas to Don Quinn and I started to look for work. It was a whole lot different from Chicago. There you could go and hang around the studios until you saw a director. Here, everyone had an agent and sometimes you couldn't even gain entrance to network studios unless you had an appointment.

I did work a few times on a program called *The Dealer in Dreams*. A young, confused person (that was me all right) would walk into his office, and it went like this:

"Oh, Dealer in Dreams, I'm so unhappy. Can you help me?"

"My dear, tell me your trouble," replied the Dealer in his rich, pear-shaped tones. Paul called the program, The Drooler in Dreams.

The second thing that was bothering us was that Christmas was coming and neither of us had ever been away from home on Christmas before, and we felt like boohooing. Babies, right? We knew we could drive back to Missouri if only we could get money for gas. One Friday afternoon, I was sitting in a sleazy little recording studio upstairs over a store on Hollywood Boulevard when I heard some men talking in an inner office. The door was open, so I guess it was no secret.

"Well, what are we gonna do? There's no script. We have to record Monday, or we lose the actors."

"Yeah, and it's not just the one script. We have to do two or three a day because we can't afford any more studio rent." Sounds like a real classy operation, n'est-ce pas?

There followed some words best described as epithets. As soon as the air cleared, I walked timidly to the open door. "Did I hear you mention you needed scripts?" I asked.

"Yeah. We gotta record *Dan Dunn, Secret Operative Number 13*. And we need thirteen scripts. By Monday."

39

"I may be able to help you," I said. "My husband and I are both writers and we can do them for you over the weekend."

"You're kiddin'."

"Absolutely not!" Then I gave them some of Paul's credits and embellished a few of mine. "We happen to be at liberty right now, and we could do it."

And so I went home with the assignment and an armload of Dan Dunn scripts to read. Paul wasn't thrilled, but it was the only thing either one of us had come up with so far. So we sat down at our dinette table and good old Paul, the constructionist, mapped out thirteen episodes. Dan Dunn was the poor man's *Dick Tracy*, and he was about to become even poorer. We each had a typewriter so one of us took the dinette, the other the living room and we went to work. We each wrote one before breakfast, another before lunch, a third one before dinner, and, hopefully, if we held out, a postprandial script. They were fifteen minutes long, and this was an emergency for goodness sakes. Not only for them but for us too.

Our pay was to be fifteen dollars per script. Figure it out. One hundred ninety-five dollars. Plenty to get us to Kansas City. We were set. The catch was they didn't have the one hundred ninety-five dollars. They paid us half and promised the rest later. Well, we figured, we could make it if we didn't stop at motels.

We did make it with only one stop and Paul drove the whole way – 1200 miles. By the time we got there, he was so tired and the weather was so cold that he was half-sick, but we were THERE. It was Christmas, and we were HOME.

P.S. We never did get the rest of our money for Dan Dunn.

5

Rudy Vallee

When we left Missouri after that Christmas of 1939, everything was snow and ice. When we arrived in California, it was all sunshine and orange trees. I wanted to get out of the car and kiss the ground. That's when I really became a Californian. I think you have to be here a while, leave, then come back to get that feeling of belonging.

We were back in our one-room apartment half underground and no sign of a job in view. That old song kept going round in my head: "What ya gonna say? How ya gonna pay?" Maybe the sheer desperation of the situation spurred Paul to act in an uncharacteristic way. He demonstrated a little chutzpah.

George Gruskin, his agent, had told him that Rudy Vallee was looking for a new format for his show. I remembered when I was in high school how we'd sit around at somebody's house and play Rudy Vallee records. "Vagabond Lover" – "The Maine Stein Song" – "Betty Co-Ed" – "If You Were the Only Girl in the World." Rudy Vallee! This was big stuff! What Paul did was to dream up an idea and all on his own go out to Vick Knight's house one evening and just knock on the door. Vick was the producer-director of Rudy Vallee's show. I waited at home, fingers crossed, holding my breath. When Paul came back, he was jubilant. Vick Knight had liked his idea very much but wanted to check it with Rudy, the ad agency, the network, etc.

We marked a little time. January 14th was our first anniversary. A big carton from the Broadway Hollywood Department Store arrived from Charlie. It was full of paper napkins, Kleenex, toilet paper, whatever they stocked in paper. "Happy Paper

Anniversary," the card said. Unpacking the box was a hoot, but I couldn't help myself – I kept picturing us out on the street selling toilet paper.

Shortly, in fact, very shortly, Paul heard from Vick Knight. Everybody liked his idea, and Vick asked if Paul would please come over and sign a contract. Would he?! He came home grinning from ear to ear.

"It's all signed!" he told me. "They're paying me two hundred fifty dollars a week."

My mouth dropped open. I nearly fainted. How could anybody possibly spend that much money? I wondered.

Most writers, comedy writers anyway, worked in pairs so Paul asked Charlie to be his partner. A couple of bright young men, Norman Panama and Mel Frank, moved over from *The Bob Hope Show*. Soon Abe Burrows was also added to the roster. As the years went by, there were others: Frank Galen, Dick Chevillat, Ray Singer, Mannie Manheim, Jess Oppenheimer, Bill Demling, Bob Weiskopf, Arthur Marx. All of those writers went on to become mainstays in radio and television comedy. More came later, but Paul always felt very close to those early writers. He truly loved them, respected them, and felt at home with them.

Early on, it was decided to take the show to New York. In radio days, they often traveled to give new studio audiences a chance to see the stars in person, to take advantage of a new pool of talent, and to get publicity. Since Paul was so busy with his new assignment, it was decided that he'd go on to New York while I stayed to close the apartment. I made a deal with the Alto Nido to store our meager possessions so that when we returned, we could move right in.

Then I flew to New York. What a high! I'd never been east of Chicago.

When I arrived, Paul was there to meet me with Ted Malone and his wife, Verila. Ted's Between the Bookends program had skyrocketed to national popularity, and he was now based in New York. They drove me around so I could get a look at the bright lights and tall buildings.

We were staying in a suite at the Essex House. Charlie also had a room there, and they worked in our sitting room, taking time out now and then to survey the tennis court with binoculars. I tried to shame them, but they only laughed and said they were doing research.

New York was exciting, but I soon had had enough of hotel living. Somebody told us about a sublease on 96th and Central Park West. It was a spacious, old apartment – just one bedroom, but the rooms were huge. We took it. There was a subway entrance right at our front door, and Central Park across the street. It was safe then – the park and the subway both. I often met actress friends there. A lot of them, seeking greener pastures, had left Chicago to move east. Paul got a permit to play tennis on the courts in the park, and there we were – a whole new life.

I'm sure they had a galaxy of guest stars on Rudy Vallee's show, but one stands out. NBC said they had a new girl singer who was doing a sustaining program (no sponsor), and they'd sure like to get her a little notice on a big show like Rudy's. It happened they were doing Stephen Foster music that week, and it also happened that I attended the rehearsal. In due time, the new girl sang her first song, and I, along with everybody else, was blown away. She was fantastic. She was Dinah Shore. Needless to say, she didn't remain unsponsored. Everybody wanted her. It's exciting to see the birth of a new talent like that.

I can't wait to tell you about the big event of the summer. The Fourth of July holiday came along, and the show was preempted (canceled) that week to make way for the political convention, which

43

nominated Wendell Wilkie. That gave everybody five days off. Accordingly, Rudy invited the writers and their wives to his famous lodge in Maine. Wow! I'd heard so much about that lodge. It had been written about and described in all the columns.

The plan was to meet Rudy at midnight in Grand Central Station. Right away you have a plot, right? We were given tickets, which entitled us each to a bedroom on the train, and as we were getting settled in, there was a knock at the door – and there was Rudy with a tray of pink champagne to drink a toast to our holiday. Wow again! This was the lifestyle of the rich and famous for sure. We changed trains in Boston and arrived in Portland, Maine, where cars met us. Paul and I rode with Rudy who showed a sense of humor we hadn't expected. After quite a long drive, we came to a little shacky place and pulled up.

"Well, there it is! How do you like it?" he asked with a perfectly straight face.

While we were sputtering around for an answer, the driver started the car, and we drove on to the sound of Rudy's laughter.

When we did get there, it was an unbelievable paradise. Deep in the Maine woods beside a large lake, Lake Kezar, was the lodge, several out buildings, and a group of tennis courts that made Paul's eyes light up. We were all assigned to rooms named for songs Rudy had made famous. Our room was "Betty Co-Ed," and it was lovely. Rudy's room was "Vagabond Lover," of course. He was accompanied by a really gorgeous brunette. She had a movie contract but no talent, so she was quickly forgotten, but that weekend she really stirred things up.

Rudy told us to change, and we'd all go out on his boat for lunch. In the meantime, he came by our room with frozen daiquiris. I'd never tasted one, and it was delicious.

44

His boat was a large Chris-Craft. There were servants aboard to serve us a picnic lunch. This became a daily thing. Afternoons were spent swimming, playing tennis, or ping-pong, or whatever. Dinners were somewhat dressy affairs always preceded by the famous frozen daiquiris. Rudy had a Waring blender, a brand new invention we'd never seen before.

The first night, Rudy's girlfriend came down for dinner wearing gauzy silk jersey pants and just a matching scarf around her neck crossed to cover her breasts – almost. All the boys' eyes bugged out, but I'll say this for her – she wasn't selfish. She came up to me, unbuttoned the top two buttons of my blouse and said with satisfaction, "That's better. If you've got 'em, show 'em!"

The food was great and after dinner each night, there was a movie, one of Rudy's naturally. The next morning the whole fabulous schedule would begin again. Paul loved to play tennis, and so did Rudy, but somebody warned the boys, "Don't beat Rudy!" The courts were floodlighted, and they often played again after the movie. Rudy's girl would get a little drunk, and someone would be appointed to take her to her room. All the boys volunteered, but Rudy would look at his watch meaningfully. They knew they couldn't dally. One night, just before the dessert course, Rudy excused himself and went out to the kitchen. After he came back, cherries jubilee was served. Rudy laughed sheepishly.

"That was dumb," he said. "I flamed the brandy in the kitchen and nobody saw it. Now why did I do that?" He could be quite endearing. Paul couldn't get over the change in him. Previously, during the show or rehearsals, he was very formal, bowing from the waist and clicking his heels and calling Paul, Mr. Henning.

The last night of our stay Rudy ran out of movies. He really hadn't made that many. So he showed us movies of his plastic surgery. He'd had a nose job and had his somewhat droopy eyes widened. We were all agog. At least three of us were. I'd always hated my nose. Marcia Panama felt the same way, and Mel Frank who'd played football in school had broken his nose several times. We all got the name of Rudy's doctor and gave each other meaningful looks.

Back at our apartment in New York, we found treasures waiting for us. A case of rum, a case of pineapple, and a Waring blender so we could make the frozen daiquiris we'd raved about at the lodge. We were astounded because Rudy had a reputation for being cheap. Well, he was. But he could have generous impulses. And that's how I always liked to remember him – the way he was that glorious weekend at the lodge.

Soon after that, Marcia, Mel, and I went to see Rudy's doctor. We went together to give each other courage. Plastic surgery wasn't so common then, and it took a lot of nerve. After our visit to the doctor, we all agreed we didn't care much for him. He'd said he patterned his noses after Greek statues and that bothered me. I didn't have a face remotely resembling a Greek statue. How would it look with a Grecian nose?

We were too hooked on the idea to give it up now, though, so we went to see another plastic surgeon whom we liked right away. We made appointments and all went to the hospital on the same day. He explained that usually you could go home right after the surgery, but since none of us had a family on hand to look after us, we'd better stay in the hospital overnight.

Well, when I got a look at myself the next day, I nearly fainted. My face was swollen until no features showed. It was black, blue green, purple, yellow – every color of the rainbow – I was petrified that I might sneeze and ruin the whole thing. Nowadays they have better methods and people don't look so bad after that kind of surgery.

Paul teased me. "If we ever split up, the nose is mine. I paid for it!"

46

A funny thing happened while I still looked like the monster from the black lagoon. Two friends of ours from KMBC came to New York. Paul met them and brought them to our apartment. I had dinner waiting, but I worried that my face would be a shock to them. When they arrived, they never said a word, hardly even looked at me. They acted as though there was nothing unusual at all. Finally, I couldn't stand it any longer.

"Aren't you going to say something?" I cried.

It turned out that on the way home, Paul had told them, "I want to explain something. Ruth and I had an argument and – well – I'm very ashamed of myself, but I hit her." Then he asked them not to mention it because I was very self-conscious about it. I nearly hit HIM then.

In time, the swelling and the bruises disappeared and I was thrilled with my new nose. I had my picture taken every which way, but mostly in profile. Before we went home to California, I bought some new clothes and decided not to tell anyone out there about my surgery. I wasn't ashamed of it, but I wanted to see if anyone would notice it. Well, they did and they didn't. Almost everyone said something, different versions of "Gee, you look good! New York must have agreed with you!" They knew I looked better yet nobody guessed the reason why.

I'm getting ahead of myself, though. While we were still in New York, we visited Lenore Kingston and Joe Conn who had recently been married. Lenore had been on *Don Winslow of the Navy* with me, and Joe had been the engineer. They had a television set – one of the first ones – in fact, THE first one we ever saw. It was a sheer marvel. But then I still didn't believe in radio or the telephone for that matter. I just had to accept them all because they were there.

Our sublease ran out, the owners came home, and we found another apartment nearby on West End Avenue. It was – what else? – one room with a Murphy bed.

At this time, Charlie had accepted another offer, and Paul was working with Abe Burrows. Paul and Abe wrote some of the funniest scenes I'd ever heard.

William Morris had sold the sponsor on a new semi-permanent guest star, none other than John Barrymore. John was brilliant – everyone admitted that – but he was also an undependable drunk, which everyone also admitted. Part of the deal was a male nurse stayed with him on the day of the show to make sure he showed up, reasonably sober.

As Paul and Abe worked in our tiny living room, writing the Barrymore scenes, they nearly knocked themselves out laughing. Abe was a large presence. He was a big man, with a big voice, a big talent, and he smoked big cigars. I just couldn't take it for long, even with the funny lines. I had to shut myself in the bathroom or go up to the roof garden of the building. They couldn't work at Abe's because he lived in Brooklyn with his wife, Ruth, and their baby, Jimmy. (Jimmy, incidentally, is the James Burrows you see listed in the credits of *Cheers* as producer-director.)

We went back to California where the idea for the Barrymore participation began. It was a sensation, the talk of the trades and the viewers too. Once they tried to get the three Barrymores on at once, John, Lionel, and Ethel. Lionel came willingly, but Ethel refused.

"I don't blame her," John admitted. "I lived with her for a while, and I stole her blind." It seems he had hocked art objects and anything else that wasn't nailed down to get money for booze.

After the broadcast, John and Lionel still sat at the table they had rigged up with a mic because Lionel couldn't stand for long – bad arthritis, I think it was – and they began to reminisce. The writers all gathered in the control room and begged the engineer to leave the mic open so they could hear the dialogue.

"Remember that whorehouse in Hong Kong?" Lionel asked, and they were off to the races – very racy races.

Once they had Orson Welles on as a guest. Orson and John were to do a scene from *Hamlet* – Orson as Hamlet, John as his father's ghost. In rehearsal, poor John stumbled along pitifully and all the writers felt very sorry for him because here was this young genius who was going to show up the old has-been. Little did they know… on the broadcast, John came alive. He was brilliant, and not only held his own but somewhat eclipsed Orson. An old pro's trick, I was told.

When we returned to Hollywood, we took a double at the Alto Nido, all above ground. Some other changes were made. Vick Knight had a previous commitment to Eddie Cantor and left the show. Ed Gardner came out from New York to take his place. He was fresh from his success as "Archy" on *Duffy's Tavern* and his marriage to Shirley Booth who had played Miss Duffy. Both the show and the marriage had been canceled, and Ed, lonely in his bachelor apartment, liked to have his writers around for company. So began an interlude when I never saw Paul. Honest, one night he arrived home from a session about midnight, had just crawled wearily into bed when the phone suddenly rang. It was Ed asking him to come right back over. There was to be yet another writers' meeting.

With all that free time, I decided to have a baby. I'd always planned to have a family and with nothing constructive to do with my time, I thought that time might be the right time. Paul agreed and in the wink of an eye – well, actually a wink had nothing to do with it – I was pregnant. Then I started looking at houses. We had good friends from Kansas City who lived in the Valley – at that time considered a distant outpost of civilization. It was before freeways, you understand. We often went to their house and lo and behold, one day we saw a charming little Cape Cod cottage for sale. It was new and when we looked at it, we were utterly charmed. It had a red and white kitchen, plate rails in the dining room, a window seat in the living room and a large copper hood over the fireplace. In short, we just had to have it. So as our grandson, Alex, used to say when he was a baby, "Want it – have it!" We moved in March 1, 1941. I was about two months pregnant.

I was warned not to climb ladders or lift boxes but this was a brand new house, it was mine, and I was dying to put in shelf paper and place every item exactly where I wanted it in my new kitchen. As a result, I had to go to bed for a couple of weeks. Paul hired a woman to unpack the boxes and it just about killed me to have somebody else arrange my new shelves while I lie in bed and nibbled soda crackers to keep from throwing up. Wherever Paul was working, usually at Mannie Manheim's apartment, he called before he came home to ask if he could bring anything. I always asked for a red pie. It could be cherry, strawberry, rhubarb, anything, as long as it was red.

I recovered and began to enjoy my house. All the furniture was new. What a joy! Paul often had the writers over to work in our den. I hired a "mother's helper" through Van Nuys High School. Her name was Leona, and I wasn't sure she'd last long. Every night I sneaked into her bathroom to feel her towel to see if it was wet, to check whether she'd taken a bath. It remained relentlessly dry. Then one day as she was serving coffee to the writers at Paul's request, she dropped a note in Bill Demling's lap asking him to meet her on her day off at a motel. Bye, bye, Leona. Too bad.

We made lifelong friends on Dickens Street. My obstetrician, Dr. Ress, told me he had a patient who was expecting about the same time as I was who lived on our street just a block away. One day, I got all dressed up and walked down the block to knock on their door – and that's how we met Kay and Jack Carson. They were charming people and we were thrilled to meet them. In Kansas City, Jack had been MC at the Tower Theatre for a couple of seasons. That was when they had movies and vaudeville together. They also had a permanent chorus line called The Tower Adorables. Can you stand it? Jack was a burgeoning movie star at Warner Brothers and Kay was the former Kay St. Germain, band singer.

There was another of Dr. Ress's patients nearby, a real bona-fide movie star, Joanne Dru, at that time married to Dick Haymes. One night, Paul took the three of us, Kay, Joanne, and me to a movie on Hollywood Boulevard. As we were walking from the parking lot, we encountered some sailors who looked at us in wonder. Paul had always thought they were thinking. "How could that little guy get so many women pregnant at the same time?"

Carol was born 23 days early, and we blamed it on Charles Boyer. The night before I went to the hospital, Paul, Charlie, and I had gone to see "Hold Back the Dawn," starring Olivia De Havilland and Charles Boyer. I was really crazy about him, and we decided he had stirred up my hormones enough to bring on early labor.

Having a baby in 1941 was a far cry from what it is today. I stayed in the hospital for ten days, dressed up each day in a fancy bed jacket, and had a room full of floral tributes. On the whole, it was a glamorous event. All the writers came to see me and agreed Carol was an unusually beautiful baby. The first day they allowed me to sit in a wheelchair and be pushed to the window of the nursery, I was gazing in abject admiration and pride at my baby when along came Cary Grant and his then wife, Barbara Hutton. They had been to see Georgie Jessel's new baby. If anything could have taken my attention from my baby, it was Cary Grant.

"That's the cutest one," he said, pointing to Carol. Barbara agreed. Talk about pride! Well, it just proved to me that Cary Grant was intelligent, as well as handsome.

51

Meanwhile, the show must go on and did. Paul went back to work, secure in the knowledge that I now had a baby nurse who came home from the hospital with me, and she came directly to us from the home of Ronald Reagan and Jane Wyman who had just had their daughter, Maureen. Since both Ron and Jane worked at Warner Brothers, we had a slight acquaintance with them because of Jack Carson. Ron hadn't gotten interested in politics yet. At a dinner party where I sat next to him, his main topic of conversation involved football and how if only they had invented contact lenses in time, he might have played for his high school team.

Our social life was almost entirely with the other writers. We loved to go to Abe Burrows' house because his wife, Ruth, was an excellent cook. She taught me to make Beef Stroganoff, a dish my Kansas City life had never introduced to me. But the specialty of the evening was Abe at the piano singing his own songs. There was "The Girl With the Three Blue Eyes" – "Strolling Down Memory Lane Without a Single Thing on My Mind" – "Waukesha Bridge" (you had to be there for that one) – and one of my favorites, which he didn't write but performed hilariously: "Rosie Rosenblatt, stop your turkey trot, Rosie, don't make a tee-ay-ter with me!" Later on, Abe had his own radio show just doing those songs. Evenings at our house were mostly a patio buffet and ping-pong.

Arthur Marx, whom we all thought of as "the kid," had begun to work on the show about then and in order to repay all our hospitality, invited us to dinner at his house in Beverly Hills. His father was Groucho Marx, and that was an evening we all remember. The house was palatial, the dinner sumptuous, the company congenial with his father at the head, his mother at the foot of the table. But what made it different was that Groucho had a girlfriend at his side, and in due time, his mother's date arrived to take her out. We later learned they were divorced but she refused to move out because of the closets.

52

In spite of the unorthodox situation, Arthur was a really nice, well-adjusted boy and we all liked him a lot.

The cast of writers changed from time to time but for the ones who remained, they developed a sort of rhythm, which didn't tax them too much. Almost every day, they met at Mannie's apartment and then proceeded to a beach club, the Sorrento. They had an arrangement with the switchboard at Mannie's apartment and the one at the Sorrento that if Dick Mack (then the producer) or Rudy called, the telephone chain would see that they were informed so somebody could call back and give reassurance that the script was coming along fine. Then they'd go back to their swimming, volleyball, or suntanning. By this time, Abe had moved on to his true calling, the Broadway stage; Panama and Frank were writing Bob Hope movies; and the core of old faithfuls included Paul, Charlie, Mannie, Jess Oppenheimer and Dick Chevillat.

Charlie liked to send funny telegrams. On Paul's birthday, the wire read: "Hope your birthday finds you out on a limb – mine. Signed, Betty Grable." Later, on our second anniversary, I got this one. "Two years wiz ze wrong man. I think I mus' go mad, but still I wait. Signed, Charles Boyer."

Of course, the big event that ended that year of 1941 was Pearl Harbor; John Barrymore was still on the show and once – I can't remember why – someone asked him, "John, haven't you heard? They attacked Pearl Harbor!"

John replied, "No! Lovely girl!"

By that time, Bob Weiskopf was working with Paul. Bob was married to the former Eileen Ito, an American-born Japanese girl. It was a traumatic situation for her. She was afraid to go out on the street alone because of the strong feeling against the Japanese. I went with her to do her Christmas shopping. Eventually, Bob quit his job, and they moved to New York.

The second traumatic event of 1941 was that Paul had an acute appendicitis attack and was rushed to Cedars of Lebanon Hospital where he was operated on immediately. All went well until about a week later, in the middle of the night, I received a solemn phone call from the doctor. Paul had had a shower of emboli and was on the critical list. I didn't know what that was, but was soon told that part of the scab from the surgical site had broken off and clots were now lodged in his lungs. Usually, this was fatal. They had bound Paul's chest very tightly, he was forbidden to move even his arms – and the only thing to do was to wait for nature to dissolve the clots. This is still a serious condition, but they have drugs to help dissolve the clots now. Also, they get patients up right after surgery, to guard against such a thing from happening.

Fortunately, at that time, I had household help: a steady, sensible girl from a farm in North Dakota who had come to Hollywood to try to find a little glamour. Her name was Orpha. I left her in charge of Carol and went right down to the hospital. Almost all the writers were there to be with me. I had no family on the west coast, and I really appreciated their loyalty. We all walked the halls most of the night. Many nights after that I spent on my knees, I looked often at my little baby and prayed that she wouldn't have to grow up without her wonderful father. A specialist was called in from the Mayo Clinic, private nurses around the clock were hired, and we waited. And waited.

All of this cost a lot of money. We had very little savings. We'd bought a house and furniture, and we'd had a baby. *The Rudy Vallee Show* was a champion. They paid Paul his salary for several weeks. Most of our relatives, just emerging for the Great Depression, had no money to spare. Mannie Manheim offered to lend me money and Paul's brother, Cotton, the automotive genius, came up with some funds. Somehow we got by. When the first emergency passed, I took one of the nursing shifts, and after eight weeks, Paul came home. That was a happy day – but I wound up with an ulcer. Small wonder.

Paul went back to work. A pre-Pearl Harbor baby kept him out of the draft – not to mention his serious illness. A Japanese submarine bombed Santa Barbara, or so they thought. Orpha, my gem, decided she'd go back to the farm.

"If I'm going to die, I want it to be in North Dakota," she explained.

With Paul's illness, my ulcer, a baby, and a house, I definitely needed some help. I decided to try Van Nuys High School again, in spite of the unwashed Leona. This time I had better luck – much better luck. A tall, willowy, blonde beauty named Wanda came into our lives. All my girlfriends thought I was out of my mind to have a girl like that living with us. I guess I was foolhardy, but it all worked out. Paul admired Wanda but remained true blue. I was crazy about her and so was Carol. And if you don't believe she was a knockout, when she graduated from high school and left our house, her next job was as a showgirl at the Copacabana in New York.

Back to Rudy Vallee. We never really left him through all the personal sturm and drang. Whenever a team of creative people work together to produce any product, especially something as personal as an entertainment, it's the personality and character of the star which sets the tone of the undertaking. Rudy was not the best singer in the world. He wasn't a good comedian, though he could play a comedy part expertly if it were tailored just for him. He got credit for discovering a lot of new people, and it's for sure they did appear on his show and get a good start, but whether it was Rudy or his production staff who discovered them, who's to say?

Rudy was the first ever crooner who used a megaphone before electronic sound systems were introduced. He was from an upscale New England family, a college graduate; he was tall, slender, clean cut, handsome in his own way, and he did croon those love songs in a soft, romantic style. Timing is important, of course. He came along at the very beginning of radio and was able to endure into television, movies, and even the stage. Abe Burrows later on remembered him when he was casting the musical he'd co-written, *How to Succeed in Business Without Really Trying*. Rudy, a bit older then, played a stuffy executive and hit it right on the nose. His reviews were great.

Rudy had his little idiosyncrasies, like always carrying a suitcase of cheap pink champagne with him wherever he went, (even to restaurants and nightclubs), refusing to go out with a girl who wore wedge shoes, or giving his faithful writers who were expecting a Christmas bonus a silly pencil called the Norma, which would write in several different colors. Still, he *did* take us to his lodge. He *was* the perfect host. He entertained us often at his home in the Hollywood Hills on Pyramid Place. Late in life, he tried to get the city to change the name of the street to "Rue de Vallee." Wisely, they refused. The last time I saw him was on stage at Sportsman's Lodge during a Pacific Pioneer Broadcasters' luncheon where he'd been honored with the Carbon Mike Award. He reacted by talking for several hours, gradually emptying the room.

Dear Rudy, bless him. He had a lot of influence on our young lives and we'll always remember him: the good, the bad, and the slightly nutty. But mostly the good.

6

Gracie and Her Husband

In the summer of 1942, a little more than two years after Paul had gotten his job on *The Rudy Vallee Show*, he had a competing offer from another show, an even bigger one – *Burns and Allen*. And so began ten of the best years of our lives.

Everybody knows George Burns now because he's lived so long and grown old so gracefully. Back then, Gracie Burns was definitely the star of the act. She got all the laughs and George would take it from there and off they'd go into the wild blue yonder of her unique brand of comedy.

A lot of younger people today don't really remember Gracie, but I do. She was tiny, delicate, and much prettier in person than on TV. She was bubbly and fun to be with but not a bit dumb or scatterbrained like her character portrayed her. She always had exquisite clothes, which usually had to be made just for her because of her size.

Also, they had to have sleeves – or in the case of formal gowns, long gloves. When she was a toddler, she'd pulled a pan of boiling water off the stove and burned one arm so badly that the scars were deep and permanent. Her health was not as robust as George's was; something none of us, including George himself, realized. Her heart was not strong, and she sometimes had severe migraine headaches. Once or twice, when the pain was so intense that she couldn't perform, their good friend, Jane Wyman, went on the show with George and read Gracie's lines.

When Paul told his mother he was now writing for George Burns, she asked him, "Who writes for Gracie? She's the funny one." Most of the public felt that way. That's the way George wanted it.

George could be very funny, of course. Paul soon found that out. On the radio show, however, he was content to be the straight man. He knew how important that was. A joke is a fragile thing. One false word, one second of wrong timing can ruin it.

In person, George was very funny. Somebody who knew that was his best friend, Jack Benny. They'd known each other from the beginning when they were Benny Kubelsky and Nat Birnbaum just starting out in vaudeville. George was half of a ballroom dancing team, and Jack played his violin. It took a while for them to find their true niches. Jack really didn't know he wasn't a good violinist, but when audiences didn't respond, he began talking to them. They laughed and laughed. His future was settled. George met a cute little Irish girl named Gracie Allen, fell in love, teamed up with her, and as they say, the rest is history.

As George and Jack toured the country on the vaudeville circuit, their paths crossed and recrossed. They got in the habit of telephoning each other late at night with funny lines. George's gag was that he always hung up on Jack before the punch line. Now, Jack often stopped by George's office in the Hollywood Plaza Hotel, and in no time at all, he was on the floor pounding it with his fists. George had only to say, "Hello, Jack" and Jack was done for.

Gracie never came to the office. She liked to stay at home, sleep late, have lunch and shop with her girlfriends, Jane Wyman or Mary Benny. She yearned to be an ordinary Beverly Hills housewife and often talked about retiring. That made George very nervous. He never dreamed he could have a career without Gracie, and at contract renewal time, he always had to talk her into signing for another year. One time he had a party the day she signed the contract. He was so jubilant. Then someone asked him, "George, don't you ever think of retiring?"

"You know when I want to retire?" he replied, "the day I die." And he's certainly made good on that statement because at 97, he's still going strong.

George ran the office and masterminded the program with a strong assist from his brother, Willie. Paul and I liked Willie. He was a funny and capable man. It isn't easy being a celebrity's brother. Willie had to do a lot of the dirty work without much credit. By dirty work, I just mean keeping pests away from George, getting George out of commitments he'd made thoughtlessly under pressure – things like that. Willie didn't seem to mind. He loved his wife, Louise, and his three daughters. He was a happy man.

At first, there were just two other writers besides Paul: Keith Fowler and Frank Galen. The draft had been gobbling up writers like a monster. When Paul first joined the show, the other fellows had told him how he happened to receive the offer from George.

"We were kicking around names and trying to come up with a writer we'd like to work with," Keith said.

"Somebody mentioned you, Paul," said Frank. "We all agreed you'd be good."

Yeah, but then somebody else said, "You can't get Paul Henning. He had a commitment to Rudy Vallee."

"What do you mean I can't get him?" George said. Challenged, George was determined. And that's how it happened. The busy people usually get the work.

At first, Paul was given the job of thinking up plots, situations, and story lines. I guess his reputation had preceded him. When they got the story set, scenes would be divided up between the writers who met every day at the office, read what they'd written, and put it together so that it all matched.

Others on the show were Bill Goodwin, the announcer, who not only did the commercials but appeared in the story as a sophisticated man about town. Blanche and Harry Morton were next-door neighbors. Blanche was always played by Bea Benaderet and Harry by a series of comedy actors, often the announcer. Harry Von Zell put in a long stint as Harry Morton, as did Hal March and Bob Sweeney. Paul always admired Bea Benaderet and her comedy talent and vowed some day to write a show just for her.

The radio show was still basically a variety show with guest stars and an orchestra. When Paul joined the show, the host was Paul Whiteman, the King of Jazz himself. The sponsor was Swan Soap. Our daughter, Carol, grew up using bars of Swan Soap for blocks. When we first took her to the zoo, her face lit up when she saw the "swan birdies."

Soon Paul was promoted to an assigned spot of the show. At first, he worked with Frank Galen, and then, after Frank was drafted, he worked alone. More and more young writers were getting "Greetings" from Uncle Sam and going off to war. Keith Fowler, the most un-athletic man we'd ever known, when he was first drafted, wrote on a questionnaire that he was in radio work, so, typical of the army, he was assigned to climb telephone poles as a lineman.

Other writers came and went. Harvey Helm, Sid Dorfman, Aaron Rubin, Hank Garson, Stan Shapiro, and, Marvin Marx. Neither Paul nor I are sure in just what order they made their appearance. Paul gradually worked his way up to being head writer, helped a lot by the draft. He was deferred for a long time because of his pre-Pearl Harbor baby, and then because George Burns pleaded "hardship." Keeping the world laughing in those troubled times was considered essential and to do that, there had to be writers to write the funny lines.

I got used to the schedule. One night was "Labor Pains" night because the next morning Paul had to show up with an idea for next week's show. Then, on the night before the broadcast, they "put the show to bed," which meant all the writers plus George and Willie met

60

in the office to put the pieces together, polish it, and added the finishing touches.

That was the night all the wives met and played gin rummy. Gracie loved gin – the card game. We'd meet at one another's houses and play. I didn't know how to play when Paul first joined the show. The brand of rummy Paul and I had played when we were newlyweds was not the same at all. If somebody "ginned" – that is, put down all their cards – and you still had a handful of high cards, you were in trouble. That happened to me often. One night, I threw down my cards and cried, "I'm schmucked!" Everybody fell on the floor.

Paul had been gradually learning Yiddish words and phrases and often used them at home. They were all colorful and expressive and I began using some of the words, too, though I didn't always know what they meant. The word "schmuck," I learned means the male sex organ. No wonder they laughed. George Burns told that story recently in one his books and made me famous for a few minutes. Friends often asked me to autograph that particular page.

Another expression we got from George and passed along to our children was equally expressive. When George or Willie really hated something, they'd say, "It's a glass!" If it were even worse than that, it was "A glass with an egg!" That one puzzled me.

"What does that mean – a glass?" I asked Paul.

"It means a glass of poo poo," he explained, though he used a more exact four-letter word.

Those gin rummy nights were fun and allowed me to know the wives and Gracie better. We played on until the boys came by after they'd finished work and then we'd have refreshments.

George and Gracie entertained often at their lovely Beverly Hills home. George called the parties sociables. They were mostly small, intimate groups, always including a piano player (sometimes Johnny Greene, composer of "Body and Soul") who was a good friend. The children, Sandra and Ronnie, would often be there for part of the evening anyway. Both of them were adopted at birth from the famous Cradle in Chicago. They were a happy family, and we liked to spend time with them.

During the summer, when the show was on hiatus, we were invited to use their swimming pool as if it were our own. There was a pool house with dressing rooms, baths, and all the important conveniences; we could just go back to the pool whenever we wanted to without disturbing George and Gracie. Gracie seldom used the pool, but George did his laps every morning, after which he went to the club – that was Hillcrest Golf Club – played eighteen holes, and then joined a big round table in the dining room for lunch. That was the comedians' table and most days included George, Jack Benny, Georgie Jessel, Milton Berle, Groucho Marx, and others. After lunch they played Bridge. No wonder George enjoyed his life. It seemed ideal to me.

Once Paul and I went to the baseball game with George and Groucho. George had a box. Paul and I sat in the front seats, George and Groucho behind us. In those days, we always wore hats, and of course, I had one on that day. Groucho spent the whole afternoon making jokes about my hat. Sometimes his humor could be cruel, but I didn't mind. I was always a baseball fan, and I was thrilled to be there with such celebrities.

George has always loved to sing and had a repertoire of old songs nobody else had ever heard of. At the sociables, he always sang after dinner. I'll admit that sometimes the rest of us would sigh and roll our eyes when it came time for the concert, but never Gracie. She always clapped her hands delightedly and cried, "Oh, good, Nattie, sing it again!" He was always Nattie to her and she was "Googie" to him.

In the summer of 1944, the Republican Convention was held in Chicago. The publicity people got the idea that Gracie should go to the convention and write a funny column about it every day for the papers. George didn't go along, but Paul did. He was the one who actually wrote the columns. They stayed at the Ambassador Hotel. One day, Paul received a call from a long-time friend, Merle Jones, formerly in the sales department of KMBC, Kansas City, and now a vice president at CBS.

"Paul, I just thought I ought to warn you," Merle said. "You were seen having a tête à tête dinner last night with Gracie, someone snapped a picture, and I'm sure it will appear in the papers today."

"Yes, what about it?" Paul asked.

"Well, George is sure to see it," Merle said.

Paul laughed and explained the situation. Gracie wasn't the only one Paul was seen with. He enjoyed having dinner with Louella Parsons, the Hearst Syndicate's popular and powerful gossip columnist, and a good friend of George and Gracie.

Paul was gone about a week, and I really missed him. I was very pregnant that summer and with a two-year-old besides, I was pretty much stuck at home. Luckily, the beautiful Wanda came to stay with me while Paul was gone.

In September, our Linda was born on her father's birthday. I had already bought and wrapped birthday gifts for him, so when I went to the hospital, I took them along, unknown to Paul. Jack and Kay Carson brought Paul to the hospital to see me and the baby that first night. Kay also smuggled in a birthday cake and when I rang for the nurse, one nurse came in with lit candles followed by another with the gifts. Paul was flabbergasted. There was even a box of new-father cigars from the baby.

With my second baby, I stayed only a week at the hospital, but it was still glamour time. I went home again with a baby nurse, this time one who had been for some months at the home of a well-known producer. Around five o'clock, she often said wistfully, "When I was at the so-and-so's, the butler always brought me a cocktail about this time." Her only other conversation that I can remember concerned the California giant redwood trees – the trip to see them being the peak experience of her life.

A month with her was almost too long. Soon I had a real English nanny, Dorothy Oldeshaw, who stayed with us off and on for many years. A real treasure!

We learned to love Laguna Beach, mainly because Keith and Fran Fowler had a house there and Paul was working with him. Paul was a sun worshiper. I really couldn't blame him because he took such a gorgeous tan. With me, it was different. I had to spend days getting what Paul could get in a few hours and I didn't enjoy it half as much. But I tried in spite of my dermatologist who warned me against it. I'd always wanted to be a blonde with a suntan – and by now, I was a blonde. An interesting comment about that is that the blonde of Chicago days (my big rival) came by to visit us one day, and I could hardly keep from laughing because now she had let her hair go back to its natural brown, and I was the blonde. Sic transit hair dye! After our son's birth in 1946, I began to notice a few gray hairs, so my hairdresser suggested that if I lightened my hair a little they wouldn't show. Well, it got lighter and lighter until I was a full-fledged blonde. Paul loved it.

Keith and Fran had a charming house in Hollywood in the Beachwood Drive area. We spent a lot of time there. Fran raised Siamese cats, and at any given time, there were ten to thirty wandering around the place. She loved to be different, daringly different. Sometimes she'd dye her hair a flaming, carroty red and wear a false blonde topknot on top. Once at a party, she wore a black hat with a very wide brim, fringe hanging down all around the edge. People stared!

Keith shrugged and said mildly, "It's the way she gets her kicks."

Fran had a cat tattooed on one hip, a mouse on the other. Her panties said "Boo!" on the seat. One summer in Laguna Beach, she bought a rather large fishing boat and hired a young hippy type who wore a ponytail and one earring – shocking for the times. He did the actual fishing. Paul and I would drive down early in the morning, spend the day on the beach with Keith and Fran, go out to a good restaurant for dinner and then drive home. We were lucky to have Dorothy, our nanny who took good care of the children.

One of our typical memories of Keith is the way he would stand patiently at the beach and calmly wait while Fran arranged a blanket, a chair back, an umbrella, a thermos, suntan oil, and whatever else was needed. Then Keith would settle himself with a book and never move the whole day. Except, of course, when the tide came in closer and closer to his blanket.

"Fran," he would call indolently, "either move me or take me home!"

Keith was one of our favorite people and a brilliant writer.

After Paul Whiteman left, Meredith Wilson brought his orchestra to the show. He featured the Les Paul Trio, which Paul and Bill Goodwin really flipped over. Once when the show was long and needed cuts, George said, "Cut the banjo player!" Paul and Bill nearly choked.

Meredith was a really fine musician. Paul confided in him that he hadn't had much education in classical music and wished he understood it better. Whereupon Meredith wrote a humorous treatise on the classics with records to play at certain points. It was invaluable to both of us.

I have another cherished memory of Meredith when after Sunday brunch at our house one day, he sat down at the piano and played and sang the entire score of his new musical, *The Music Man*.

Among the guest stars who appeared on *Burns and Allen* was my heartthrob, Charles Boyer. Paul invited me to come to the rehearsal and meet him. I'd studied French – even tutored it during the depression years – and all the way to the studio I worked out in my mind what I'd say to Charles Boyer when I was introduced.

"Je suis très heureuse de fair votre connaissance, Monsieur Boyer," I'd say in my perfect Parisian accent.

When the great moment came, he took my hand, looked down at me with those soulful bedroom eyes, clicked his heels, bowed, kissed my hand, and said in vibrant accents, "Madame! I'm charmed!"

I stared like an idiot and never uttered a word, either French or English, the rest of the day.

Another kick was to see Frank Sinatra in the flesh (not much of it) when he was just coming into his own. He sang "Sunday, Monday, and Always" – a popular number of his. In the middle, where he sings, "No use to tell me now what makes the world go round," he always did his little trademark up and down on the same word – "rou-a-ound" – and that's when the girls lost it. They screamed and fainted by the dozens. He was young and skinny and adorable, but I could have talked to him. He didn't strike me dumb.

Cecil B. DeMille was also on the show. This one I heard about – didn't see in person. The great DeMille brought his secretary who did all the talking for him all day. He'd whisper in her ear and then she'd say, "Mr. DeMille wonders if perhaps he could change the line at the top of page seven." We never knew why he didn't talk for himself. The same thing happened once when we were in a small party with Gary Moore at Ciro's, who whispered messages to his wife

66

all evening. It seemed unbearably pretentious to me and I never liked him much after that, although he was at the height of his popularity.

And then there was the night I was sitting in the control room watching the show through the glass. Everyone was joking and laughing until suddenly there was utter silence. I turned around and there was Cary Grant in all his glory. His looks were so blindingly gorgeous, it struck you like a blow.

We did a lot of traveling with *Burns and Allen* – usually on the train since Gracie hated to fly. Sometimes when we were in a strange city and Gracie needed to do some shopping, I'd go along as a sort of protection. She would invariably be surrounded by fans wanting her autograph. Graciously, she would oblige them but after a while, I would speak my lines.

"Miss Allen," I'd say rather sternly, "we must go. You'll be late for your appointment."

Then Gracie would smile and shrug helplessly like, "What can I do? They won't let me be free!"

I didn't mind doing that. I'd seen George in the Brown Derby try over and over again to get a bite of food to his mouth. Somebody always interrupted him – even grabbed his arm and demanded an autograph for Aunt Minnie.

We had a lot of fabulous trips on trains. Trains were luxurious in those days, and we often crossed the country on the Super Chief and the 20th Century Limited. I remember one trip when Gracie, Louise Burns, Elvia Allman, Mrs. Paul Whiteman, and I spent the whole time in Gracie's room playing gin rummy. Our breakfast was sent in and we went on playing. Coffee. More playing. Lunch. More cards. Cocktails. More games. Exhausted, we finally joined our husbands for dinner in the diner. Nothing could be finer.

That trip we were headed for Philadelphia. We all went backstage at the big theatre studio for the rehearsal. We wanted to hear the guest star, Jose Iturbi, play. And boy he did he. Not only did he play his numbers for the show, but he graciously fulfilled all our requests. What privileges we enjoyed! I never got used to all the glamour and privilege, never tired of it, and never failed to be grateful to Paul for providing me with such a world!

7

London, Paris, Television

In 1948, we moved to a beautiful, big house in the Toluca Lake area. It had more than an acre of ground and a pool. We had our three children by then: Linda, Carol, and Tony. I was ready to retire from the pregnancy derby, and we hired a couple to help us ease into the gracious life. As often happens though, just when everything seems perfect, life reminds you that you're human, and this is reality. What happened was I got sick. I had to have a very serious surgery on a kidney. It was painful and miserable, with a long convalescence. I was just regaining my strength and had begun to feel that maybe there was, after all, a rose garden in my future. Paul came home one day, and there it was, sure enough.

"How'd you like to go to Europe?" he asked. Before I could manage to say anything he continued, "With George and Gracie!"

"You mean really? Europe? George and Gracie?" There was an echo in the room.

"They're appearing at the London Palladium, and they want me to go along in case they need a writer."

"That's wonderful, but where do I fit in?"

"Well, Sandra and Ronnie are going along, and they thought maybe you and the kids could do some sightseeing while we're working." Sandra and Ronnie, George and Gracie's children, were in their early teens at the time.

That was very much okay with me, but I was sure they were asking me not only to be a companion for the kids but also because they were the nice, generous people they were. Either way, I was beginning to smell the roses.

We'd leave in July, sail on the Queen Elizabeth I, and stay at the Savoy Hotel. I shopped for clothes, because you had to dress for dinner every night on the ship. Maybe you did that in London at the Savoy too. As usual, I economized. I'd been raised that way – it was too strong a habit to change now.

One day I was lying by the pool in my bathing suit when Paul made a quick, unscheduled trip home, handed me a large box, and rushed back to the studio. The box contained a lovely dark, mink stole. I put it on over my bathing suit and it felt so gooood! When I phoned Paul, he said, "I can't let you go on that trip with Gracie, dripping furs and jewels – and you without a single fur to your name." This was before we all become conservation-minded and gave up wearing furs.

Paul's mother and sister came out to California to visit, and it was decided to leave our son Tony in their charge, along with our nice couple, and on my way to New York, I'd take the girls to Kansas City to stay with my mother.

And so – joy divine! We sailed at midnight from New York harbor. Everyone said, "Be sure you are on deck to see the Statue of Liberty as you sail. It's a thrill you'll never forget."

An hour before we sailed, I took two Dramamine capsules, just as my doctor ordered. I had always been subject to motion sickness, and I certainly didn't want to spoil this voyage by being seasick. Well, I wasn't seasick. What I was… was asleep. I'd never had Dramamine before and didn't realize how susceptible I was. So I missed the Statue of Liberty at midnight.

Our first-class stateroom was huge, with twin beds and a complete bath with tub, just like in the A movies. The first night out, Ronnie, who was only twelve, filled his tub to the brim and the water sloshed out all over his bathroom. Help had to be summoned.

There were definitely classes on that ship. We were given a tour, and I couldn't help feeling that passengers in third class, though their quarters were cramped, were having more fun than we were.

We had our own reserved deck chairs, and every day at teatime we all assembled to be served tea by waiters in satin knee breeches and silk stockings. The tea was accompanied by silver epergnes of scones, watercress sandwiches, and little pastries. After that, Paul and I usually attended the movie, being the fans we were, and then it was time to dress for dinner. Each night, Gracie wore a gown more lovely than any I'd ever seen, and Sandra was beautifully dressed for a young girl of thirteen. I wore my little bargain formals, but with my mink stole on top, I felt like a queen. What's more, after dinner there was dancing, and I got to dance with George. He's a fantastic dancer. After all, he got his start as part of a ballroom dance team. As for me, I'm a dancing fool.

I should mention that in our party were dancer-comedian Ben Blue and his wife. They were to be in George and Gracie's act. Ben had been gone for a long time, but he was a unique and funny performer with a special quality nobody else had.

On the last day of our voyage, I got up at dawn to look out one of our portholes and watch the passengers disembarking at LeHavre board the tenders manned by French sailors in striped shirts and berets, bound for France. I could actually see it – France! I don't know why, maybe because of my love for the French language, but I've always had a special feeling for France, and now there it was, right before my eyes!

The Savoy was wonderful – old and elegant and British and wonderful – but I couldn't resist stomping down the corridors now and then so I could boast that I'd been "Stompin' at the Savoy."

London was shocking – whole blocks bombed out during the Battle of Britain. Many things were scarce. A friend of ours who had visited us in the states, arrived one day with a special gift for us, two fresh eggs, which she carried in her coat pocket. It was possible to get the room service on our floor to cook them for us. We ate mostly at private clubs since we were well-connected. One night there was excitement in the air. Steak – real steak was on the menu. Of course, we ordered it, and it turned out to be as thin as cardboard and about as tasty!

Most of the time, while George and Gracie rehearsed at the Palladium, and Paul stood by to make changes or write new scenes, the kids and I had a ball. George had hired a car and a chauffeur-guide to take us simply everywhere. Sometimes Paul was free to come with us. We were all invited for cocktails at the American Embassy – fancy that! I'd had good advice before I left home, so I took lots of new nylon stockings with me, which I used as tips everywhere we went. They were really appreciated.

After their opening at the Palladium, the manager, Val Parnell, threw a big party for George and Gracie at his townhouse. Jack Benny was in town, though George didn't know it. He'd flown in just to see their act, and that night at the party, by arrangement with Val Parnell, he telephoned George from a second phone in one of the other rooms. When George answered, and Jack began his conversation, George, as usual, hung up on him. Just at the moment when George was laughing and telling us about how he'd hung up on Jack who was way out in California, Jack walked into the room. Jack had the last laugh. Jane Wyman was with him. She was in town on some business and after that, Jack and Jane were in our party everywhere we went.

We went to Paris for a week. It was a very short flight across the English Channel. One man said the only thing good about London in those days was that it was so close to Paris. I didn't quite agree with him. I loved London, even bombed out and with the scarcity of food. But Paris – ah – Paris! We stayed at the Georges Cinq, very near the

72

Arc de Triomphe. We went everywhere and often as we entered a room, the musicians played "California, Here I Come." Paul had a couple of days in bed with the well-known Turista, but as soon as I saw to his comfort, I was off on tours with American Express. Paul occupied his time watching out the window as the rats frolicked on the rooftops of Paris.

One thing I promised myself: I would never again travel to Europe, especially Paris, without a glamorous nightgown. I had taken along a practical, cotton, shortie gown, but still every night it was laid out in splendor on the bed for me. How embarrassing! I thought, I had to shop – though shopping was not my thing. Still, I did buy a Paris hat with a plume, two frilly blouses, gloves, and lots of perfume for gifts. In London, I'd bought cashmere sweaters and scotch plaid in the Stuart and MacBeth clan tartans. I had them made up into pleated skirts for me and the girls when we got home.

When it came time to leave, we were sad, but anxious to see our children. I was still awed by flying. To have dinner in Paris one night and the next night be in Kansas City at my mother's just boggled my mind.

Very shortly after we returned to Hollywood, my cousin, Martha, visited me from Missouri. I took her to Romanoff's for lunch. That's where I took all visitors if I could get in, because you were sure to see very big stars there. That particular day was no exception. The stars were there all right – Gary Cooper and Greer Garson, among others – but the big thrill was that Jack Benny came in and clear from the doorway he called, out, "Ruth! Didn't we have fun in London?" Every head turned to look at me. My cousin was impressed.

Back in Hollywood, all the talk was about television. At every radio show, the big question was to convert or not to convert and when. It was a whole new ball game. Performers who could read lines from a script, could not necessarily act in a visual medium. Of course,

73

for George and Gracie, it was natural. Years of vaudeville had prepared them. At first, Gracie was apprehensive about having to memorize all those lines every week, but soon it became a necessity if you wanted to compete at all.

After weeks of discussion, they finally came up with a format they thought would work. It was very loose and informal. George could step in and out of the scene and set up a situation or comment on it directly to the audience. A kind of *Our Town* approach.

They had to go to New York to start the new series because New York in 1950 was the center of television. The west coast was three thousand miles away from where things were happening.

"I've been trying to think of a way to do television," Fred Allen said, one day, when he, Paul, and George met in New York. "Now you fellas have come up with it."

It really worked beautifully. For instance, when the character of Harry Morton made one of its many cast changes, George would simply step out of the scene and say, "Oh, by the way, tonight Blanche Morton is going to have a new husband." The people didn't seem to mind.

In New York, the whole gang stayed at the Algonquin, beginning a long-time our love affair with that hotel. At first, they did the TV show only every other week because television seemed too formidable to tackle every single week. Bea Benaderet flew in every two weeks for the show, and I suppose some others did too, but most of the regulars settled in.

After weeks away from my husband, I made arrangements to fly to New York for a visit. I, too, was charmed by the Algonquin. It was small enough to be intimate, all the employees remained year after year, and like in *Cheers*, everybody knew your name. They served tea every afternoon in the lobby, and an after-theater supper that made you feel as though you were at a private party.

Besides that, they had a resident cat. In the beginning, it was Rusty whose small door from the lobby is still there. For years though, the Algonquin cats have been called Hamlet I, Hamlet II, and Hamlet III. Most of them are gifts from the Algonquin's good friend, *The New Yorker* magazine.

We met the magazine's owners, Mary and Ben Bodne, who told us about how they'd come to the hotel on their honeymoon, fallen in love with it, bought it, and have lived there ever since. I was glad Paul had a homey place to stay, though he didn't eat many meals there. To economize, he walked about a block to the automat. It fascinated him since he'd never seen anything like that before.

After my two weeks visit, I had to go back home, and I began to think. It looked like the move to New York might be permanent, so with Paul's agreement, I put our house on the market. Among the prospective buyers who came to see it were Bette Davis (it was so close to Warner Brothers), Debbie Reynolds and Eddie Fisher (they were newlyweds), and Gordon and Sheila MacRae. We didn't sell it and I was very glad because, in due time, the show moved back to Hollywood. Lucille Ball and Desi Arnaz had begun filming their show, the idea caught on, and that took a lot of the pressure off. You didn't have to worry so much about forgetting a line or tripping over a cable.

Our easy, pleasant life resumed, and we were very happy. I don't mean it was easy for Paul, but at least they had to do a show only every other week. And he was at home. He had some free time and wrote an episode of *Mr. Blandings Builds His Dream House*, a radio show starring Cary Grant and his then wife, Betsy Drake. Of course, it was good and Don Sharp, the producer, kept calling Paul urging him to write another. Paul really didn't have the time, because *Burns and Allen* was rapidly deciding to go every week, but still the producer called. I had done quite a bit of radio writing so, all on my

75

own, I wrote a script for Mr. Blandings. I thought if there was anything I knew something about, it was houses. I'd always wanted to build my dream house. When I showed the script to Paul, he liked it.

"You know, this is good!" he said in surprise.

"Well, you don't have to act so shocked!" I answered.

"I think I'll show it to Don," he said.

"Well, for goodness sakes, don't tell him your wife wrote it. That's the kiss of death!" I said.

So Paul turned in the script. He didn't put any name on it. Soon he got a call from Don.

"You didn't write that script, did you?" he asked.

"No, I didn't. Do you like it?"

"Yes, I do. I'd like to buy it, but I have to know who wrote it."

So that's how I sold my script. They paid me two thousand dollars for it, a far cry from the fifteen dollars I got for *Dan Dunn*. I was jubilant until I got a call from Don.

"Could you come over to my office, Ruth? We have a few simple rewrites we want to talk to you about."

I went. What they asked for didn't seem too difficult. "I'll go home and work on it and have it for you tomorrow," I said.

"Better still," Don said, "we have an empty office with a typewriter right across the hall. Why don't you just go in and do it now?"

I agreed, but I was a little nervous about it. I had counted on asking Paul's advice. I settled myself at the typewriter in the vacant office and tried to think. Pretty soon I heard footsteps and felt a presence in the room. I turned around and there was Cary Grant looking over my shoulder. Gad! I seemed destined to run into Cary Grant!

"Hello," I quavered.

76

"Hello, Ruth," he answered, sounding just like Cary Grant.

If I was nervous before, now I was in shock. "You know, I've forgotten an appointment," I said, gathering up my things. "I'm going to have to take this home and bring it back tomorrow."

When I got home, I called Paul and said just one word, "HE-L-L-P!"

Of course, Paul helped me rewrite that night, and I was saved.

In no time at all, *Burns and Allen* was sailing along on television weekly, so when Paul got an interesting offer, he seriously considered it. Dennis Day, who was very hot at that moment, wanted to leave *The Jack Benny Show* and do a show of his own. If Paul would create a show for him, he could produce it and own part of it. That was tempting. So far, Paul had worked only on well-established shows – *Fibber McGee and Molly, Rudy Vallee, Burns and Allen* – but he knew the only way to advance his career and make more money was to venture into ownership. Dennis was a clever comedian who, besides his glorious tenor voice, was a really good mimic.

Paul had a talk with George. Ten years on the same show was a long time. A fellow could get stale. A fellow might need a change. A fellow could also do a lot worse. George Burns was one of the nicest, kindest bosses Paul had ever known. He didn't want to lose Paul. He offered inducements. In the end, Paul had to take the chance – so, regretfully, in the spring of 1952, he made the break.

8

Dennis Day, Ray Bolger, Ed Wynn

Everything was different now – exciting, scary, and unknown. Writing ten years for the same show, the same stars, the same boss, had given Paul and me, too, a sense of security. Now Paul was out there in the deep water again, taking a chance. He'd never created a big show from scratch. Dennis was well-liked but untried as the star of his own show. All the decisions were up to Paul now. He couldn't do it by himself, of course. He definitely needed writing help, so he hired Stanley Shapiro, a young writer he'd known and worked with on *The Burns and Allen Show*, a writer he considered brilliant.

They spent all that summer of 1952 working out the format, the setting, the characters, and the general story line. Dennis would be himself, Dennis Day, the singer. He would live in an apartment house. A beautiful girl also lived there. Dennis wanted to date her but was shy. Hal March played a handsome bachelor who also lived there and had no trouble wooing the girl. She had a little sister, however, played by little eight-year-old Jeri Lou James. (Later, she played Zelda on *Dobie Gillis*. She was Sheilah James then.) The little sister much preferred Dennis and tried to help him.

A very important character was the funny old janitor of the building. Paul wanted Cliff Arquette for that part. Cliff had created the character of Charlie Weaver for himself – a funny, eccentric, old codger, just right for the janitor. The trouble was nobody could find Cliff. He had moved without leaving a forwarding address and nobody could find him. When they finally did run him down, he admitted sheepishly that he was trying to hide from his ex-wife who kept demanding more alimony.

The Dennis Day episodes usually ended with Dennis singing a song to the little girl. It was funny, but it also had charm and heart. That was typical of Paul's writing style.

The new *Dennis Day Show* went on the air in October of 1953. Dennis, the network, the sponsors, and the critics all liked it. Allen Rich, TV editor of the *Los Angeles Times* wrote: "There is a growing school of thought around town to the effect that Dennis Day has a h--l of a show." That's the way it was in 1953. You couldn't say "hell."

We were all happy. Little did we realize the hazards that lie ahead – not around the corner, but right there in plain sight on another network. Opposite *Dennis Day* was another fairly new show that was catching on like wildfire: *I Love Lucy*. *The Hollywood Reporter* reviewer slighted *The Dennis Day Show*, "Opposite *I Love Lucy*, it's a little like the Dodgers meeting the Yankees. It's a good team, but the odds favor the champs." Allen Rich wrote: "Oddly enough, almost everybody I talked to had seen *The Dennis Day Show,* and this is very unusual indeed because according to the ratings, most people are supposed to be watching *I Love Lucy* at the time Dennis is on." What a lousy break! A brand new show with a brand new, untried star going up against a blockbuster like *Lucy*!

Dennis and company all worked hard and held on to enough of their audience to be renewed for a second season. Things looked pretty good, so they decided to go to film. But there was a fly in the ointment – there always had to be one, it seemed – and that was that Stanley and Dennis had some major personality conflicts. Paul managed to smooth things over time and again, but one night he came home, sat down in the den by himself and actually cried.

"What is it? Oh, darling, what is it?" I asked when I discovered him there in the dark.

"I'm just so sorry for Stan," he sobbed. "He was fired today." Stan and Dennis had finally reached the breaking point, and there was nothing Paul could do about it. He admitted Stan had been tactless and Dennis difficult, but Stan was very young, he explained, and Dennis was understandably nervous about Stan's new status. Paul had always thought that things would settle down. Only now, it seemed they wouldn't – at least not for Stan – and as I've said, when Paul liked someone, there was no halfway.

Now that they were filming the show, Dennis began to change. He was getting the adulation from the entourage who always surrounded a film star, and he was becoming temperamental and demanding. Far from being the modest, hardworking fellow he was the first year, he was now beginning to believe his publicity. It happens to a lot of people, particularly when they're young and perhaps haven't had to work their way up through hardships and disappointments.

The situation became too difficult and unpleasant even for Paul, the most agreeable and peace-loving person in the world. Regretfully, he left the show in mid-season – the first and only time he ever did that. It was too bad. We liked Dennis and his wife, Peggy. We loved to hear him sing, we had partied together and enjoyed each other's company. Both agreed there were no hard feelings, but it was over.

One nice residual affect was that we made the acquaintance of a lovely girl named Marian Rees, who was Dennis' secretary at the time. Now she is one of the most successful women producers in television who has won awards for Hallmark Hall of Fame dramas. She and several other girls shared a rented house near us and often came over to swim. One of her housemates, Norma Haglund, became Paul's secretary during *The Bob Cummings Show*.

It was the spring of 1954, and there we were at liberty again, only this time it was vastly different. This time we had more to worry about than paying the rent and getting home for Christmas. We had a big house, three children, and world-class living expenses.

William Morris began to hustle and soon Paul was writing for *The Ray Bolger Show*. He didn't stay with it long, but apparently he had an impact. A *Variety* review said: "A few more like this one and Ray Bolger will be leaving his imprint on the home sets of a Thursday night. It remained for Paul Henning to come up with a story line that called up Bolger's comedic talents heretofore relegated to lesser importance than his nimble footwork." That's my boy!

As for me, I've always been partial to dancers, and Ray was one of the best. Once at a party at our house, I told him how our daughter Linda wanted to be a dancer and was starting ballet lessons. He picked her up – she was only six – and danced around the room with her. I tell her about it, but she can only remember it vaguely and probably didn't even realize she was dancing with one of the most famous dancers in the world.

Meanwhile, William Morris was still hustling. They thought they might be able to sell a show starring S.Z. Sakall, the sweet, old character actor with the jowls and the Hungarian accent. "Cuddles" he was called. He was always in Deanna Durbin pictures being quaint and funny and sweet, helping the young folks with their romances. A trademark of his was to slap his jowls and say, "Nah! Nah! Nah!" Paul and I were invited to the Sakalls' for dinner, so Paul could get better acquainted and get an inspiration for a pilot.

What an evening! I love food and have been known to pig out now and then, but those Hungarians! I never saw the like of it before or since. I don't mean *they* necessarily overate – maybe they were used to it – but the goodies they provided just about put me under the table. We started out with a modest cocktail and a few simple hors d'oeuvres, nothing especially fancy. Then we went to the table. There was soup – delicious, but I don't even remember what kind it was.

Next came a course Paul and I thought was the entrée, stuffed cabbage served with sour cream. It was so good we eagerly took second helpings when it was passed. Little did we know that was just the beginning – the appetizer. I could have gotten up right then totally satisfied. But no! Next came the main course, a big, beautiful roast, accompanied by vegetables, noodles, salad, rolls, everything. When we had eaten ourselves into a stupor, there was homemade cake – rich with chocolate, custard filling, nuts, whipped cream – whatever you can think of that tickles the taste buds, it was there. Jenny Craig, hide your eyes! Weight Watcher, stop your ears!

We all stumbled into the living room and collapsed in the nearest chairs. The evening's entertainment consisted of Cuddles passing around pictures he'd cut out of magazines: pictures of babies, kittens, puppies, all darling, the kind you ooh and ah about. While we were politely exclaiming over the collection of cutouts, Mrs. Sakall passed – guess what! – a box of chocolates. We finally made our excuses and went home early, fell into bed, and the next morning my bathroom scales recorded a five-pound overnight weight gain.

If we were ever invited back, we decided we'd practice restraint, as well as a couple of days of fasting before the event. We also agreed they were charming people, warm, friendly, and unpretentious. Paul thought he might very well be able to write something nice for Cuddles. Alas, it never happened! Paul worked on it until he had a rough draft to show the Morris Agency. That was as far as it went. Somebody discovered, a mite late, that Cuddles simply could not memorize a script, so that was that. We never got another Hungarian dinner. Too bad.

There was a weekly variety show on the air then, an hour long, alternating comedy stars. I wish I could remember who they all were. I do know Ed Wynn was one of them because Paul wrote one for him. It was fun for Paul, or so he said, but hard work, too, because it was a total change from what he was used to doing. Ed Wynn liked sight gags, short and funny. All through the show, characters would walk across the stage with funny bits of business. One night at the dinner table, Paul mentioned that he was trying to think of some sight gags. Our daughter, Carol, who was ten at the time and fancied herself a future writer (she was, actually) asked how much he'd pay for a gag if it was used. They settle on a fee of five dollars.

Next day, Carol submitted a bit and it was used on the show; she was thrilled and made her first money as a writer – as anything, for that manner. At that time, women were wearing their hair in all over curls, which was called a Poodle Cut. Carol's gag was to have a poodle wearing a woman's wig walk across the stage on its hind feet and Ed Wynn would comment, "Oh – a poodle with a woman cut!" It got a laugh. Carol was ecstatic and so was Paul. He was raising a collaborator right in his own home.

Hustle! Hustle! There were some more might-have-beens. Donald O'Connor was one of them. He came out to the house to talk to Paul about it one day. They sat in the den, and I served lunch to them. As soon as they were settled, Donald spied a picture of Paul's automotive brother, Cotton.

"That's Cotton Henning!" Donald cried excitedly.

"Yes, he's my brother," Paul said.

From then on, Donald couldn't talk about anything else. He was a mad racing fan, and Cotton Henning was one of the legends of the auto-racing world. I don't know whether they ever got back on the subject of a TV show for Donald. At least, one never happened.

Another might-have-been involved a big CBS special to star Victor Borge. He wanted to spend time at his home in Denmark and invited Paul and me to visit on his estate while the show was being written. Yum yum! I was practically packing when the deal fell through. CBS and Borge couldn't come to terms on the contract.

Hustle-hustle – still hustle time – but with a difference! Paul and I get a lot of laughs remembering that time – pleasurable memories, too! I like to call it "Duel of the Giants." Paul's contract with the William Morris Agency was set to expire, and of course, they were pressing him to re-sign. At the same time, MCA, Morris' chief competitor in the talent agency field, was well-aware of Paul's track record, and they wanted him to sign with them. The duelers were Sammy Weisbord of William Morris and Mickey Rockford of MCA, both high-powered charismatic representatives of their agencies. Both of them, en garde, faced each other across the Sunset strip, épée's at the ready.

Paul and I were invited to dine at least twice a week at the most expensive, stylish, "in" restaurants, or to nightclubs like Ciro's or Mocambo. Both Sammy and William were charming; they were well schooled in handling much bigger stars than Paul. They flattered him. They flattered me. They painted castles in the air. They talked about building a Henning Dynasty. We loved it. We knew it was hype, but we loved it anyway and were almost tempted to believe it.

MCA got in the first thrust with a list of important clients of theirs who were in the market for a television series. The names were all impressive. William Morris, perhaps a little over confident, didn't offer any bait.

"If you write a show for an MCA star, would you have to sign with them?" I asked.

"I don't think so," Paul said. "And I feel loyalty to William Morris. They took me on when I was nobody, and I'll always respect George Gruskin."

"Do you have to sign with either one of them?" I asked. I kind of liked things the way they were. To change metaphors in midstream, it was like a young girl being wooed by two rich suitors who both plied her with jewels and promises.

84

"I guess I have to have an agent," Paul said. "I need somebody to negotiate contracts for me. I don't know anything about that."

We began to study the MCA list. One name on the list looked awfully good to Paul: Bob Cummings. I agreed. We'd seen him in the movies and liked his work. He was a good actor and certainly handsome. We hadn't cared for his first television show, *My Hero*, but figured it probably wasn't his fault.

MCA was delighted and arranged a meeting immediately. Bob was crazy about Polynesian food so he chose The Tropics in Hollywood for our meeting place. We had some fancy rum drinks with little umbrellas and slices of pineapple sticking out the top. Dinner was lovely, and we all got along great. Bob and Mary were enthusiastic about the new show Paul would create for him and I was thrilled to be sitting there at an intimate table with a movie star I'd seen on the screen with the likes of Hedy Lamarr and Grace Kelly. After dinner, Bob suggested we all go to their house and see some videotapes of *My Hero*. Since we didn't know where they lived, it was decided that Mary would ride with Paul and I with Bob.

The Cummings lived in the Hills of Beverly (like *The Beverly Hillbillies* theme song would describe it some eight years hence). We sat through *My Hero* tapes and tried to laugh. Actually, having smoke come out Bob's ears whenever he kissed the girl wasn't our idea of great wit. Still, Paul wasn't too worried since he knew there would be no more such gimmicks. The evening began to be more friendly and informal. I demonstrated my unique ability to touch my nose with my tongue, a trick I don't usually consider very chic unless I've had rum drinks with umbrellas. By the end of the evening, everyone was feeling no pain.

That is, everybody but William Morris. They didn't like the idea at all and had a big pain in their commissions. Even if Paul did sign with them, the package would belong to MCA and that's where the big money is – in the packaging. Sammy Weisbord's comment to Paul was, "Never go to bed with a fallen woman."

"What does that mean?" I asked Paul.

"It means Bob has had one unsuccessful television series – he's no longer a virgin, so to speak," Paul replied. But since there were no specific offers forthcoming from Morris, *The Bob Cummings Show* seemed a done deal… except that in show business, like any other business, there are various elements which have to be coordinated and brought into harmonious agreement. MCA made mention of ownership, distribution, screen credits, money – all that stuff. Bob Cummings mentioned a lot of the same things from a different point of view. Paul got a word or two in here and there, but frankly, he was mainly eager to get started writing the show. Because of all this wrangling around, Paul thought of George Burns whose company, McCadden Productions (named for the street where Willie lived), was eager to produce some other shows besides *Burns and Allen*. Paul knew that George had the reputation, diplomacy, and clout to gather up all the elements and put them together so they'd spell Mother. And so he did.

9

The Bob Cummings Show

Paul spent the summer of 1954 writing the Cummings pilot. Bob was to be cast as a photographer with lots of beautiful models posing for him and making a play for him, and vice versa, but neither managing to succeed. Some of the critics likened the show to a more acceptable version of *Playboy*. I don't think Paul had anything like that in mind. All he knew was that once when he had approached the publicity people for *Burns and Allen*, complaining that the show wasn't getting its share of attention in the media, they had told him it would be a lot easier if there were some pretty girls around. This time, he vowed, he would provide the girls. As a contrast, Bob would have a plain-looking secretary in love with him, who pines for him but knows she hasn't a chance. A character like that would touch a responsive chord in a lot of women. At home, Bob would live with his widowed sister, Margaret, and her teen-aged son, Chuck. They would keep him down-to-earth and show his finer side.

Rosemary DeCamp was an easy choice for Bob's sister, Margaret. She was a proven actress, a beautiful woman, and I thought she even looked enough like Bob to be his sister. Dwayne Hickman, her son, Chuck, was a nice, clean-cut American boy who would worship Uncle Bob like a hero, but he was kept in line by his old-fashioned mother.

The secretary, Schultzie, was harder to find. Paul spent hours looking through Screen Actors' Guild books, interviewing a lot of prospects, but none of them seemed just right. Then one night at an intimate little night spot on Sunset Boulevard, Cabaret Concert, located east toward the city rather than west on the upscale Strip, we saw Ann B. Davis. Paul was interested. She was asked to come to the office. They tested her and Eureka! They had their Schultzie! She was a fine actress, a little on the plain side, but she was so loyal, and so in love with her boss, hopelessly, she knew, that everybody liked her and kept hoping against hope that one day she'd get her man.

The show was done in a radically different way – keeping it all in the family, so to speak. Paul would produce and write. Bob would star and eventually direct. They would use two cameras shooting from different locations, thereby eliminating the need for constant repetitions of shots to get new angles and close-ups. What's more, they had plenty of rehearsal and shot it in one day. Very economical. It worked. By the time they got everything ready though, there was no room for the show in the fall lineup, so they made their debut in January 1955 as a replacement for one of the season's failures.

There was the big question of the laugh track. Doing funny lines to absolute silence is depressing and takes away from the audience's enjoyment. You're not as apt to laugh if nobody else is laughing. It's catching. Back in the *Fibber McGee and Molly* days, I had been hired as a shill. I was paid five dollars to come to the show and laugh out loud at the jokes. The theory was that other people would join in and they did. There may have been about six of us strategically placed. My own problem was that if I brought a friend along, I felt a little embarrassed laughing raucously – not my usual style – and I couldn't explain, due to my contractual promise.

The use of recorded laugh tracks, however, was getting a lot of criticism. Some shows overused them, and there'd be wild laughter after lines that weren't particularly funny. Besides, you can't really tell what people are going to laugh at. They decided to preview the filmed show every other week, two at a time, for a live audience. That way the actual laughter was recorded and far from having to add laughter, they often had to take some out when it was so loud or

88

prolonged that it interfered with the lines. It's interesting that in the *Hollywood Reporter* review, it said, "Series can also boast one of the most hysterical laugh tracks ever unleashed on the public." He didn't know, of course, that those laughs were real.

The reviews were good. They gave Bob Cummings most of the credit, which, of course, he deserved. But Paul had not made his mark yet with the critics and received barely a mention at the end of the reviews. The show got an overnight rating in Trendex (in the days before Nielsen) of 12.1; that wasn't good. It was largely attributed to three things: first, it was a mid-season opening, which is never helpful; second, it was opposite the very popular *What's My Line?* in the East, and their rating was 16.9; and third, it was on quite late on Sundays in the West after audiences who were still around had their fill of comedy. Most important though, everybody seemed to like it.

It was nominated for a Best New Comedy Series Emmy that very first year. The show received more nominations for Bob as Best Actor, Paul as Best Producer, Stanley Frazan and Guy Scarpitta for Best Editing, and Ann B. Davis for Best Supporting Actress. They were on the air for five years and reaped dozens of nominations, but the only one who won the prize was Ann B. Davis for "Schultzie" – two or three times.

The *Variety* review later on (alas it isn't dated in my scrapbook) began: "Ciggie sponsor (Winston) of *The Bob Cummings Show* must've taken the tack 'if we can knock off *What's My Line?* at 10:30 p.m., we should do as well or better against Groucho Marx at an earlier hour of 8 p.m.'" In the same review, it said Cummings has a rating of 23.5 and Groucho has 33.7, "which is in nose-bleed territory." By this time, Paul and his co-writers, Dick Wesson, Shirley Gordon, Bill Manhoff (at various times) got a lot more credit. It remained for Charles Mercer of the Boston Daily Globe, in 1959, to write an article about Paul: "One of the chief reasons for the success and health of *The Bob Cummings Show* is that it is as solidly constructed as one of those gold vaults at Fort Knox." I've been saying that Paul was a great constructionist. It made me feel good to know somebody else recognized that fact.

Bob was a character. Aren't we all? Bob was a health nut, first and foremost. He took about fifty vitamin pills a day and shot himself in the fanny at lunchtime with a special supplement. He exercised a lot, mostly swimming, but he was a good, all-round athlete and kept in extremely good shape. He must have been pushing fifty at the time but looked twenty years younger. He became involved in a lot of health fads and was constantly trying to convince others to try them.

One night, we were invited to their house for dinner with the proviso that we eat whatever they served without complaint. We agreed. It was a lovely, balmy night. A small table was set by the pool, the outside lights were low-key and romantic, the scent of jasmine was in the air. Of course, no cocktails were served, so we sat right down to partake in our first course. Before each place was a silver dish shaped like a seashell, filled with pills – all shapes, sizes, and colors. In the middle of the table was a large pitcher of court bouillon. Bob led the way. He poured himself a tall glass of bouillon and swallowed all the pills with just a few gulps. We all tried to follow suit but I had to keep refilling my glass to get them all down. That over, my stomach felt a little odd, but Bob assured us we'd be in great shape as soon as the pills had time to metabolize and do their thing.

The main course was a small New York steak, broiled. Nothing else. No potatoes, no vegetables, no salad, no bread. I didn't mind. That steak tasted like heaven to me and sort of pushed those capsules down my gullet. There was dessert; they explained it was only in deference to us, since we were guests and probably expected it. It was ice cream. Oh boy, I thought, really surprised. But this ice cream was different. It was made from protein powder and carrots. It

90

really didn't taste much like ice cream, but it wasn't bad either. Somehow, a little sugar or honey must have sneaked in.

After dinner, a new performer came on stage – Bob's trainer. He was a muscular young man who put Bob and the other members of his family through their paces several times a week. We all adjourned to the living room where we were entertained with a demonstration. We were urged to try some of the exercises, but mostly we made excuses since one of the procedures was for Bob to lie down on the floor and let the trainer walk up and down his back in his bare feet.

I hasten to add that Bob didn't eat that way all the time. We often had dinner at their house or other people's houses or at restaurants where there was regular food. But he always did take the vitamins. One of Robert Junior's jobs was to count out the different pills every day and put them in separate bottles, morning, noon, and night, so that his father wouldn't have to interrupt his busy schedule to take on such a time-consuming chore.

Another of Bob's big passions was Astrology. Everybody was called by his or her Zodiac sign. He termed himself "Two-faced Gemini," Paul was "Nit picking Virgo," and I was "Passionate Sagittarius." Carroll Righter, Astrologer for the stars and the *Los Angeles Times*, was his mentor and guide. Bob gifted Carroll Righter's book to Paul in hopes that Paul could insert some of the wisdom into the show. Paul was appalled. The first thing he noted was that a Gemini (Bob) and a Virgo (Paul) should never enter a business venture together. The next little gem of wisdom was that a Virgo (Paul) and a Sagittarius (me) should never marry. There went the ball game! To my recollection, he never put anything more in the script than a casual reference to the stars.

Bob's wife, Mary, was a bit more realistic. Once when it was extremely important for Bob to go to New York one weekend (something about getting his picture on the cover of a magazine), everything was planned and then Bob flatly refused to go. Carroll Righter had said the stars were not right, or the moon, or whatever. Paul tried every persuasion in vain. Then there was a call from Mary.

"How important is this trip to New York?," she asked getting right to the point.

"Very important," Paul answered, not mincing words.

"Don't cancel anything," Mary said, "I'll get back to you later."

She did. "Carroll Righter is going to change his prediction," she said. And he did. And Bob went to New York. Everything was fine.

I don't mean to downgrade Astrology. I presume there is something to it. When I read my own horoscope and it says nice, complimentary things about Sagittarians, (Winston Churchill and Frank Sinatra are fellow Sagittarians), I think there definitely is something to it. But when I read that I'm stubborn, and opinionated, and a few other bad things, I don't believe it anymore.

But I have to admit that my life is intimately entwined with three Virgos, and it's hard not to see the nit-picking elements in them all. Paul is nasty clean. You'll have to take my word for that. My sister washes her dishes and THEN puts them through the dishwasher. My daughter, Linda, gift-wraps a package so precisely, so tightly, there's no need of a card. You just know it's from Linda. I try to keep an open mind.

In June of that year, 1955, our social life was definitely on the fast track. On June 4, George and Gracie gave a really, really big party in a private room at Romanoff's. We were invited and spent the whole evening sitting on the sidelines and gawking at movie stars. As they say, Tout Hollywood was there. (Or maybe that's only Tout Paris.) Every big star I'd ever thought or dreamed of was there, all except one – Clark Gable. They said he almost never went to parties. I don't know why. Everyone was dressed to the nines and they all looked fabulous, but I'll tell you the one who impressed me the most, Lauren Bacall. She was class personified! Another really stunning lady was Merle Oberon.

Just one week later on June 11, the Cummings had a big bash at their house for seventy-five guests. We got acquainted with some of their best friends: the Art Linkletters and the Milton Berles. I remember sitting on the floor next to the Berles' and laughing a lot at Milton's stream of jokes.

And to prove that June was bustin' out all over, toward the end of the month, we all went to Hawaii. They planned to film some commercials there, which was probably a good idea, but mainly, Bob loved Hawaii and since I was going along, I thought it was a brilliant inspiration. We even planned to take along our daughter, Carol, then thirteen and with a teenage crush on Bob. We stayed about three weeks – plenty long to eat more pineapple than your stomach could stand, to lie on the beach until you were burnt to a crisp, to listen to more steel guitars and jungle drums than Dorothy Lamour, and to watch lots of hula dancers going to a hukilau until you longed for a tango or even the Charleston. I'm only kidding, of course. I loved it and had a wonderful time. So did Carol. It was a popular vacation spot, and we met a lot of stars there. Carol got to have her picture taken with Red Skelton on the beach. Katy Jurado, fresh from her triumph in *High Noon*, was in our party most days. And Lew Wasserman, head honcho of the Music Corporation or America or MCA, was very much in evidence. At lunch one day, I admired an unusual ring Mrs. Wasserman was wearing and asked her what kind of stone it was.

"Don't you know, dear?" Lew answered for her, "That's the kind of ring we always give to the wives of men who sign with us." Obviously, Paul hadn't signed a contract yet.

We ate dinner at a different restaurant every night, dressing to the teeth in sarongs or strapless cottons that would show off our new tans, wearing flower leis and a flower over one ear. We ate poi (rather gummy and tasteless but edible) and raw fish (sorry, not for me, I barely like it cooked) and coconut ice cream, which was one of the best things I ever tasted. During the day, they did film some commercials on the beach, but Paul had plenty of time to do his sun worshipping. Mary and I took dance lessons every day at a regular dance studio with a professional teacher. I loved that. We learned to do several hulas and would have liked to get into Tahitian dancing, much harder and more lively, but there wasn't time enough. When we had to leave, our teacher presented us with records of our dances and real grass skirts she had fashioned from tiki leaves. They were in plastic bags, which she said the airline hostess would keep refrigerated for us on the trip home. I kept mine all summer and all our guests had to endure my hulas until it finally wilted.

One thing we found out about Bob while we were there was that he was really attracted to Polynesian women. He said one reason he married Mary was for her Hawaiian cheekbones. They seemed to fancy him, too, the Polynesian women. He received some sizzling fan letters in his hotel box while we were there.

After we were home, we had a catered Hawaiian luau for our friends – doesn't everyone? – where we all sat on the floor and I did the hula while my grass skirt was still fresh.

Then it was back to work for Paul getting scripts written to start the second season. He had learned from experience that you can never make up a name for a character that somebody real doesn't have. That's why he often named his people after friends or relatives.

94

Then if anybody complained or threatened to sue, he could always say the character was named for his cousin who had given him permission. A male character on the show, a pilot from an airline and somewhat of a womanizer who had eyes for Bob's sister, Margaret, was called Paul Fonda after a dear old friend of ours from our Kansas City days. Lyle Talbot was the actor who played the part, and I couldn't help remembering our first little apartment on Whitley in Hollywood when he was the only one in the building with a real acting job, and therefore, much too important for us to know. It was fun getting the real and the reel Paul Fondas together. Another character was a pretty teenage girl, whom Paul called Carol Henning after our daughter.

During the run of *The Bob Cummings Show*, our son, Tony, got a taste of show business. Paul had written in a part for a newsboy who would have a long speech to deliver, filled with big words. He thought he might have a hard time casting it. Hesitantly, timidly, I said I thought that Tony could do it. He was quite young and small for his age, as all members of our family are, and would look even younger than his years. Paul agreed to audition him, and of course, Tony did it brilliantly. They hired him… after I took him down to the Board of Education and got him a work permit. He was so good that we had calls the next day from several agents who wanted to handle him. Tony declined.

"Who wants to be a movie star?" he said.

Later in the series, there was another part for a small boy, Tony, again. This time it was with Bob playing Grandpa Collins and part of the scene called for Tony to eat a piece of birthday cake. They did several takes of the scene and each time, more birthday cake. Tony rather liked that part.

Other things came along, calls from hopeful agents, and Tony, who still had no show biz ambitions, was beginning to like the idea of paychecks involved. He had decided to take what came along and save for his first car when he reached sixteen. He did a small part on *Those Whiting Girls*, a short-lived series starring singer Margaret Whiting and her sister.

Then there was a big cattle call audition to cast a boy for the son of Claudette Colbert in a pilot where she'd be elected president of the United States. I picked Tony up at school, we rushed home, and I made him take a bath and put on clean clothes before we went to the studio. He hated that part of it. What small boy loves baths?

Anyway, we went, it took hours, but he survived the first elimination process. The next day we went again, and we repeated the same routine – bath, clean clothes, studio. Tony was disgusted, but the excitement was contagious. They eliminated a lot more, but Tony was still in the running. He began to think that a part like that could earn him enough money to get a really great car. Several more baths and clean shirts, and it was down to three. Tony didn't get it. The kid who did was a cute, freckle-faced boy who smelled to high heaven – just boy smell. Tony was really disappointed and I caught a lot of flack about all those unnecessary baths. He did work in the pilot as a consolation prize. The show was never sold, so it was all academic anyway.

Some years later, a representative of Disney Studios came to our house to ask if we would allow them to film there for a short time. It seemed they were searching the neighborhood for a house that didn't look typically "Californian." It was to be the home of an eastern man, and our house was authentic English architecture and very solid looking. The film was *Moochie of the Little League*.

"I suppose you'll use a lot of boys on Moochie's baseball team," I asked craftily.

"Oh yes," he replied.

"Well, I have a son about the right age...." You know the drill. The result was that I agreed they could film the outside of our house at one hundred dollars a day if they put Tony in the picture. Was I a stage mother? You bet! Incidentally, they pay a lot more now to use a house.

I enjoyed going to the studio with Tony as his guardian. All kids who were underage had to have one. However, it did get boring for me – and for Tony, too. That ended his thespian career. He didn't earn enough to buy a fancy car, but we helped him get a Volkswagen. Also, the films we have of *The Bob Cummings Show* in which he appeared are invaluable now. He shows them to his sons, and they marvel at their dad. Alex, his older son, looked exactly like him at that age.

Working for a major star includes a lot of perks. You rub elbows with many interesting people. I've already mentioned Art Linkletter and Milton Berle, close friends of Bob's, but there were others – like Ken Murray.

We met Ken for the first time in Las Vegas where he was playing during one of our quick trips. We went for the shows, which were choice! We never gambled except for a few coins in the slots. A lot of the daytime was spent by the pool in the sun, and that's where we first met Ken. He and Paul hit it off right away and met the next day for brunch and talked for hours. It was the beginning of a long friendship. Ken was well-known not only because of his comedy talent and his long running show, *Blackouts*, but also for his home movies of the stars. It had been a hobby of his ever since he'd arrived in Hollywood. He used to show us some of them at his house, and by now the collection is invaluable and much in demand.

It was through Ken that we met Paul's early singing idol, Gene Austin. Paul had a high tenor, not unlike Austin's, whom he shamelessly imitated during his short singing career. The first time we went out together with the Murrays and the Austins, we wound up at the Murray's house, and I was bold enough to ask Gene to play two numbers, which had provided a romantic musical background during my early teens: "Forgive Me" and "Someday Sweetheart." Gene was not a well man and died much too soon. Paul was asked to deliver his eulogy at his funeral, which he did beautifully to Gene's recording of "Lonesome Road." In the hospital, during Gene's last stay, he had jokingly told us that he had enough ex-wives to be his pallbearers.

Las Vegas brings to mind Joi Lansing, one of the gorgeous models who graced *The Bob Cummings Show* regularly. She was appearing there, and one day came over to visit and sun with us by the Desert Inn pool. We were lying there with our eyes closed, but it was no trick to guess when Joi made her entrance. There was a chorus of male "Ahhhhhs." Joi was blonde and beautiful, with long legs, narrow hips, and a very large bosom, thanks to plastic surgery. Even if I hadn't known about that, I would have guessed because when she lay down, her bust still stood straight up. Nature simply doesn't do that. Joi was a nice girl. The figure enhancement helped her to make a living, and nobody can be blamed for that. Unfortunately, she died much too young of cancer.

And of course, there was Fred Allen. We went to New York almost every year on business but also for fun because we loved the Algonquin Hotel and the Broadway plays. On one of those occasions, Paul and Fred were introduced by Bob Weiskopf who had at one time worked for Fred. Paul never did, but Paul and Bob quickly formed a mutual admiration society. We became good friends with him and Portland. Whenever we were in New York, we always had dinner with them and usually went to a play.

Once when we were with old friends from Paul's school days, they couldn't wait to see Fred. They were just sure he'd say something funny right off the bat. Paul worried about that. He explained that comedians aren't necessarily funny on their own time. They need a rest sometimes. At that moment, there was a knock at the door of our suite, and there stood Fred and Portland. They walked into the room, saw the management's complimentary basket of fruit on the TV set, and Fred remarked drily, "That's the only good thing I've seen on TV all day." We all had a good laugh, and our friends could never be convinced that comedians aren't always funny.

When we walked to the theatre, it seemed to us an awful lot of bums and panhandlers approached Fred. He had a five or ten dollar bill for each of them. They always knew where he'd be and managed to cross his path with palms outstretched. Fred knew that and made sure to have the ready cash available.

When Fred and Portland came to California (and it wasn't often enough for us), we always had them over. One night, our dog embarrassed us by barking constantly.

"That's the first time I ever heard a dog barking on spec," Fred remarked.

To explain that remark, writers often wrote on spec, which meant on speculation that the script would be sold. So our dog, Patsy, was barking just in case we had a prowler.

The friendship deepened over the years and when Fred died, he left his collection of joke books and comedy books to Paul in his will. We were honored and proud of those shelves of books.

Ken and Bette Lou Murray had a lot of parties with some fascinating guests. Loretta Young was there once. She looked so stunningly young – I couldn't believe it. People said she slept sixteen hours a day in order to keep her youthful appearance. I don't know if there was any truth to that, but she was lovely.

One night, I met one of my early crushes, Maurice Chevalier, at Ken's house. He was old by that time, with a pink-cheeked complexion and a head of snow-white hair – and he was just as charming as ever.

Sometime during *The Bob Cummings Show*, Paul wrote a pilot for Peter Lawford. We neither one can imagine why Paul did that in the middle of a series but can only surmise it was an urgent request from the William Morris office. Besides, Peter was young then and quite attractive and talented. He wanted very much to sing and dance, so Paul tried to do a light-hearted musical with Peter as the prince of a mythical European Kingdom, a real fairy tale. In fact, for the lack of any partner on the enterprise, I worked with Paul on it. I loved it.

I have a special feeling in my heart for Howard Duff. Sam Northcross, the agency representative for our sponsor, R.J. Reynolds, knew Ida Lupino and her husband, Howard Duff, from some other show, and so did Dick Wesson, who was working with Paul at that time. One night we all wound up at their house – Ida's and Howard's, I mean. Everyone was having drinks at the bar and being very merry, and I felt totally out of it. It was one of my ulcer periods. Once you have one of those suckers, it tends to return from time to time. During those times, drinking is definitely not recommended.

I sat down in the living room and started thumbing through a magazine. Is there anything more boring than to be the only sober one in a group? Howard came to my rescue. We talked a while. He told me he'd had my same problem and knew just what to do. He fixed me a tall drink made of milk, a tiny bit of bourbon, ice cubes, and a cherry. He called it a milk punch. It tasted good, and made me a part of the group. You don't forget kind gestures like that.

Rose Marie played a regular part on the show. She was warm and friendly and often invited us, as well as Dick and Wini Wesson, to her house for dinner. Her mother lived with them. Rose and her mother were Italian and enthusiastic cooks. They served almost as much food as the Hungarians but with this difference: Rose and her

100

mother never sat down; they just kept bringing more food to the table, passing it, heaping our plates, and watching every mouthful we ate. If we slighted even one dish or didn't take a second helping, they looked woebegone and insisted we didn't like the food. It was a tough job, but somebody had to do it. We enjoyed being her guests.

Rose Marie had started as a child actress when she was called Baby Rose Marie, in case you don't remember. Even as a tot she could belt out a song. Later she learned to become a skilled comedienne and a good actress.

Every year when we went to New York, Sam Northcross (our sponsor's rep) invited us to come out on his boat. Boats were a passion of his, and I'm sure he felt there was no better way to extend hospitality. I think I've mentioned I'm inclined to have motion sickness and on a small boat, that can mean murder. We always found a good reason to decline those boat invitations until one year when Ann B. Davis (Schultzie) happened to be in town and was also invited.

"I think this is the year we go on the boat," Paul said.

"Why this year?" I asked. It was Sunday, and I had been picturing a nice walk up Fifth Avenue, possibly brunch at the Plaza, a lazy afternoon reading the papers, doing the Times crossword puzzle, and tea in the lobby.

"This is the year we have to get a renewal signed," Paul explained, and I could see he wasn't joking. He called Ann and we arranged to take a train to Old Lyme, Connecticut where Sam's boat was moored. There was a wonderful old inn there, Sam's wife, Kitty, had told us about. It was an inn where we could have a fabulous brunch first. That part sounded good to me.

The brunch was fabulous... if not lethal. First, we had champagne. Then other preposterous preliminaries, and finally, lobster. It was topped off with a heavenly, rich pecan coffee cake.

101

Then it was Hi Ho! Off on the bounding main, Yo Ho! Sam, Kitty, Ann, Paul, and I, and Sam's dog.

Right from the beginning, I knew it wasn't going to be my finest hour. The sound was choppy, the horizon moved this way and that. Even the dog threw up on deck, and he hadn't even had the lobster and pecan cake. I managed to hold everything down, but I know I must have turned a beguiling shade of green.

As if that weren't enough, one of the engines conked out. Sam stripped down to swimming trunks, dived under the water and tried to see what was wrong. He couldn't fix it, and we putted along on one engine for a while.

Pretty soon we came within sight of New Haven harbor – land, thank God – and Sam suggested we'd better go ashore where we could get a train back to New York. That was the best idea I'd heard, so that's what we did. Sam and Kitty, true to the code of the sea, stayed bravely with the boat until it sank. They were rescued, the boat was eventually rescued, and the renewal was signed – all in due time.

Seems like a lot of my memories are about food… and my own over indulgence. Why did I do it? I have no answer except to repeat what the mountain climber said when asked why he had risked his life to climb to the top of Mount Everest.

"Because it was there," he replied.

In the spring of 1959, *The Bob Cummings Show* ended. We felt sad about it. When you work so closely with people, they become your family, and you hate parting from them. As much as you promise to get together and keep in touch, you know you never will. You have to earn your living, go on to another show, and begin a new family.

10

The Norwegian Connection

Something significant happened during *The Bob Cummings Show* – something that had nothing to do with Paul's career but changed and enriched all our lives. One evening in 1957, we were having our dinner in the breakfast room – the whole family for a change – when Carol dropped a bombshell.

"We're having two exchange students at Hollywood High School next year," she began, "one boy and one girl."

"That's nice," I said, not really thinking much about it.

"I've volunteered to have one of them live with us," Carol added, watching us carefully to see how we were taking it.

"What?!" I cried.

"You what?" Paul also cried.

"Neat!" exclaimed Tony.

If she'd wanted to announce the news for maximum effect, she'd certainly done it.

"Where will the student be from?" asked Linda. "Will it be a boy or a girl?"

"A girl, dummy," Carol said. "She has to room with me. And we don't know yet where she'll be from."

The talk turned to bedlam. What we gained from it all was that this was all to be handled through The American Field Service, that the student would live with us for a whole year and go to Hollywood High School with Carol, and that in a few days a committee would call on us to see if we were suitable.

"Good lord! It's like adopting a child!" I said. "They'll never accept us."

"Why not?" Paul protested.

"Because we're not a typical American family," I replied. "You're in show business, you're not home very much, we rarely all sit down to the table together, and I don't think I've ever seen you carve the meat."

"Who do you know who does that?" he asked.

"Andy Hardy's father. He always sits at the head of the dining room table and everybody says Grace, and then Judge Hardy carves the roast."

"Oh for goodness sakes, they don't expect us to be the Hardy family. I'm sure Ma Hardy didn't spend half her time at the ballet school."

Touché!

"Well, of course, if you don't want a student, I suppose I can tell them at school – but I really thought you'd be glad," Carol said, piling up guilt.

We all hastened to reassure her and spent the next several days getting used to the idea and preparing ourselves for the visit of the committee.

All of our worries were for nothing since the committee loved us. They claimed we *were* the typical American family and that the girl would be lucky to live in a home like ours. The die was cast. I still felt nervous about it, but after a few meetings with other prospective parents around the city, we began to look forward to the experience. Several months later, we learned that our student would be Bente Dahl from Alta, Norway – way up north of the Arctic Circle.

She arrived in August, we all went to the airport to meet her, and although we made a supreme effort to make everything go smoothly, that first evening was strained and the girl didn't seem very happy.

"Maybe she's homesick," I whispered to Paul in the kitchen.

"I think she's just tired," Paul said. "It's been a long trip. She doesn't seem to feel very well."

That was the understatement of the day! She had pneumonia! What she and everyone else had thought was that she had caught cold. But when she didn't seem to get any better, I took her to the doctor. That's when we got the diagnosis.

Back home, Bente looked up "pneumonia" in her Norwegian-English dictionary, seemed frightened, and then went to bed willingly. She had a couple of weeks to get used to us from her bed, having meals on a tray and watching television. It was probably the best way in the world to create a transition period from the Arctic Circle to Southern California. Later, she told us that the commercials on TV were a big help. They showed the product and then talked about it. Soon, she was better and her true personality began to shine out. She was a darling! Bright, it goes without saying. Only the brightest kids get to come. Charming, lovable, eager to cooperate, and ready to like us.

Bente was fine by the time school started. Paul took the girls, Carol and Bente, to Hollywood High every morning on his way to the studio. In those days, they put kids from our end of the valley in the Hollywood High district to make up for the population, which was moving out of their usual area. Before long, Bente made a lot of friends. I bought her some new clothes. It wasn't supposed to be in the deal, but I didn't care. I couldn't let her go to school not looking as well dressed as our own daughter. She was thrilled. And we were totally thrilled with her.

It was a busy, happy time for me. Daily I packed four lunches now and took the younger two to their school. Our house was full of young people all the time. And so was the pool. Additionally, there were a lot of social occasions planned for the exchange students. The boy was from Argentina. His name was Adolfo, and he played the guitar. All the girls were agog.

We introduced Bente to American lifestyle and helped her perfect her English, and in turn, she taught us a few words of Norwegian and told us many interesting things about her homeland. Her father, Birger, managed a string of resort hotels, and in Alta where she lived, they had midnight sun in summer and no sun at all for a while in winter. The Lapps (or Sami people) lived up there and were a part of their culture with their folk dancing and native costumes.

I wrote letters to her parents regularly and hoped they knew enough English to read them. Our eating habits were different. I know we didn't have as much fish or boiled potatoes as she was used to, but we more than made up for it with our glorious fruit – and ice cream. She adored ice cream! She was a tiny girl, about a size four, and a little weight really showed.

"Oh – I'm getting too wide," she said, looking in the mirror.

Elvis Presley came to town, and I took Bente and another exchange student to see him. Of course, I saw him too. My only time. They giggled at his pelvic movements. They were glad to have seen the number one star but had no desire to scream or faint. Neither did I.

Both Bente and Carol joined sororities at the high school, and we had to go through two initiations simultaneously. One of the pledges' requirements was to bring lunch every day. There were all sorts of other stunts they had to undergo, like wearing necklaces of garlic and onions. That just meant I had to string them. I didn't mind. I remembered my high school days and how much fun it all was.

During Easter vacation, I took all the kids to Hawaii. Paul didn't go. He couldn't get away. But we had a wonderful time. A Tahitian dancer on the ship – one who danced with knives and flaming swords – fell for Bente, and we teased her about taking him back home to the Arctic Circle.

When it came time for her to leave for home, she cried and clung to us. We cried and hugged her. It was like parting with a member of our family.

Of course, we wrote often. She went on to the university and became a practicing sociologist, working for the government, helping to improve the lot of immigrant workers among other projects. And then she met Gudleiv Bø.

On her wedding day, Bente wrote me a letter. "I know I'll have a happier marriage because of living in your home and seeing your example." What a lovely thing for her to say – and for me to hear. I cried.

Gudleiv Bø, when we met him, proved to be every bit as charming and lovable as Bente. He had his doctorate in Scandinavian languages and taught at Oslo University. The first thing we noticed when we met him was that not only was his English impeccable, but it just may have been better than ours. I mean, he always had just exactly the right word for the occasion.

We visited back and forth many times. Gudleiv's parents, Bente's parents, assorted nieces and nephews – all of them visited. Now they are a rounded out family of four daughters – each one very blonde, very blue-eyed, and very rosy cheeked. Also very beautiful. The second daughter, Ingvild, is my godchild. I think of them all as our grandchildren. Gudleiv has his tenure at the university now, which makes them secure. Bente has risen in her field to ever more responsible jobs, writing learned articles for publication and being interviewed on radio and television. Yes, I'll have to say we did fine with our Norwegian daughter.

All our children have visited Norway. Carol particularly likes it. She is our nature girl who enjoys the outdoors and roughing it.

"If you're hiking and you come to a fork in the road," Carol explains, "if one fork is dry and smooth and the other is up to your hips in mud, the Norwegian will take the muddy one every time." She finds it a challenge.

The first time Paul and I visited there, we saw all the sights of Oslo and especially enjoyed having dinner at the Dahls' apartment located on a fjord. They moved down from Alta while Bente was in the United States. We had a delicious dinner of roast whale (tasted just like roast beef) and all the trimmings, accompanied by aquavit, a Norwegian liquor. Many toasts were made, speeches were given – that's the custom – and we ended up on the balcony watching the sunset over the fjord. I casually looked at my watch, and it was about midnight. We went back to our hotel, very tired, a little intoxicated – that aquavit is potent – and went to sleep only to be awakened by the sun shining through a crack in our drapes at 3:00 a.m. It's very strange and different to get used to that skewed sort of time. But what fun!

And what wonderful people! We love them all dearly, and we can't help thinking that there must be a lot of fabulous, interesting people living in other parts of the world too! What a pity we can't get to know more of them. Maybe we could all get along. Do you think that will ever be possible?

11

The Cinema

After *The Bob Cummings Show*, Paul was very tired in body, tired in mind, and also tired of television. He badly needed a change, so what did he do? Go fishing? Camping? A health spa? Europe? None of the above. He took his mother-in-law on a long motor trip. Now tell me that wasn't unusual!

Paul and Liza, as he called my mother, had a lot in common. They were both fascinated with history, especially the history of this country. My mother had never been a movie fan. When you got past Mary Pickford, Douglas Fairbanks, and Rudolph Valentino, you lost her altogether. But she was a very big fan of political figures: George Washington, Thomas Jefferson, Abraham Lincoln, Woodrow Wilson, and Franklin Roosevelt. She also had a love of the South. She always said if she could live her life over again, she'd like to be a southern belle sitting on a verandah, surrounded by white columns on a plantation, wearing starched petticoats, drinking lemonade, and listening to the field hands singing as they picked the cotton.

She'd never had much chance to travel, so Paul invited her to be his companion on a trip to all the places they both loved and had heard about. He drove to Kansas City and picked her up and off they went. They visited Washington, D.C., Mount Vernon, Monticello, Hyde Park, and the battlefields of Williamsburg and, Gettysburg. Along the way they stopped to see relatives who happened to be in their path. They were completely compatible. Paul liked to get up at dawn. So did Mother. He liked to go to bed with the chickens. So did Mother. He hated to wait for people. Mother was always on time. In fact, as I was growing up, she taught me that if you were on time, you were late. They were gone three weeks and covered 19,000 miles.

I stayed behind to keep the home fires burning (more like the air conditioner humming) and to ride herd on three teenagers, aged 18, 15, and 13. I hadn't outgrown my carsickness. I hadn't learned the "early to bed, early to rise" habit. I had a very busy life helping Carol to decide on a college, helping Linda to become a dancer, taking Tony back and forth to Art School and Judo classes.

Besides, I'd started my own ballet classes. Always a frustrated dancer, I finally got up the courage to enroll in a Mothers class. I nearly died working up the nerve to go out on the floor in leotard and tights, but once I did it, I loved it as I always knew I would.

When I was little and wanted to take dancing lessons, I wasn't allowed to. My grandfather was a deacon in the Baptist Church and considered dancing a sin. My mother didn't exactly think it was sinful, but it didn't seem quite ladylike. Piano lessons, on the other hand, were almost required. When I progressed far enough to play "Hovering Butterflies" and "The Happy Farmer," I was always asked to play for company. As soon as I struck the first note, they'd all resume their conversations. Nobody listened at all, and I finally begged to quit lessons I wasn't particularly good at.

But dancing – ah, dancing! I started with one class a week, then it became two, three, and finally six, every day but Sunday. I was in Natalia Clare's "professional" class. I never thought for a moment I'd be a professional, but it was the only adult class there was. I danced alongside Alexis Smith and some other excellent dancers. I branched out and occasionally took classes from Victor Moreno and Bert Prival.

I was also active in the Toluca Lake Little Theatre, making my stage comeback in *Rebecca* as Maxim de Winter's sister – not a great part, but I was trodding the boards! I could smell that grease paint! Later I had a really good role in *A Roomful of Roses*. Linda was also in it, but I didn't play her mother – I wasn't considered the type. I was the next-door neighbor with all the funny lines.

By summer, Paul was back at home and "at liberty" again. I began to remember what my mother had said when I told her I really wanted to marry Paul.

"I like him a lot," she said, "but I kinda wish you would marry someone with a steady job." By that, she meant working for one company all your life and then retiring with a gold watch and a pension.

"Don't worry, mother," I told her confidently. "Paul's going to be on top one of these days. I know that."

I did know it, and I still knew it, but it wasn't paying the bills, which never seem to take a vacation. So that fall he signed to write an hour long Art Linkletter special, *Secret World of Kids*. He knew and liked Art, had read his book about kids and liked that, too. So how hard could it be to make a TV show of it?

And the answer – it was very hard. You had to assemble a whole new staff and crew, get guest stars, write a script, and please a lot of people you didn't really know and who sometimes didn't even know each other. Everybody was jockeying for position, and some of them would drop out, while others you were counting on found they weren't going to be available. Then the struggle came for replacements. The final cast included Ed Wynn, Vincent Price, Ann Blyth, Mickey Rooney and his son, Danny Thomas and his TV daughter, Angela Cartwright, Jerry the Chimp, and even vice president Richard Nixon! Lord help us! That was a mixed bag if ever there was one! However, *Variety* said: "No show of this young season was more spirited, with novel innovation, buoyant with smart comedy, and enough of a story line with running gags to keep the laughs cascading." Again Paul was barely mentioned in the last line of the review.

Dick Wesson was his co-writer and how they did it, I can't imagine. Paul got a telegram from Eddie Cantor: "Dear Paul, to these old eyes, the Art Linkletter *Secret World of Kids* was the fastest hour I can recall on television. It had warmth, good fun, and comes from a different kind of format, which we televiewers appreciate. Congratulations!" I don't remember the program very well, but I do remember Paul swore that "never again" would he do an hour special. It just wasn't his cup of tea.

So now what? Paul enjoyed his liberty, and so did I. We spent a lot of time together and with the children. The holidays came and went, we were into a new year, 1960, and liberty didn't taste quite as sweet as it had. That's when Paul got a call from writer Stanley Shapiro.

"How'd you like to work with me on picture?" he asked.

"Sounds good," Paul said. He'd always liked Stanley and liked to work with him. Their minds seemed to mesh well. Stanley had been very successful at Universal Studios first writing *The Perfect Furlough* and then *Pillow Talk* with Maurice Richlin. For that, they won an Academy Award for best original screenplay.

Stanley continued. "Television is such a grind," he said. "You're always under the gun, working toward a deadline. In pictures, it's different. You have plenty of time to develop characters and a story."

Stanley went on with his sales pitch. "Very little stress and strain. Leisure time. A chance to do something really good."

By that time, Paul was sold. He went over to Universal and visited Stan in his bungalow office on the lot. It was luxurious: a reception-secretary's room, two private offices, and a private bar. He shared the bungalow with Rock Hudson who had the same type of suite on the other side. Stan was eager to continue the successful partnership of Rock and Doris Day.

112

Universal Studios were a far cry from the big conglomerate you see today. No tall black buildings, no hotels, no amphitheatre, no studio tours, no cinemas, and no restaurants. Stan's bungalow was near the front of the lot with handy room for parking. Paul took me over to see it on April 22. It's in my Daily Reminder. I was impressed! Television was wonderful, but this was real movies, the way it used to be, and the way I'd always pictured it. Big sound stages all around, people in costume and makeup strolling along the streets, famous faces visible here and there.

There was a problem though. The Writers' Guild went on strike. All ready and excited to begin work, and Stan and Paul weren't allowed to. So Stan came over to our house, and the two of them sat around in our Guest House. They never touched the typewriter, but they thought of ideas and sort of worked out a plot. As soon as the strike was over, they presented their idea to Universal who authorized them to do a screenplay. And so it began.

Paul went to the studio every day and came home for dinner every evening – just like a real, average workingman – the kind my mother had envisioned for me. Once in a while I dropped by the studio – it was within walking distance of our house – and whenever I did, I could hear the laughter before I even went inside. Paul and Stan constantly broke each other up with their funny ideas. They really liked working together. Paul was older than Stan, and where once Paul was in charge, giving the young kid a break, now Stan was the one with the track record in feature films. He was not only writing, but his company would produce the picture. Stan was happier and it was all fine with Paul.

Yesterday, Paul and I had lunch at the Music Center before a matinee at the Mark Taper Forum. It's one of our favorite forms of recreation. We dress up in our best, have a leisurely lunch with a glass of wine, and if there's time before the curtain, we walk down to see the pigeons that gather around the outside tables on the Plaza hoping for crumbs. I call them my birds – because pigeons are city birds and so am I – a city bird. But yesterday, while we were at lunch, I opened up the subject of his collaboration with Stan on the movie.

"Do you remember any special thing that you feel you contributed to the script?" I asked.

"No, I really don't. I think everything was just what we said – a collaboration."

I thought I could detect things here and there, little touches that seemed typical of Paul, others that seemed more in character with Stan's writing, but maybe I'm wrong. It doesn't really matter.

"Did you use your own private bar very much?" I asked.

"No. Certainly not when we were working. Once in a while, somebody – Rock Hudson or someone Stan knew – would come by just before quitting time."

"Did you eat lunch in the studio commissary?" I asked trying to stimulate his memory of that time.

"Yes, sometimes. Other times, we had them deliver our lunch to the office – sort of like room service."

"Sounds like a very nice way to work," I said. "And you had a parking space right there?"

"Right next to the office. I didn't have to walk more than fifty feet. I had my little Mercedes then, the 190." He smiled fondly, remembering that little blue two-seater, his first Mercedes. Paul has always been fond of cars. They're very important to him. It's a streak that runs in his family. I've mentioned his brother, "Cotton" Henning, the race driver and master mechanic. His oldest brother, Bill, had his own garage in Kansas City. During World War II, when mechanics were needed so much, Bill was offered a really fine job at a factory at a salary much larger than what he was making at his garage. He turned it down. When Paul asked him why, he shook his head. "Nobody's worth that kind of money," he said.

Another brother Leonard, always called "Major," made his living selling Cadillacs to the wealthy oilmen in Tulsa. And I'll never forget when early in our marriage, his sister, Jane, came out to visit us. I wanted her to see Hollywood in all its glamour, so I took her to a big premiere at Grauman's Chinese Theatre. I kept trying to edge through the crowd closer to where the stars were being interviewed, but Janie kept pulling in the opposite direction.

"Janie," I protested, "come on. We can see them better over here." There was Hedy Lamarr just arriving in white fox fur to her ankles and orchids cascading down her front.

"I'd rather see their cars," she said, and I gave up. To me a car was something to take me there and bring me back, nothing more. If it started and stopped when it was supposed to, that's all I required. Not the Hennings. They all did love their automobiles.

Getting back to our original subject – the Universal movie. I asked about the casting and other production details. Paul said they talked everything over and most decisions were joint decisions. When the film was finally finished, it turned out to be *Lover Come Back*, starring Rock Hudson and Doris Day, featuring Tony Randall, Edie Adams, Jack Oakie, Jack Kruschen, Ann B. Davis, and in a tiny part, a lovely blonde, Donna Douglas. Of course, after the script was finished, the movie had to be filmed. That took a while, then postproduction work, editing, scoring, all of those dozens of things that make up the finished product. It wasn't until August 2, 1961 that they previewed *Lover Come Back* in Inglewood. Undoubtedly, they made some changes after the audience reaction and the preview cards. Then in December, it was previewed again.

It was released in early 1962. Paul wasn't used to that kind of time lag. He missed the excitement of television where you write something and see it in the following week. This way, you lose some momentum – in fact, you almost forget it before you finally see the finished product. Some adrenalin was missing. A writer may think he's done a good piece of work, but until audiences see it (and of course, the critics), he can never be sure. But once the movie was out for all the world to see, the momentum came back, also the adrenalin and the enthusiasm because it was a smash! Here's what Bosley Crowther of the New York Times had to say:

"*Lover Come Back* is one of the brightest, most delightful comedies since *It Happened One Night*. Stanley Shapiro and Paul Henning have contrived some of the sharpest and funniest situations you could wish and some of the fastest, wittiest dialogue in years. Delbert Mann has directed at such a pace that *Lover Come Back* is the shortest hour and three-quarter film we've ever seen. Hudson and Miss Day are delicious. Mr. Randall makes a wonderful nitwit. Funniest picture of the year!"

Paul and Stan were nominated for an Academy Award that year for Best Story and Screenplay written directly for the screen. They sent us tickets for the third row at the Santa Monica Civic Auditorium. I bought myself a dress. It wasn't the greatest dress I ever had. Why does this happen to me? On all really important occasions of my life, I can't find a special dress. I never was crazy about my Mother of the Bride dress or my Mother of the Groom dress. Other times, when it really doesn't matter, and nobody's looking at me, I'm a knockout! (You don't have to believe that.) Still, it was a new dress, the best I could do.

When we arrived, we ran the gamut between bleachers of cheering fans. They looked puzzled as we were ushered in. I'm used to that. Nobody recognizes writers. Sometimes I'm convinced fans think the actors ad lib the lines.

All through the evening, I watched big stars presenting and accepting awards – and then our turn came. Paul and Stan didn't win. William Inge won for *Splendor in the Grass*. I was disappointed but not too surprised. Comedies rarely win. And here was a really eminent playwright who had written his first screenplay. It kind of figured he'd be the odds-on favorite. I'd like to see *Splendor in the Grass* again to see if it was really that good. But if you think Paul is shy and retiring, and I've certainly given you that impression, wait till I tell you about Stan. The year before, when Stan's name actually was announced as the winner, he was nowhere to be found. He was hiding in the men's room because he couldn't bear to make a speech. Maurice Richlin had to accept the award for both of them. Writers are a different breed.

After the awards show, we went to the Board of Governors' Ball at the Beverly Hilton. Everybody came by our table and gave their condolences. They also congratulated Paul on being nominated. That was really the honor, they all said. That's what they always say when you lose. But it's true. Since then, I don't think I've ever missed an Academy Awards night on television except once when we were in a small town in France. Even there, they knew about it and could tell us who had won.

In the fall of 1960, Paul and I started night school at North Hollywood High School taking a class in German. Paul feels an ethnic attachment to Germany since his grandparents came from there. Some of mine did, too, but with me, it was mostly that I love languages. I had already studied Latin (four years), and French (three years), so I felt I had a head start. We enjoyed it, and I got to feel important because during the coffee break, I was surrounded by other students asking me to explain the subjunctive. We got well-acquainted with our teacher and had a lot of fun in the class, but we came away with very little German. We still say to each other now and then, "Wo fliegt das flugzeug?" The answer is "Uber den bergen" – or "Where flies the plane?" "Over the mountains." This didn't come up much in ordinary conversation. But we still enjoyed it.

Sometime in 1961, Paul and Stan began writing another movie. Same studio, same bungalow, same pleasant working conditions. This time, it was to be about two clever confidence men (Paul has always been fascinated with such scoundrels), one older, one younger, and both irresistible to women to be played, hopefully, by Cary Grant and Tony Curtis. The working title was *King of the Mountain*. But you know what they say about the "best laid schemes o' mice and men" (and movie writers): they "gang aft agley." The title *King of the Mountain* was already registered with the Writers' Guild, which meant somebody else got it first, and it turned out Cary Grant and Tony Curtis were feuding. Paul doesn't remember what it was all about, but it certainly made that ideal casting notion "gang agley."

They had to know who they were writing for before they could begin because the roles would have to be tailored to fit. They wound up with David Niven and Marlon Brando – quite a different pair, I'll admit – both fine actors but not what the writers originally had in mind. Shirley Jones would be the girl. She just had to be pretty and sweet and innocent.

When the script was finished, it had become *Bedtime Story*. It opened in June 1964 to mixed reviews. Everyone was surprised and delighted by Marlon Brando's comedic acting. One thing I love is that in his *Playboy* interview some years later, Brando said, "Those were some of the funniest lines I ever did," referring to *Bedtime Story*. The quote was in a box, so nobody could miss it. Some critics did say it was "dirty," but that's a laugh by today's standards – even by those long ago standards. I've always thought that at least one reason it wasn't as popular as *Lover Come Back* is that it didn't have a really strong love story.

Never mind.

118

Several years ago, it reappeared with only slight changes under the title *Dirty Rotten Scoundrels*, starring Michael Caine and Steve Martin. I was glad because our grandsons, born rather late in our lives, had never known their grandfather, except as an "old man" who was hard of hearing. They saw *Dirty Rotten Scoundrels* during one Christmas vacation when they were visiting us from their home in Berkeley. The younger one, Jesse, came home and hugged me jubilantly. "Grandma! Grandma! We saw Papa's name right up there on the screen!" Jesse cried. That made it all worthwhile, even if the residual payments didn't. Just as the payments were beginning to trickle in, Orion Home Video went into bankruptcy. C'est la show biz!

12

The Beverly Hillbillies
(The Beginning)

From conception to birth, it takes nine months to make a human baby. Before that, people often say the baby was just a gleam in his father's eye. *The Beverly Hillbillies* was certainly Paul Henning's baby, and it took every bit that long to create it. As for the gleam in his eye – that had begun a long time ago.

Paul had always been fascinated by hillbillies. It probably stared when he was a Boy Scout and went on camping trips in the Ozarks where he met people who didn't even know who was president or who'd never been ten miles away from home – they didn't see any reason to go. Early in his career, he'd seen the play, *Tobacco Road*, at the Kansas City Orpheum Theater. I was with him, and I remember how he laughed. Later on, he began to look forward to the Bob Burns' spots on *The Bing Crosby Show*. I remember some of the things we laughed at. Bob said he'd taken some bananas to his Aunt Boo, but when he went back to see her, he'd found all the peeled bananas on the front walk.

"Didn't you like the bananas, Aunt Boo?" Bob asked.

"Naw – they was mostly all cob," she replied.

Another time, Bob told how his grandfather offered him a cup of coffee.

"Here, take mine," he said, "it's already been saucered and blowed."

And then there was the motor trip in the spring of '59 – 19,000 miles of it – with my mother in the South and the East. As Paul expresses it, they were cruising along the highway in Kentucky or Virginia, one of the southern states, talking about some of the

120

historical figures they admired, and a thought came to him that he just had to express.

"What if a person from a hundred years ago – someone like Abe Lincoln – were in the back seat of this car cruising along the highway in a high-powered car? What would he think of modern life?"

They discussed it as they rode along. The idea really fascinated him; he couldn't get it out of his mind. He doesn't believe he thought specifically of a television program on the subject because there would be no way to do it unless you made it science fiction. Soon after that, however, he read that there were pockets of people living in isolated places like the Appalachian Mountains and the Ozarks – people for whom time seemed to have stood still. They had no modern conveniences, not even a radio. What would they think if they were transplanted to a sophisticated environment? He put the half-formed idea on the shelf, and they went on with their trip.

Meanwhile, real life intervened – real life in the form of bills to pay, the Art Linkletter special, German classes at night school, family life, and writing a movie with Stan Shapiro. And then one day early in 1961, he got a phone call from his old friend, Al Simon.

Ever since Paul's *Burns and Allen* days, Al had had a production company working out of General Service Studios. Recently, he'd been made president of the newly-formed Filmways Television Corporation. Filmways had been doing commercial films in New York for a long time, and lately, feature films from MGM, but so far, they had only one television show, *Mister Ed*. They needed more – lots more.

"How about creating a new television series?" Al asked.

"I'd like that," Paul replied. "I may do it one of these days."

The next day Al would call again. "Are you thinking about that television series?"

121

"Oh yes – yes, I am," Paul would say, but he couldn't be specific because he didn't yet know just what he was thinking of. To tell the truth, he was thinking mostly of another feature film with Stanley Shapiro. *Lover Come Back* was in production and they'd been kicking around ideas. Still, there were days when Stan was occupied with production details, and Paul would stay home, go out to our guesthouse which he used as an office, and think about a television series.

That's when the idea on the shelf came back to him. He took it down, dusted it off, and gave it some serious consideration. The more he thought about it, the more he loved those simple hillbillies. There was just one problem. They were usually poor – and drab. The setting would be poor and drab. The costumes would be poor and drab. A person could get tired of that very quickly. Ahhh! But not if they were transplanted to some other location, like New York City.

He really didn't have a lot of time to dwell on it. Most days, he'd be back in the bungalow at Universal working with Stan on a new feature film. Nights he'd work in the guesthouse thinking about the *Hillbillies*. Back and forth, back and forth –
enough to make a man dizzy. Meanwhile, *Lover Come Back* had opened, was a big hit, and he and Stan were nominated for an Academy Award. That's the way it always seems to happen in show business. For a long time, you don't have anything to do, and then it all happens at once, and you have to try to do it all because the chance may never come again.

I was seeing very little of Paul those days – you can imagine. He worked late a lot of nights and began to miss some of our German classes. I was still driving the kids around, teaching a Sunday School class, doing publicity for the Toluca Lake Little Theatre, taking a ballet class every day, and even trying to do a little writing of my own. I'd been selling short stories to the women's magazines. Besides her

122

dancing, Linda had been rehearsing at the North Hollywood Playhouse for *Gidget*, a role that seemed just right for her. Carol was going to college in Berkeley, and often I drove her back and forth on weekends. Tony was learning to drive, and it was my turn to yell and scream when we went for practice drives together. It was a very busy household.

Through it all, Paul kept getting daily calls from Al Simon. One day, Al asked him to have lunch at The Brown Derby. Marty Ransahoff was there, too. Marty was Filmways' Chairman of the Board. He was the one with the office at MGM who presided over those feature films. The conversation turned to TV series without much preliminary chitchat. That's when Paul told them he wanted to do a show about hillbillies.

Marty seized on the idea right away. "I'll buy the rights to Ma and Pa Kettle," he said eagerly.

"No – no – I don't want to do anybody else's characters," Paul protested. "I want to create my own."

"You don't have to worry about Paul," Al told Marty loyally. "Anything he writes will be better than anything you can buy." Al has always been one of Paul's biggest boosters.

Paul began talking about his vision for the show and about the idea that would eliminate the problem of drabness. They could strike oil on their property, become rich, and move away from the hills, starting a whole new lifestyle mingling with other rich people.

They all loved the whole idea, and by the time they finished their lunch, they were so excited about it they could hardly wait for a pilot to be written. Then Paul became very busy indeed, trying to work with Stan on the screenplay and on the pilot at the same time. He wanted to write the pilot alone. He really didn't know any writer who would understand those people as he did. Most comedy writers come from New York, and hillbillies are just not part of their experience.

123

Besides – and he insists this was only a secondary motive – he wanted the show to be his and if he had a co-writer, it wouldn't be all his.

In any television show, Paul always tries to write the first few episodes alone to "set" the characters. With the *Hillbillies*, he felt he had to do more – maybe twelve or thirteen episodes because these characters were different.

So he started to visualize his family. He likes to get to know each character in-depth. Usually he writes a short history of each one. Those details may never come up in the script, but if HE knows where they're coming from, he can do a better job.

To quote Paul from an interview he gave to Professor Ronald L. Davis of Southern Methodist University: "I learned early on that the *characters* are the important thing in television. In a movie, you can have people you wouldn't want to meet again and still have a successful movie. But in television, you're hopeful that the people will become interested, that they will begin to care about your characters and will welcome them back the following week, and the week after that. And knowing that, you write for characters. Because that's the secret of a popular show, I think. You get to *like* the people. You get to know them and like them – there are certain performers that people simply *love* – and they don't have to be hilariously funny to entertain the viewers – and I think that is the secret of success in television."

He started with Jed Clampett, patriarch of the Clampett Clan. Here's a part of the biography he wrote of Jed right in the beginning. "Jed is the seventh generation since the family migrated west from Virginia in the early 1800s. Almost completely isolated in the rugged hills, Jed and his family have lived much the same life as their pioneer ancestors. Consequently, Jed is a man completely lacking in formal education but powerfully developed in the areas nurtured by close contact with nature – that is, physical and spiritual strength. He is

124

simple, honest, and friendly but with a pride and independence born of complete self-sufficiency."

One bit of dialogue from the pilot that I always remember – and which seems to set Jed's character – is with Cousin Pearl after she tells him he's now a rich man and can do anything he wants or go anywhere he wants.

"What do you think, Pearl? You think I oughta move?"

"Jed, how can you even ask?" Pearl says. "Look around you. You're eight miles from the nearest neighbor. You're overrun with skunks, possums, and bobcats. You got kerosene lamps for light – a wood stove to cook on winter and summer – you're drinkin' homemade moonshine, washin' with homemade lye soap, and your bathroom is fifty feet from the house! And you ask should you move?"

Jed thinks a moment and then answers soberly, "Yeah, I guess you're right. A man'd be a dang fool to leave all this!"

Next Paul thought about Elly May. To continue his character sketches, he writes: "A widower at an early age, Jed was never remarried. He has raised his only child, a beautiful daughter, as he would have raised the son he wanted but never had, teaching her the lore of the woods and streams but neglecting the more civilized aspects of her education. She is a wild but beautiful tomboy. At the age of 17, Elly has never known any life but that of the hills – nor any clothes but those of a boy. Like most hillbilly boys, she is adept at rough and tumble "rasslin'" and throws rocks with uncanny accuracy. She loves nature and critters, and nature has been bountiful in return. But Elly is naively unaware of her fabulous physical endowments." You see, Paul had never forgotten what he learned from that P.R. man way back in *Burns and Allen* days. You need a beautiful girl to get media attention.

125

Granny, of course, has been almost everybody's favorite. According to her biography, she is a very "wiry, indestructible little woman whom no amount of contact with urban life will change from a pure and intractable hillbilly. She is a typical of the 'granny women' of the hill country who are skilled in the preparation and application of 'mountain medicine' – first cousin to the 'folk medicine' of the eastern seaboard. Granny's remedies consist mostly of herbs, barks, and roots, and the produce of her still – and probably have some real as well as psychosomatic medical value. Granny is kindhearted and God-fearing but to say that she is 'set in her ways' would be an understatement."

This scrap of dialogue from the pilot illustrates Granny's character. The family is loading up the truck to drive to Beverly Hills, but Granny is still sitting in her rocking chair on the back porch, shotgun across her knees.

"Now what's this nonsense about you not goin' to Californy?" Jed asks.

"Ain't no nonsense to it! If the Good Lord had wanted me in Californy, he'd a *put* me in Californy."

"Mebbe he's just gittin' 'round to it. The Book says he moves in mysterious ways."

"Well, if HE moves me, I'll go. But you and Big Jethro ain't budgin' me."

There's a dissolve, and we next see Granny, still sitting in her rocker, mounted on the truck.

Jethro is Cousin Pearl's son, a hulking, powerful teenage giant, not too long on brains but fortunately good-natured and anxious to be helpful and friendly. He's going to Californy with the Clampetts because he's the only one who can drive the truck, and as Pearl says, to get an education. She also has an ulterior motive. If her son is there, she'll have a good excuse to visit.

126

Well, there's the core of the family. Now all Paul had to do was write it and cast it. Both were important, but to him, casting was almost more vital than the lines. As he wrote and thought, one actor kept coming into his mind to play the role of Jed Clampett. Paul had recently seen Buddy Ebsen in a television drama in which he'd played a rural man with a beautiful daughter. Buddy was about the right age, he was a fine actor, ruggedly handsome, and had a certain grace about him which Paul decided came from his being a dancer. From the very beginning, Paul never thought of anyone else for the part. If Buddy had been unavailable or had turned it down, I don't know what would have happened. Would there have been a *Beverly Hillbillies*?

I should mention here that when Paul first thought of moving the hillbillies from the hills to a sophisticated setting, he had been thinking of New York. Soon, however, he realized how foolish it would be to have to make location trips to the east when Beverly Hills was right close at hand.

By this time, Stan knew what Paul was doing and agreed to postpone work on their second screenplay until the pilot was written. Paul was welcome to work in their bungalow offices, and that's where most of the first episode was written. I have it in my diary that on several occasions I worked with Paul whether at the studio or in our guesthouse. He was writing alone, you know, which he wanted to do, and yet he hated it, too. He needed somebody to talk out ideas to, somebody to test things on, somebody who would respond and be encouraging and maybe even occasionally contribute something.

As the script began to take shape, he naturally thought more about casting. His good friend, Bea Benaderet, who Paul had always liked and admired and had even pledged himself to do a show for, wanted very much to test for the part of Granny. Paul didn't feel she was quite right but agreed to the test. Of course, they hadn't come to that yet – the actual testing. They were interviewing, reading, and looking over talent, but making no decisions. Yet nobody had come along who seemed right for Granny.

We started going out to western nightspots like The Palomino and other places that featured western musicians and singers. Actors and agents began besieging Paul and Al and Marty proposing their clients. And then one day an actress named Irene Ryan came by the bungalow to say hello. She knew both Paul and Stan slightly since she'd worked on *The Dennis Day Show*. Naturally, she'd heard about the show Paul was writing – the grapevine is swift and active in Hollywood, if not always strictly accurate. She knew it was about country people and wondered if there might possibly be a part she could play.

It was hard to tell. She was much younger than Granny, but she did have the build for it – small, thin, wiry. Using a lot of imagination, Paul could see her as a possible Granny. He began asking her questions about her experience, and she told him about an incident he's never forgotten. It seems she was with a small stock company, which was to appear at a country theatre in Arkansas. The play was ready to start, but the audience was still waiting outside the theatre.

"Why don't you let the people in?" Irene asked the manager.

"I don't let 'em in till the show is ready to begin," he said. "If they have time, they whittle the seats away."

They all had a good laugh about that and something in the way Irene told the story gave her chances a little boost.

By this time, it had been decided to do the tests and the pilot at General Service Studios. Al's office was there, and Paul had worked there with *The Bob Cummings Show*. Paul finished writing the script and began in earnest interviewing actors for the four major parts. When they tested Irene, Bea Benaderet was there and watched it. Afterwards, she came to Paul.

128

"There's your Granny," she said indicating Irene. "I'm not right for it, but she IS Granny." She was right, of course, right and very generous. You can see why Paul was so fond of her. Not many actresses would give up their own chances willingly for the good of the show. Irene was ecstatic! Ever since she and her ex-husband, Tim, had split up their act, she had been working here and there without any regular job and this looked like – at last – her big break!

They tested a bevy of beautiful girls for Elly May. That was a pure pleasure. All the men at the studio offered to help. You'd think, with all the beautiful girls in Hollywood, it wouldn't be hard to find the right one. But it was. Some had no talent. Some couldn't do the hillbilly dialect so it would sound natural. Some were too sophisticated looking. They did find one girl, a redhead, beautiful, and an excellent actress. Paul says she wasn't as "right" for the role as Donna Douglas, but she was the best they found. They had practically signed her when she accepted a job at another studio. Paul was furious. After all the time they had spent on her, he thought that was most unprofessional. Then he got a phone call from Donna Douglas. He knew her from the small part she'd played in *Lover Come Back*. Donna was in the hospital for some minor surgery.

"Paul please don't make up your mind until I get out of the hospital!" she begged.

He promised, and the next Sunday morning she came out to our house to see him. He went to the door and ushered her straight to our den.

The children and I were all having our breakfast at the kitchen table. We were disappointed not to get a look at her. So I fixed a tray with coffee, rolls, and dainty napkins and carried it to the den. When I returned to the kitchen, the children were all eager.

"What does she look like?" they all wanted to know.

"She looks like Doll Face," I told them without the slightest hesitation. Doll Face was one of our cats – white, with just a few grey-blue hairs mixed in, fluffy, beautiful, with big, round eyes.

That may seem derogatory or at least strange to most people, but we all understood it, the children and Paul, too. We are a family of cat lovers. We think they're all beautiful, but especially Doll Face. She looked sweet and innocent, too, not sly and wild as some cats do. Donna is like that. Her face is symmetrically perfect, her skin is peaches and cream, her hair is long and blonde, and those eyes – so big, so blue, so sort of innocent and trusting. Besides that, she was born and raised in Louisiana and had the perfect accent. To this day, she calls me "Miss Ruth," or affectionately, "Missy Ruth." And I don't have to tell you that in those tight jeans she was certainly something for the boys. And for the media.

And now about Max Baer. It must have been Paul's lucky day when Max came to the studio on a sort of cattle call audition. He was big and handsome – definitely a hunk. He'd had a stock contract with Warner Brothers where he'd done parts in B pictures that faded into the background. He needed a break. Years later, when we shared a flight from New York, he told me about that audition.

"I was there reading the script with all those other guys. They were all good looking. Some of them were a lot more experienced than I was, and I figured I'd have to do something unusual to make anybody notice me at all. So I decided that no matter what anybody said or did, I'd just have this big, dumb grin."

And that's what he did – and it worked. Max is terrific, the perfect Jethro. And he's not dumb. Because of the part he plays, you can get confused sometimes, but Max has a college education and is really quite sensitive and intelligent. He could be difficult at times, but – well, that's another story for later.

On December 13 of 1961, Paul invited me to the studio to look at all the tests. That was fun. I think Paul and all the rest of them knew pretty much whom they were going to cast, but this was like the final exam. So that was pretty much it. Paul had written in Cousin Pearl, Jethro's mother, for Bea Benaderet, and the president of the oil company was to be played by Frank Wilcox.

When Paul read the script to Al and Marty, Marty (always ready to do things in a big way) said, "Let's go to the Ozarks to film it!"

Paul said that would cost a lot and wasn't necessary. He'd heard about a place called Franklin Canyon near one of the Beverly Hills reservoirs. It looked wild and uninhabited. So the crew built Jed's mountain cabin right there in Beverly Hills, up over Mulholland Drive and down the road a bit.

They filmed the pilot in December of that year, 1961.

13

The Beverly Hillbillies II
(Waiting for the "Go")

Once a baby is born, after nine months of anticipation, hard work, and finally the pain of delivering it, you have to name it. Sometimes you have a name all picked out beforehand, but often you have to wait and see the child before you can choose a name that fits. In the case of the *Hillbillies*, at first Paul called it *The Hillbillies of Beverly Hills*. CBS rather liked *Head for the Hills*. Seems ridiculous now that anybody even thought of anything but *The Beverly Hillbillies*. It's such a natural. It was so natural, in fact, that somebody else – a group of musicians – was already using it. They played on a radio station owned by Gene Autry. Paul remembers going to see Gene Autry and explaining the situation to him. He was real nice about it.

"I don't feel I have any hold on that title," he said.

The musicians, however, didn't feel that way. They filed suit in Superior Court for over a million dollars damages and an injunction against the TV performers using the name.

The musicians weren't very well organized. Members came and went, and it was hard to get them all together. At any rate, there was never too much of a threat. A settlement was made by the studio, and that was that. The new show was officially *The Beverly Hillbillies*.

That's the way it goes. One at a time, elements come together. Next, they had to think about music. For the pilot, Paul had used a recording of bluegrass banjo and guitar music by a couple of his favorites, Lester Flatt and Earl Scruggs. Of course, everybody knew they couldn't continue to use their music without permission, and besides, they needed their own theme song. Al Simon hired a team of songwriters – Paul doesn't remember their names – to write a theme. When they brought it to him at his office out at Universal Studios, it wasn't what Paul had in mind at all. Next, he talked to Perry Botkin, a former neighbor, whose work Paul liked a lot. He was thinking of asking him to be musical director of the show anyway, so he consulted him about the theme.

"I want something that goes sort of like this," Paul said, ad-libbing the words and the tune. Not the finished product, you understand – just the general idea.

"Look, you don't need me," Perry said. "Why don't you write it yourself?"

"Me? I can't write music. I can't even read it," Paul protested.

But he did. He wrote "The Ballad of Jed Clampett" all by himself – words and music. Then he asked a friend of ours, Martha Jamieson, a fine musician, to help him get it down on paper. He went to her house and sang it to her while she took notes and wrote it out on music paper.

Perry Botkin suggested Jerry Scoggins to sing the song, then went to Tennessee to see Flatt and Scruggs, and they all got together to record the theme, which has been so popular all these years.

On January 17, 1962, they previewed the pilot for a live audience to record the laughter, just as they had on *The Bob Cummings Show*. Later, when they listened to the recorded laughter, they knew they couldn't use it. The audience had laughed so hard and so long that you couldn't hear the dialogue. Nobody felt bad about that though. They knew now that they had a really funny show and that's what mattered.

That was such an exciting time for our family – 1962. Lots happened. Paul had a successful pilot ready to go in the fall. He was working with Stanley Shapiro again on their second screenplay. They would meet at a motel in Hollywood to work. Sounds weird and mysterious, doesn't it? Well, it was. It was Stan's idea. Now – thirty years later, Paul doesn't have any idea why. When I ask him, he just says, "You know writers. They're odd." I'd have to agree with him.

We were seeing a lot of Sam Northcross, Al Simon, Jim Aubrey, and Marty Ransahoff. Dinner out almost every night. At the same time, Linda was being seriously considered to play the lead in the picture, *Bye Bye Birdie*. Some agent had seen her at the Playhouse in *Gidget* and took her to the studio – Columbia. There followed a short period that was exciting and in the end, heartbreaking for her. After a weeklong series of auditions, they told the agent they had secured Ann-Margret for the part. They'd been trying to get her all along but weren't sure she'd be available. After Linda received the news, I had to stop the car on the way home and let her out so she could throw up. I began to wonder whether I should have encouraged her to seek an acting and dancing career.

Carol was still at school in Berkeley, and Tony a sophomore at North Hollywood High, waiting impatiently to get his driver's license. I was doing my usual three-ring circus act.

During Linda's Easter vacation that year, Paul and I took her with us – first to Missouri, then to New York. While in Paul's hometown, Independence, we went to visit the new Truman Library and were asked to President Truman's office for a visit. He remembered Paul and other members of his family from long ago. What a thrill! He was such a wonderful, down-to-earth man, no pretentions at all, and he talked to us in such a friendly manner. Paul had bought a new camera for the trip and snapped lots of pictures. When he took them to be developed, it was found that the film had not engaged, and he had nothing. I don't think Paul ever tried to take pictures again. Mechanical things, even something as simple as loading a camera, defeated him, so he just didn't try. I'm pretty much the same way, and the children all tease us about having to call a serviceman to change a light bulb. It's almost true.

While we were in Independence, Paul rented a movie projector and showed *The Beverly Hillbillies* pilot to all his relatives at his mother's home. After it was over, the reaction was enthusiastic. Everybody had laughed but his mother, Sophia. She looked sober and serious as usual.

"They pay you for that?" she asked.

What's that they say about a prophet being without honor in his own country? It always seemed that way for Paul.

We met Carol in New York. She had flown in from San Francisco to meet us at the Algonquin Hotel where we had a suite. The girls loved that hotel as much as we did. They learned about room service there and liked to order the famous Algonquin cheesecake late at night after the theatre. If there was any left, they just put it on the windowsill outside. It was cold enough to keep it.

During the New York trip, we saw *How to Succeed in Business Without Really Trying*. Our old friend, Abe Burrows, had written libretto and another old friend, Rudy Vallee, played one of the leads. Both were excellent, and it was good to see them again.

Back home again, Paul immersed himself in his writing, missing most of the German classes, even the final in June. I went on and finished the course, but sadly, I don't remember much of it.

Linda worked on *Mister Ed* and began filming *Bye Bye Birdie*. They'd given her a small speaking part and hired her as a full-time dancer as a consolation prize. Thus, I began my stage mother routine again, going to the studio with her as her guardian. A lot of it was filmed on the back lot at Universal. That was very convenient for me since we lived so close, but it took up a lot of time, too. My mother and other relatives stood in for me. When I became acquainted with Kim Darby's grandmother, we'd take turns acting as guardian for

135

both girls. Kim was only fifteen at the time, but she was an excellent dancer.

On July 17, a lot of the studio people went to a big birthday party for Joe Depew at his house in Pasadena. Joe was Assistant Director on the *Hillbilly* pilot and would perform the same duty for the series. One of the other guests also had sold a new show which was to debut in the fall.

"How you doing with your show, Paul?" he asked.

"Slowly – very slowly," Paul answered.

"I've got my first thirteen episodes written," the other fellow said triumphantly.

Paul congratulated him, but I noticed on the way home he was very quiet.

"Anything wrong?" I asked.

"Sometimes I wonder if I can cut it," he said, sounding very down and discouraged. "I have to work so hard. I have to really struggle to finish a script, and here he already had his first thirteen written."

I tried to say encouraging things, but the proof of the pudding was that the other guy's show was a total flop – canceled before they even used those thirteen episodes. And Paul's show – well, you know what happened to it.

A couple of days later, I went to the studio to see the *Hillbillies* set. It was quite elegant; the exterior copies from a real Bel Air home they had scouted – a lavish mansion owned by some very wealthy people. Of course, they got permission to shoot exteriors there. Little did the occupants know what they were in for later. It's interesting to note that the house is now Ronald and Nancy Reagan's next door neighbor, if you can call anything next door with such spacious grounds.

Besides the exterior, they had the "cement pond" – a real, albeit shallow swimming pool built right on the set, provided with a filter and everything. There was the front hall, the living room, the kitchen, the "fancy eatin' room" (a billiard room), and some bedroom sets. The whole thing began to seem very real.

About a week later, Paul received the news that his mother, Sophie, had died. She was 94 and had been ready to go for quite a while. Paul was glad she'd seen the *Hillbilly* pilot but sorry she never lived to see his big success. We flew back for the funeral but stayed only two days.

I have to tell you about another incident that happened that summer because it has a bearing on things that happened later. Paul and I were lying out by the pool sunning ourselves – our favorite way to relax – when Linda came out and told us she was going to play the lead in *Bus Stop* at the Playhouse.

"You mean the Marilyn Monroe part?" Paul cried, not believing his ears.

"Yes," Linda said. "Isn't that wonderful?"

Paul started to laugh and nearly fell off his chaise. He simply couldn't imagine Linda as "Marilyn Monroe." She was tiny, and though she had long, pretty dancer's legs, the rest of her figure was roughly the shape of a pencil. Besides that, he thought of her as a mere baby.

A little hurt, Linda said, "You have to remember, daddy – the part was not written for Marilyn Monroe. The way it's written, she's a poor little waif from the country, and she really has no talent. She's rather pitiful. That's the way I'll play the part."

Paul tried to restrain his amusement. "You'll have to have a country-western accent, won't you?" he asked.

"Yes," she said. "I can do that. The hardest thing will be to sing just a little off-key in the nightclub scene."

Paul now had his own suite of offices at General Service Studios. A period began when he really worked all the time. He'd be up and gone from home by six at least and never home before dark. Sometimes he even slept on the daybed in the office. Once in a while, I went to the studio and "worked" with him. You know what that meant – kept him company while he worked. Other times, busy as I was, I felt very lonely and deserted. Often at the end of the day, a whole group of people involved with the show would drop in at his office, have a drink, and talk over the day's events. I'd have dinner ready at home and call to see when to expect him, and I'd hear the noise, chatter, and laughter, and it all sounded so exciting – all those people involved in a project together that everyone thought would be successful. One day I got an idea.

"Paul, why don't you give me a job at the studio? Surely I could do something to help you – anything to be part of the gang – to be near you, to see you sometimes."

He thought it through for a long pause. "Gee, honey, I wish I could, but I don't know what it would be. This is going to be hard work, and I need trained people, people in the business who already know their jobs. I don't have time to train anyone else."

I just sat there, not saying anything.

"Besides," he added, "I hate nepotism. You're always criticized when you hire your relatives. People would resent you. They might not show it, but they would."

"Okay," I sighed. I knew he was right, and I had to accept it. We'd been in this kind of spot before. I was used to his work habits. I was used to making my own life. Only now the children were growing up. Carol was already away at school. Linda was old enough to drive and was planning on going to California State College at Northridge. That, with all her other activities, would keep her plenty busy. Tony had turned sixteen in May, had his driver's license and a

138

steady girlfriend. I think he'd been keeping her on hold until he could drive. I wouldn't have all that chauffeuring to do – so what *would* I do with my time? You can't make a life out of ballet classes, not at my age. And volunteer work is fine but not too thrilling as a way of life. I couldn't even get interested in writing the short fiction I'd been selling. The "slicks" as they called the women's magazines were folding one by one – I wondered if I'd helped to kill them – and there I'd be, sitting in my big, beautiful, empty house thinking about all this excitement going on at the studio. Sure, I could come down sometimes, but I would be an outsider – I wouldn't be part of the team.

That was about the time I went with Linda to Cal State to enroll. It was a fairly new campus and very attractive. We saw a lot of her friends and all had lunch together in the cafeteria. What fun! I wished I were a student again. I had always loved school. I was one of the few who was sad on the last day of school in June and tickled pink when it started again in September.

Fresh from high school, I'd gone to Junior College in Kansas City but hadn't been able to go away to finish college – the Depression, you remember – and anyway, I wanted to get into radio. So I'd never graduated and gotten a degree. Why not do it now?

I won't go into details – just to say I took a French class because that was something I loved. It was five days a week and I thought I'd see if I could do it. I'd find out if my brain had atrophied or if I would even enjoy it. There wasn't too much red tape involved in just taking the one class. And I simply adored it! And just to put a finish on the subject, in December of 1961 I took my SAT test and also a language placement exam and was accepted as a regular student.

Everybody loved the idea. I had done something right. I was keeping busy at something worthwhile, and I wasn't messing in my husband's business where I didn't belong. Paul made jokes about

139

sending four children to school and there it was – a fait accompli. Even Linda approved. I didn't want her to be embarrassed by having her mother on the same campus. I promised to stay strictly away from the Theatre Arts Department. My French class was every morning at 8:00 a.m. After that, I'd have coffee in the cafeteria with one of my new classmates, and then I'd go home. If she wanted me, she knew where to find me, but I'd not bother her.

On September 26, 1962, two days after I started college, *The Beverly Hillbillies* made their debut, nine o'clock Wednesday on CBS. Paul's baby had grown strong enough to walk and talk – and it had teeth!

Young Paul Henning in Independence, Missouri.

Henning Children front row (left to right): Paul and Jane. Back row (left to right): Drusilla, Rose, and Patti.

Paul Henning spent his early career at KMBC radio in Kansas City, Missouri. It was at KMBC where Paul and Ruth first met.

Paul Henning interviewing Bernice Claire; flanked by
Ruth Warrick and Dick Berger at the Kansas City Airport for KMBC, 1937.

Ruth (Barth) Henning.

Henning family Christmas card photo from the 1950s
(from left): Carol, Paul, Tony, Ruth, and Linda.

Henning family Christmas card photo 1966 (from
left): Linda, Tony, Ruth, Paul, and Carol.

The *Saturday Evening Post* featured *The Beverly Hillbillies* and
Paul Henning as the cover story in the February 2, 1963 edition.
The cover image (above) featured Max Baer, Jr., Irene Ryan, Bud-
dy Ebsen, and Donna Douglas dressed in character.

Paul Henning (right) reviewing and editing an episode of *The Beverly Hillbillies*. This picture was also part of the *Saturday Evening Post* cover story.

Paul Henning met Harry Truman long before either were nationally known. The future president encouraged Henning to study law. The two exchanged correspondence several times throughout their lives.

Images are copies of letters between Henning and Truman. Photograph is from the Henning's 1974 visit to the Truman Library.

Ruth and Paul Henning came back to
Independence on March 1, 1974, with
Buddy Ebsen to visit the Truman
Presidential Library, and to present a
painting by George L. "Shag" Shultz of
President Truman. Following the
presentation, they toured the museum
with museum director Benedict Zobrist.

14

The Beverly Hillbillies III
(The First Year)

The Beverly Hillbillies! Some people loved it. Some people hated it! Nobody ignored it. Everybody was talking about it. Some of them were honestly puzzled by its popularity. Others explained it philosophically. People were tired of world problems – crime, violence, poverty! They wanted something light that they could laugh at. The timing was right! It was social commentary. The class struggle! It was slapstick! It was corn! People liked it because they could feel superior to the *Hillbillies*. It was a gimmick! A fluke! The officials of NBC and ABC admitted they probably wouldn't have bought the show if it had been offered to them. It's the poor slobs against the world! Their assorted adventures did not merely strain credulity – they crushed it. Each half hour seemed as if it contained sixty minutes. It was the arch symbol of a degraded mass television audience. The plots and gags were out of the fourth grade set. No culture – no message – no heart. Well, that's enough of that. You realize those words are quotes and I could fill up another page with them, but you get the idea.

But it wasn't all negative. Some writers actually liked it, some were crazy about it, or they at least had the good sense to know it would be a hit. Vance Kind, writing for the *Hollywood Reporter*, said, "Writer-producer Paul Henning has come up with a real winner in *The Beverly Hillbillies*. It bids fair to become one of the funniest filmed series ever to hit the TV sets." Jack Hellman of *Daily Variety* said this: "For laughing out loud, this is your show – the season's sleeper." Two smart men, Vance and Jack. They were right, of course. It hit number one in the ratings the third week. I heard that the cast and crew formed a conga line on the set chanting, "We're number one! We're number one!" Paul was so elated he went out and bought me a present, a lovely topaz ring – my birthstone. I still have it and wear it often, and it always reminds me of that sweet success.

When *The Beverly Hillbillies* wound up in Nielsen's number one spot, phone calls began coming in from New York. Jim Aubrey at CBS wanted another Paul Henning show as soon as possible – yesterday, hopefully. Paul was worn out from writing those first episodes by himself, dizzy from going back and forth between television and cinema, pretty hurt by all the nasty things the critics were writing, but at the same time, deliriously happy at the way the viewers were receiving the show. Of course, he told Aubrey he'd like to do another show but didn't know when he'd have time to write it.

"You don't need a pilot," Jim told him. "Anything you write is definitely on the schedule next season. I have the day and time all reserved for you."

That was pretty heady stuff. People in Hollywood began to say that Paul Henning could copy a page from the telephone book, and CBS would put it on the air.

"I tried that," Paul told me. "It didn't work."

Nobody really believed that, of course, least of all Paul who knew all too well the hard work involved in creating a new show. He was burning the midnight oil, not to mention the before-dawn oil, getting *The Beverly Hillbillies* off to a good start.

"What in the world will you do – about another show?" I asked Paul. You can't always tell when Paul's hatching an idea. The wheels keep turning and sometimes you don't know what he's thinking till the idea is completed.

"I can't do anything," Paul said. "I have so much work to do on *The Hillbillies*. I really can't think about anything else."

The day came, however, when Paul came home and announced, "Jim Aubrey will be in town tomorrow. He's coming to my office to hear about the new show."

"Good grief!" I cried. "You're really on the spot!"

And he was. But he ad-libbed an idea to Jim about a widow, three beautiful daughters and a train. Does that sound anything like *Petticoat Junction* to you? Jim loved it. He came out to our house and brought me the most beautiful flower arrangement I'd ever seen. "What a nice man!" I thought. I couldn't understand why people called him "The Smiling Cobra."

Meanwhile, the cameras kept grinding out *The Beverly Hillbillies*. People had said it was a one-joke show, but Paul had more ideas than he knew what to do with.

Early on, he had one of his less successful ideas. He wanted to flash back to scenes in the hills with Bea Benaderet playing Cousin Pearl, so he introduced Jethro's twin sister, Jethrine, played by Max Baer in drag; the voice dubbed by our daughter, Linda. I thought it was hilarious. Max did a wonderful job as the mincing Jethrine in curls and ruffles. And Linda, chosen because she was an expert at dubbing, had a sweet little girl voice as Jethrine. Dubbing, you know, is watching a film and putting in the voice to match the character's mouthing of the words. Maybe I was prejudiced. Maybe that's why I liked it – because it involved Linda – but even when I see repeats of that sequence today, I still think it's funny. I know Max enjoyed it. Sometimes you'd see him walking down a studio street, bare chested, wearing ruffly petticoats and twirling a bra around his finger.

Phil Gordon played Jazzbo Depew, a feisty little fellow in love with Jethrine – and the two of them together were a scream. The character didn't last long. It made Paul uncomfortable. He wanted to keep the characters, as unusual as they were, real and true. Max in drag was kind of burlesque.

151

Animals were big in the show. Paul had worked with animal trainer, Frank Inn, before and thought he was a genius – what's more, a kind genius. He trained his animals with love. Using Linda as a model, Paul made Elly May a lover of "critters." Donna loved animals, too, and got along great with them. She was absolutely fearless working with dogs, cats, mountain lions, bobcats, a chimp, an ostrich, a kangaroo, and a hippopotamus. Once the chimp bit her, but she swore it wasn't his fault and after treatment, insisted on going right ahead with the scene.

Frank Inn had taught some cats to swim. I made a special trip to the studio to see the swimming cat, Rusty, a big yellow Tom. He swam the length of the cement pond. Then Frank's assistant would quickly dry the cat's fur with a hair dryer, while an understudy took his place for a second take. There were several yellow cats – all expert swimmers – and by the time they'd used them all up, the first one was dry enough to do it again.

There was a flamingo, flown to California from its native habitat in Florida at great trouble and expense by Frank Inn. Jethro sees it and thinks it's a pink chicken. On Thanksgiving, they had a turkey dressed in a Pilgrim's outfit. I visited the set, and one of the funniest sights I ever saw was the turkey's agent, squatting on stage reading *Variety* while his client stood at his shoulder, craning his neck forward as turkeys do and looking for all the world as though he were reading *Variety*, too.

Once there was a kangaroo that Granny mistakes for a giant jackrabbit. The kangaroo was trouble right from the start. They're trained to box, they're strong, and they have a powerful kick. He wasn't at all in the mood to be photographed and the story called for Granny, thinking this is a huge rabbit she can cook, to capture it and get into a boxing match with it. The director had an awful time trying to get those scenes without injuring Granny. Paul called me frantically

152

and asked me to start looking at toy stores for a life-sized, stuffed kangaroo that they might possibly use in long shots to save some time. Of course, I tried to do it, but they only had giraffes, bears, dogs, cats, lions, elephants – no kangaroos. Somehow they did what they had to do, but I don't know how. I'd like to see that episode again.

And then there was the time Mr. Drysdale, the banker next door, got the idea to paint an advertisement for his bank on the side of a hippopotamus and have the animal march in a parade. Seeing it in the Drysdales's backyard, Granny is excited to think it's a big hog that she can enter in the country fair and win the prize. All well and good except for one thing: the hippo had a best friend – a baby elephant. They were inseparable. The hippo wouldn't go anywhere without his friend. The director had to devise some unusual camera angles to get the hippo in the picture without the elephant.

"Go try to hide an elephant!" he said at the end of the day.

The television audience loved the show, and soon fan mail started coming in. There were boxes and boxes, most of it for Elly May. Our daughter, Carol, who had taken a leave of absence from Berkeley in order to do some traveling, filled in the time by working on fan mail. It was a mind-boggling task. By this time, Paul had added a couple more secretaries besides Gloria. There were now Janet and Candy – both stunning. They all went to work on Donna's fan mail. I don't know if they ever answered all of it, but Carol left for Europe in March 1963.

In January 1963, I started my first semester at college as a regular student. I never took more than six units at a time. I had too many other duties, and I was eager to do well. I continued my French course and added Psychology. I went to school only Monday, Wednesday, and Friday. That relieved some of the strain.

Other events were coming along thick and fast. I'm getting these from my Daily Reminders. March 4, Linda had a screen test.

153

That indicates to me that *Petticoat Junction* was by now more than a vague idea in Paul's head. On March 9, Paul had a kidney stone – a painful malady he suffered from periodically. *Bye Bye Birdie* opened at the Paramount Theatre March 5. You could see Linda in some of the scenes, though most of her lines landed on the cutting room floor. On May 8, Paul and I flew to New York for the CBS Affiliates meeting. The cast of *Petticoat Junction* came, too, to be introduced. It was an exciting affair.

One thing stands out in my mind. Judy Garland who was to do her own show on CBS the following season sang a popular song of the day, "Call Me Irresponsible" with special lyrics. It ended, "Call me undependable. Say I'm unreliable, but it's undeniably true – I'm irrevocably signed with you." It brought down the house, given Judy's reputation.

That's the year Paul saw hordes of press people to talk about his new show. One day he invited a bunch of them to our suite at the Algonquin. I wondered what in the world he'd say about *Petticoat Junction* because at that point, it seemed to me there was nothing particularly unusual about it. Algonquin suites at that time separated the bedroom from the sitting room only with double louvered doors – so I stayed quiet as a mouse in the bedroom and listened. Paul served coffee and drinks and then began talking. I was absolutely knocked out! Paul was usually so quiet, so reserved, never tooting his own horn, always letting the other guy do the talking, but this was different. The chips were down. He had to do it, and he was positively brilliant.

"This show is about a way of life rapidly disappearing from the American scene, when people lived simple lives. They took time to enjoy each other, they helped their neighbors, they weren't completely dedicated to making money!" And on it went. I don't know whether he convinced the members of the media, but he certainly convinced me. Then again, I'm always a pushover where Paul is concerned.

The Emmy Awards were held about a week after we returned home. It's the one I mentioned in the first chapter of this book. *The Beverly Hillbillies* was nominated as Best Comedy Show, and there were scads of individual nominations, but they didn't win a one. *The Dick Van Dyke Show* won. That was the show *The Beverly Hillbillies* had saved from cancellation. We were sitting at a table right up front. Max Baer and his date, Sharon Tate, were right across from us. When they announced the winner, I cried. I couldn't help it. Paul had worked so damned hard, he'd done such a great job, the show was breaking all records, and still the Academy didn't see fit to give him an award.

The season ended, and Paul got another unpleasant shock. Irene Ryan's agent asked for an enormous jump in her salary. "If you don't meet our demands, you'd be doing the second year without Granny," he threatened. Paul was hurt. Irene was practically an unknown when he cast her as Granny. It looked like the others might join and ask for more money. Agents! By this time, Paul didn't have an agent. His attorney, Norman Tyre, negotiated his contracts, and he didn't need an agent to get him a job.

Jim Aubrey came to the rescue. He had a little dinner party that included Marty Ransahoff, Al Simon, and Paul at the Bel Air Hotel. I don't know how he knew it, but Irene's agent was having dinner there at another table. Jim said loudly so his voice would carry, "Fellows, the show is renewed for next year with or without Granny!" There was no more trouble from Irene's agent. None of it was Irene's fault. She was still in heaven playing Granny and would have been glad to do it the rest of her life.

15

Petticoat Junction

Petticoat Junction made its debut September 24, 1963, just one year after *The Beverly Hillbillies*. It was the most successful of the season's new shows, rating number five in the Nielsens. Everyone was surprised because it was on opposite what they called "blockbusting" competition, the new *Richard Boone Show*. Allan Rich wrote in the *Valley Times*, "Paul Henning may have another hit to go with his smasheroo, *The Beverly Hillbillies*." Cecil Smith commented in the *Los Angeles Times*, "Henning's magic touch has apparently extended to his new project, *Petticoat Junction*, one of only four shows to make the Nielsen golden list of the top fifteen. Neither Jerry Lewis, Danny Kaye, nor Judy Garland made the list."

The show didn't get terrible brickbats like *The Beverly Hillbillies*, nor did it get raves. Everybody seemed to think it was a pleasant, charming show – a nice change from psychiatric problems and violence. One writer said it was just "too innocent to pick on." Still they said it was a "property not to be underestimated. For Paul Henning, producer, it was his second smash."

This was the show. Paul had written, goodness knows when, right in the middle of *The Beverly Hillbillies*' first year. When he finally told me about it, I was thrilled and surprised that the inspiration had come from me – all unknowingly. Here's how.

My grandparents had owned and operated a small hotel in Eldon, a small town in mid-Missouri. The Rock Island Railroad ran between St. Louis and Kansas City stopping at all the little towns along the way. The Burris Hotel was within sight and walking distance of the railroad station. Every summer, my mother and I spent a lot of our vacation there. Mother had four sisters, three of them with daughters who also came to Eldon. We cousins had a ball. When the hotel was full of paying guests, we'd all sleep in a row on the floor of the family's apartment. As children, we played together, and as we grew older, we began to enjoy walking uptown and having a coke or a phosphate at the drugstore to let the local boys look us over. As soon as we'd get home, the phone would start ringing. They'd ask for my Aunt Tamar, the youngest sister, still unmarried and not a lot older than I. She'd be the go-between to arrange dates for us. Our grandparents had to approve them, of course. One rule they insisted on was that we were never – under any circumstances – to date one of the drummers (travelling salesmen) who were their regular customers.

Dinner was served much like at the Shady Rest Hotel in *Petticoat Junction* – at a long, family-style table in the dining room and the food was wonderful home cooking. In fact, a lot of people who had no need for a hotel room came for dinner. I think they were charged the outrageous price of fifty cents for a meal. Of course, that was in ancient times as my children like to remind me. There was a second table for the family, and I remember how we kids would peek in the window and worry when one of the guests at the first table ate too much or had a second piece of pie – for fear there wouldn't be enough for us. We should have known Mama (as we called our grandmother) had some put back for us.

So, that was the seed planted in Paul's mind by my memories. It took root and grew into *Petticoat Junction*. From the beginning, Paul wanted to call it *Whistle Stop* because that's what it was – a whistle stop on the railroad, and the double meaning was that the guys would whistle at the pretty girls. Again, he was thwarted because someone else had already registered the title with the Writers' Guild. One day we sat around in Paul's office – lots of us – trying to think

157

of other names. *Ozark Widow* was one of them. *Dern Tootin* was another. (Ugh!) *Petticoat Junction* won.

We had recently been re-acquainted with some very old friends and associates, Curt and Edythe Massey, from b.ack in the KMBC radio days. Curt had been a staff musician. His band played at Kansas City's Plamor Ballroom where I went at least twice a week, being the dancing fool I was. Curt was a tall, handsome, versatile musician who could play many instruments, and one of the sweetest guys we ever knew. His wife, Edythe, had been a beauty queen and had been in some of my classes at Kansas City Junior College. More recently, Curt had had a TV show with Martha Tilton. What I'm getting around to is that Paul hired him to do the music for *Petticoat Junction* – and *The Beverly Hillbillies*. Perry Botkin had gone his way after the first season. Paul and Curt wrote wrote the *Petticoat Junction* theme together – Paul the words and Curt, the music.

Come ride the little train that is goin' down the tracks to the Junction
Petticoat Junction! (said softly by the girls)
Forget about your cares, it is time to relax at the Junction
Petticoat Junction!
Lots of Curves – you bet – Even more when you get – to the Junction
Petticoat Junction!
There's a little hotel called the Shady Rest at the Junction
Petticoat Junction!
It is run by Kate – come and be her guest at the Junction
Petticoat Junction!
And there's Uncle Joe – he's a movin' kinda slow at the Junction
Petticoat Junction!

It was a catchy tune, sung and arranged by Curt, and it just fit as background for the little train, which was always in the opening shot. The train, the Hooterville Cannonball, was an important character in the show. Some people might have said it was the star. I think everybody loves trains. They're romantic – they make us dream of faraway places. Paul used to lie in bed when he was a boy and listen to the train whistle as it went through Independence. Some folks are absolutely crazy about trains. I even heard that one man who didn't care a thing about television, didn't even own a TV set, used to go to his neighbor's just to watch *Petticoat Junction*, not for the action, the plot, or the pretty girls – just for the train.

One day, doing postproduction work on *The Beverly Hillbillies*, Paul and some of the crew were at the Todd-A-O Studios located conveniently right at the back gate of General Service. Postproduction includes some editing, putting in music, sound effects, laughs, etc. Thinking aloud, Paul remarked that he wished he knew more about trains. Right away, somebody recommended he get in touch with Jerry Best who worked at Disney Studios. Jerry knew all about trains – he'd written several books on the subject. Through Jerry, they found the little train up at Sonora, California. It was just right for what Paul had in mind. The first year, they made all their long shots of the train up in Sonora. It was considerable trouble and expense to take a crew up there, so before long, they had a miniature made in Japan to exact specifications so they could take the long shots any time they wished right there at General Service. They also built a mock up (reproduction) of the train (with open sides for filming) on a sound stage. A lot of action took place there.

I've read scads of publicity about how the three girls were picked for the show. Here's the way it happened as Paul and I remembered it. Marty Ransahoff had put Sharon Tate under personal contract. She was a beautiful girl, and Marty planned to groom her for movie stardom, but he thought it might be nice for her to get a little experience on television first. So he asked Paul if he'd be willing to cast her as the blonde, Billie Jo. She was beautiful, so Paul saw no objection. Pat Woodell was found in the usual way, through the casting people. It was a bonus that she could sing. Some of the group went out to The Horn, a nightclub in Santa Monica to hear her. She was the brunette, Bobbie Jo. That left only the redhead. So how did it happen that our daughter, Linda, got the part when her father was so against nepotism? Of course, I was biting my tongue the whole time to keep from saying anything. It was Bea Benaderet who did it. She had seen Linda the previous summer in *Bus Stop* at the North Hollywood Playhouse and in some showcases in which her son, Jack Bannon, had worked with Linda.

"What are you looking around for?" she asked Paul. "There's your redhead."

Linda came down to the studio and had a screen test. Dick Wesson, the producer, thought she was fine. Paul worried about it, but he knew Linda was good – he knew how hard she had worked and how much she wanted the part. Besides that, he simply adored her. And besides that, he had some strong feelings for Linda's mother who also wanted Linda to get the part. So what was the poor man to do?

The crew getting ready to film the first episode, in the summer of 1963, and had taken some publicity stills, when they found out Sharon Tate had posed for some semi-nude photos, and that made a difference. This was a family show. They couldn't have those photos come to light after the show was on the air. Everyone was distressed. Seemed they'd have to start all over with the casting. Then Ozzie Nelson saved the day. He brought Jeannine Riley to Paul's office and introduced her. She had worked on their show, and he thought she was a good actress and she sure was pretty – so in short order, they had their blonde.

It was a happy set. Bea and Edgar Buchanan were old pros. Two other old-timers, Smiley Burnette and Rufe Davis, were the trainmen. Frank Cady was Sam Drucker, owner of the General Store and an old friend of Kate Bradley. The girls all got along beautifully. Some members of the Press tried to drum up a feud between them, but it just didn't happen. They all had equal parts, they knew they were very lucky to be on a hit show, and they were eager to make good. Off screen, they were not close. They all had their own lives and not much time to live them now that they were in production. Later, they traveled a lot making personal appearances at state fairs, charity events, and talk shows – and as they got better acquainted, they began to enjoy each other's company.

Late in November of 1963, when they were filming the Christmas show, the writers had a lovely idea to decorate the little train with lights and have all the folks in the area ride through the valley singing Christmas carols. When Curt Massey began to edit the music, he was pretty disappointed. The Christmas Carols just didn't come across. Hardly anybody seemed to be singing very well. What was the reason? They filmed that scene on November 22, 1963, the day President Kennedy was assassinated. Nobody had the heart to sing.

Curt had a complete music studio in his home in Beverly Hills. His recording setup had many tracks, so he could play several instruments, one at a time, then put them all together to sound like an orchestra. So here's what we did. Linda and I went to his house. Curt was there with his son. We all sang the carols doing different parts and sang them several times, each time on a different track. That way, all together, it sounded like a crowd of people singing. It worked.

That was a sorrowful weekend for everyone. I was in class when we got the news. I'd like to explain that this class was very difficult for me at first. It was called History of French Civilization and was taught by a charming French woman with a fine Parisian accent. She lectured to us, in French, and of course, I had to take notes in French and try to read them when I got home. I didn't think I could do it. Early in the semester I told Paul that I thought I'd drop the class. It was too hard. I'd never get an "A" grade in it.

"I'm surprised at you," he said. "I never thought you were a quitter."

"But it's too hard," I wailed. "I'm not used to listening to a lecture in French, and when we have exams, there'll be essay questions. Not only will I have to know the content of what she's saying, but I'll have to write about it in French."

"So you'll work a little harder. You'll get used to it."

"I'll never get an A," I moaned.

"Now that's the silliest thing I ever heard you say," Paul scolded. "You're there to learn, I thought. Not to get a grade."

I reacted just the way he knew I would. "All right," I said, clenching my teeth. "I'll take the damn class. What's more, I *will* get an A." And I did. But sometimes I asked a couple of native-born French women, who were in the class to get their teaching credentials, to help me after class with something I'd missed. They turned their backs on me. I think they resented that I, a mere upstart, was trying to compete in their own native language.

That day, after we heard the news of the shooting in Dallas, miraculously, it all changed. Class was dismissed. No use trying to go on with it under the circumstances. I ran out to the hall and couldn't help crying. One of the French women came up to me.

"I'm so sorry," she said, putting her arm around my shoulder. "You know, we loved him, too."

After that, they were helpful and friendly. But at what price? I stopped on my way home at the Little Brown Church, whose doors were always open, and went up to the altar to pray for Kennedy's life. I didn't know it, but it was already too late.

We all grieved, but life goes on. A week later, there was a sneak preview of *Bedtime Story*, Paul's second film with Stanley Shapiro. On December 12, Carol returned from Europe. We celebrated Christmas. Johnson was President, and the war in Vietnam began to escalate.

Meanwhile, back at the studio, both Paul's shows were swimming along, and one day, Frank Inn (the animal trainer) came to Paul's office.

"Paul, I'd like you to meet Higgins," he said and led a cute little dog in on a leash. He was what is known as a cockapoo.

Paul and his co-writer and the secretaries all raved over Higgins and petted him, and then Frank got down to business.

"I found this little fellow at the animal shelter," he said. "I took him home with me just because he was so cute – but when I started to train him and found out how smart he was, I went right back to the pound and got his sister and brother."

Then he began to put Higgins through his paces. It's hard to explain the clever things he did, but he was amazing! Paul wasn't sure yet how they could use him, but he definitely wanted first chance.

"Don't show him to anyone else, please," he asked Frank. "I know we'll have a place for him on one of the shows."

And that's how *Petticoat Junction* got "Dog," which was all they ever called him. He followed Betty Jo homed after school one day and won his place in the household. Uncle Joe pretended to think he was a lot of trouble, but secretly he was just as smitten as everyone else. None of them realized they were working with a future superstar of the animal world, the famous Benji.

In one scene of the show, weeks after Higgins made his debut, Betty Jo wrote a play in which the dog played the part of a private eye. He had a long scene in which he makes his entrance in a little toy car. He gets out, goes to the safe, removes some papers, gets back in the car, and drives off. He did it right on the first take just by following hand signals from his trainer. The director was so impressed with him, he almost cried.

"I've worked with a lot of members of the Screen Actors' Guild who couldn't do that in one take," he said.

Higgins became a regular member of the cast. He had his own dressing room right on the set. It was a small doghouse with a small yard of artificial grass and a little picket fence. There was a sign in the yard, "Cats and people, keep out." He went there to rest sometimes between takes. On rainy days, his trainer fastened plastic baggies on his paws with rubber bands for galoshes. A star couldn't perform with wet feet, could he?

Years later, when he won such fame and fortune as Benji, he was already an old dog, but we were all so proud of him. Paul and I used to go out and visit Frank and his wife, Juanita. Benji would jump up in my lap and lick my face. How many other people can claim that kind of relationship with a movie star? In subsequent Benji films, his sister, son, granddaughter, other relatives who looked like him, did the work. They were good, but none equaled the original Higgins.

In the spring of that first year, the *Petticoat Junction* girls made a big hit as "The Ladybugs." The Beatles had just been a sensation on *The Ed Sullivan Show*. Everybody was talking about the four boys from England with their crazy long haircuts and their wild music. Paul had the idea to have Uncle Joe try to cash in on the Beatles' publicity and get up an act for the girls. They wore scraggly wigs, black tights, and long sweatshirts with big ladybugs on the front and sang, "He was just seventeen – you know what I mean!" They were good. They could all sing, and Pat was a soloist who could belt out a song. Linda played the part of Ringo Starr, the drummer,

164

dancing around and drumming wildly. The other girls held guitars. Since they needed a fourth girl, Uncle Joe got Selma Plout's daughter to join them. The role was played by Sheila James (Zelda on Dobie Gillis). They were so good and caused so much talk that they were asked to be on *The Ed Sullivan Show*. What a thrill! They made one appearance as The Ladybugs and then came back in their lovely dresses with all the crinoline petticoats. A short time after that, they were on *The Tonight Show*. Business was booming.

I stayed out of school that spring semester of '64 – too much else was happening. Paul and I went to New York in February on business – don't ask me what. I think Paul was lobbying CBS to do the shows in color the following year.

In May, Pat Woodell married her steady, Gary Clarke, of *The Virginian*. Linda was a bridesmaid. Pat was fabulously beautiful. Shortly after that, Paul and I went to Europe.

Back home again in June, just in time for Tony's graduation from high school. We were very proud of him. He was president of the student body and had won a scholarship.

Linda opened at the Pasadena Playhouse in *Best Foot Forward*. Jack Bannon, Bea Benaderet's son, was in it, too. Carol was working for CBS at the Republican Convention in San Francisco, the one that nominated Barry Goldwater for president.

Amidst all that was happening, in August, Gracie Allen died. The funeral was at Forest Lawn, and the crowds were so great they had to install microphones outside the chapel for them to hear the service. It was a sad day. We had loved Gracie for such a long time. We grieved for George. He'd be lost without Gracie. We wondered what on earth he'd do now. He so loved show business, but without Gracie, the act wasn't much. It was the end of an era.

16

Double Your Pleasure

On Tuesday nights, you could watch *Petticoat Junction*, and on Wednesday, there was *The Beverly Hillbillies*. Lucky viewers! Lucky Paul! Workin' his buns off keeping two shows high in the Nielsens. And just so he wouldn't get lazy, CBS was hinting that if he should happen to come up with a third show, they wouldn't exactly throw rocks.

Lucky daughter Carol! She enjoyed working in the Publicity Department of General Service Studios, had sold two *Addams Family* scripts, and bought herself a bright red Chevy convertible she named Rosario.

Lucky daughter Linda! *Petticoat Junction* was in its second year, she was guesting on game shows, and bought herself a yellow Porsche named LeRoy.

Lucky son Tony! He had begun his college career at Stanford, become a cheerleader, and joined a fraternity. (The latter two were only temporary – he was a serious student.)

Lucky me, too, ha! Now I really felt "de trop." Hardly anybody was ever at home anymore, and the answer to "Guess who's coming to dinner?" was "Nobody!" Doggedly, I started another year at Cal State. Besides my usual French Lit course, I took Drama. It had nothing at all to do with getting my degree, but once in a while, you have to do something just for kicks. Now I could read Stanislavski and find out why I had always done the things I did when I acted.

A lot of perks go with a successful TV show. I got the advantage of one. All the cars used on *The Beverly Hillbillies* were Chryslers. Therefore, we got to use a new Chrysler every year just for the price of license and insurance. Since Paul was by that time addicted to Mercedes Benz, I got the Chryslers. They ranged yearly along the line from an Imperial, a station wagon, a New Yorker, and finally, a Roadrunner in poison green with a horn that honked "Beep" like the roadrunner in the cartoon. I got a lot of attention from young guys in filling stations and car washes. They always asked me if I wanted to sell my hot rod. But I didn't.

When the show was finally canceled and I had to give up the Roadrunner or buy it, I kissed it goodbye reluctantly because Paul wanted to get me my own Mercedes. I certainly didn't mind that. There was that snobbish little frisson when you tell a valet parking attendant – "The blue Mercedes." Other than that, I stubbornly maintained I didn't care so long as it took me there and brought me back. I meant it at the time, but I'm just as corruptible as the next person. I grew to like those cars very much. After the blue one, I had a red one, and I'm just waiting to inherit Paul's white one after he gets a new one.

The Beverly Hillbillies were still flying high and the critics were still complaining. The audience remained faithful, however, and that included a senator; a big business tycoon who adjourned board meetings in time to watch *The Beverly Hillbillies*; a jet setter who was on first name basis with waiters in Paris and Rome; President Ike, who had been known to keep an important visitor waiting while the show was on the air; even the renowned Shakespearian actor, Maurice Evans, along with big stars, professors, psychologists, and plenty of just plain folks.

They had a lot of interesting and famous guest stars. Some of them actually volunteered their services. The widely read gossip columnist, Hedda Hopper, was a big fan. She had written in her column the very first year: "It's ridiculous that Henning's *Beverly Hillbillies*, the number one show, has never received an award. Could it be jealousy? Or don't the people who vote on TV awards watch

167

their competition?" She was thrilled when Paul asked her to guest on the show.

Jed Clampett had bought himself a down and out movie studio, and in an effort to save it was planning to produce his own pictures, the really good kind like the picture palace in Bug Tussle used to show silent films. So Hedda, wearing one of her famous hats, starred in one of the films.

Another guest star, one that everyone turned out to see, was Gloria Swanson. The Clampetts read in the paper that Gloria is auctioning off some of her possessions, and not realizing it's for charity, they think she's destitute. Naturally, they want to come to her aid. Jed feels the best way to do that and not hurt her pride is to offer her a job. So they offer her the lead in *Passion's Plaything*, another silent picture. They all appear in the picture, too. The outcome is pretty funny.

Phil Silvers appears on several episodes as a slick confidence man who appeals to Jed's community spirit by offering to share his secret for eliminating California smog. He will drill a large hole through the San Bernardino Mountains, install a powerful blower, and blow the smog right out to the Pacific Ocean. Of course, he doesn't have the money to finance this plan, and that's where Jed comes in.

Later, in New York, Phil sells them a plot of land in Central Park. When they try to pitch their tent there and build a bonfire to cook vittles, they are arrested by an Irish cop, played by Sammy Davis, Jr.

In Washington, D.C., Senator George Murphy played himself, and Rich Little impersonated President Nixon on the phone. Bob Cummings judged a beauty contest in Beverly Hills, which Elly May almost won. Rob Reiner was a hippy musician. Leo Durocher, then the manager of the Dodgers, scouted Jethro for his strong pitching arm. Rosemary DeCamp played a society lady friend of Mrs.

Drysdale's. Roy Clark, fresh from his triumphant performance at the Bug Tussle Hilton, was in Hollywood to try to find an agent. Louis Nye was Sonny Drysdale, the banker's son, who courted Elly May. Wally Cox was a bird watcher. That's the way it went. If your favorite star hadn't yet made an appearance, all you had to do was be a little patient. When a show is as popular as *The Beverly Hillbillies*, it's not hard to get guest stars.

Perhaps the most famous cameo appearance was by John Wayne. Granny, for reasons too complicated to explain, is convinced the Indians are surrounding the mansion. At the crucial moment, John Wayne rides to the rescue to save the helpless women from a fate worse than death. It was a great pay-off, and Wayne refused any compensation. He said it was a pleasure to do a favor for his friend, Buddy Ebsen, and besides, he loved the show. Paul sent him a bottle of his favorite bourbon.

Petticoat Junction was doing quite all right on its own. As one critic said, it was "a top audience grabber simply because it was about a group of identifiable and endearing people – folksy foolishness."

Uncle Joe is forever trying out get-rich-quick schemes, one of which involved a buffalo. When Frank Inn, the animal trainer, was given the job of finding a buffalo, he went on a real safari in the Western plains. They're not easy to find, and when you do find one, they're not easy to catch, acquire, and transport. Frank did find one, however, put it in his trailer, and started for home. He was a long way out on the lone prairie and just had to stop overnight. Since motels don't welcome buffalo guests, he parked the trailer out back behind some shrubbery, checked in, and got a good night's sleep. Alas! When he went to get his trailer, half of it wasn't there. The buffalo had kicked it apart and split. He was no doubt halfway back to his herd by now – or do buffalos have homing instincts like cats and dogs?

Frank Inn really hated to be defeated. He rented a bull, had a buffalo costume made for it, and it worked. I don't believe it had any really dramatic scenes to play. There was a representative from The Humane Society on the set the whole time though, to make sure "Buffalo Bull" got the proper treatment.

The three girls had a good act whipped up by now and were very much in demand for personal appearances at fairs, telethons, talk shows, game shows, nightclubs, parades – they even entertained at the top of the tram in Palm Springs. They were young, enthusiastic, and really enjoyed it.

Linda, as Betty Jo, the tomboy, learned to pitch horseshoes, play football, and drive the Hooterville Cannonball. A choreographer made up a dance called The Hooterville Hop that became popular. The girls often had their friends to the Shady Rest where they sang and danced and livened things up.

And then Linda became a finalist for the Deb Star of the Year, chosen by Union Local 706, a branch of the International Alliance of Theatrical Stage Employees (IATSE), more popularly known as the Makeup Artists and Hairstylists Guild. The awards were presented on TV at the Hollywood Palladium in January. Steve Allen and Jayne Meadows were co-hosts and the judges were five prominent members of the entertainment industry. Linda and I went shopping for a smashing dress, beautiful, sexy, and loaded with class. We chose an all-white sheer wool, trimmed with bands of white fox (we were still wearing fur). If I do say so myself, and I do, she looked stunning! Newspapers reported that of the *Petticoat Junction* actresses, Linda had had the most acting success so far, but the title went to Swedish actress, Sivi Aberg, a tall, blonde, typical Scandinavian beauty. We heard, through reliable sources, that Linda came in a close second. Ah well, Sivi was never heard from again as far as I know.

170

Higgins, Petticoat's "Dog," won the Patsy award that year for Best Performance by an Animal. Broadcast Music awarded a citation to *The Beverly Hillbillies* theme, "Ballad of Jed Clampett," in recognition of the great popularity attained on the Country and Western charts.

Other minor awards trickled in, but never the big one. Never an Emmy. Say it again, Hedda Hopper!

17

A Pig, a Pancake, a Pretty Woman

Sometime during *The Beverly Hillbillies'* third year, *Petticoat Junction's* second year, Paul Henning stopped goofing off and came up with a third show. Strictly speaking, it was Jay Sommers' baby, an idea he'd turned into a radio show some years earlier, but he needed Paul's help and track record with CBS to get it on the air. Paul helped in the casting (one of his special talents) and became Executive Producer. Gossip around Hollywood was that "Paul Henning had done it again!"

The show was *Green Acres.* It was about a big city lawyer who longs to get back to the soil, buys a farm, and moves his sophisticated city wife out to the sticks. It was sort of a reverse situation from *The Beverly Hillbillies*, only if the critics thought *The Beverly Hillbillies* was far out, they hadn't seen nothin' yet!

Activity began early in 1965. Jay, who had been writing for *Petticoat Junction*, now spent all his time on the new project. Dick Chevillat entered the picture early on to collaborate. They started looking around at talent. There was one actor, formerly a very big star, who led the pack being considered for the lawyer. One night, Paul and Jay took him to dinner at Chasen's to discuss the deal, and unfortunately for him, he broke his plate. I don't mean he dropped Chasen's crockery on the floor – his table manners were fine. But he was a complainer. Nothing was right. The service was too slow. The food wasn't to his liking. The wine was fruity instead of nutty. Their table was in the wrong location. Bitch – bitch – bitch!

"I wouldn't work with him for a million dollars!" Paul said to Jay when the evening was over.

"He's a fine actor," Jay said.

"He's trouble," Paul insisted, and Jay agreed.

They got busy with the casting people and found a much better star – amiable Eddie Albert.

A lot of actresses had been interviewed for the role of the wife, and a few tested. I overheard a discussion among some of the men at the studio. One actress seemed to be favored above all others and as far as I could tell, her chief qualification was that she had a big bosom. Men!

Paul had a different idea. He remembered a play we'd seen on Broadway some years ago – a charming comedy, *The Happy Time*. The teenage son of the family gets a big crush on the French maid, played by Eva Gabor. We loved her performance; in fact, we loved everything about the play and were pleasantly surprised that she was such a good actress. So far, the Gabors had been known only as personalities on talk shows.

When Paul suggested Eva for *Green Acres*, everybody thought he was out of his mind.

"She can't act!"

"Those temperamental Gabors!"

"She'll cause trouble!"

"Nobody will understand her Hungarian accent!"

And so on.

"Just give her a try, huh?" Paul said. So they did. After all, he was the executive producer.

Pat Buttram was to be Mr. Haney, a rural confidence man, and Tommy Lester would be Eb, the hired man. Paul remembered him from a showcase at the North Hollywood Playhouse. And oh yes, *Green Acres*, like *Petticoat Junction*, had a non-human star. In *Petticoat*, it was the train. In *Green Acres*, it was Arnold the pig, treated as the adopted son of Doris and Fred Ziffel.

The talk of the town that fall involved a new term, "Cross Pollination." *Green Acres*, the farm, would be located in the Hooterville Valley, the very venue of *Petticoat Junction's* Shady Rest Hotel. Cross Pollination meant that the characters of both shows would meet now and then in the general store, the train, or anywhere their plots took them and appear on each other's shows. "Birds do it – bees do it – even actors on TV do it!" Cross Pollination!

Paul thought up the word and was pleased with it and the idea it represented. This hadn't been done before and some pundits looked on it as a dangerous gamble. I don't know why. Go explain a pundit! To me, it sounded like a very good idea. Even *The Beverly Hillbillies* might come to visit from time to time. On one Thanksgiving episode, they all celebrated together at the Shady Rest Hotel – all three shows. Why not? They were all blood relatives – Paul Henning's blood. That's what he'd given to get them all going.

Green Acres started off strong to the minor accompaniment of critical booing. It remained that way along with the other two shows, and to this day (1993), it's very popular. In fact, it has a big cult following.

Eva Gabor proved all her critics wrong. After an initial skirmish when she demanded her own makeup man and hairdresser (both expensive), she was a dream. Totally professional, she was always on time, always knew her lines, and always looked the part. She had never cooked but now that she was on the farm, she started her cooking experimentation with pancakes. They turned out to be as hard as manhole covers, but her husband ate them bravely, and so did everyone else. She never caught on that they weren't delicious, so they remained her specialty. Her gowns were gorgeous, whipped up by famous designers like Dior, Scassi, and Count Sarmi. Once in a while, they had a little problem about her Hungarian accent. She lost

174

it. If she spoke a line with all the "V's" and "W's" in the right places, they had to shoot the scene over.

"Back to Accent-Retaining School for you!" the director would tease.

Eva was no fool. She'd been in this country long enough and knew how to speak good English, but she always tried to stay true to her legend – a beautiful, crazy Hungarian!

Her husband – the fourth, I think, but who's counting? – Richard Brown was his name – was a stockbroker in New York, but when he got tired of flying back and forth, Filmways offered him a position. Wisely, he took it. Eva needed him. And just between you and me, Zsa Zsa needed him, too. Zsa Zsa Gabor wasn't currently married, and once in a while, she had to have a big, strong man to get her out of scrapes. I liked Richard. I thought he was attractive and strong – no gigolo, he. I was sorry when they split up, but I guess it wouldn't be easy being married to a Gabor.

Strangely enough, Eva and I became good friends. I say "strangely" because no matter what else, she IS an international glamour girl, and I'm well, I'm just me – an ordinary housewife who happened to have married some kind of genius. Now when I took guests to the studio, I had another set to visit. I loved to take them to the *Green Acres* set. Eva never let me down. She always rushed over to me, embraced me with glad cries of "Dahling!" and ordered somebody to bring chairs for me and my guests. In no time at all, tea and cookies would be served to us. My guests became firm fans.

Eva's house was something out of a storybook. All her furniture pieces were authentic antiques, all of the upholstery and wall covering in her living room was powder blue satin brocade. A perfect background for her pale beauty.

There were a lot of events we attended together in those days: charity balls, award banquets, the types of events held at the Beverly

Hilton Grand Ballroom with stars galore, both on and off stage. The only problem for me was that no matter how hard I tried, she always made me feel like a little brown mouse. She really was gorgeous.

One time, I thought I had it made. I had a new ball gown, all white lace, form fitting, covered with silver sparkles and a midriff of flesh colored chiffon made to look bare. Shoes to match, white mink stole, sparkly earrings – the works. Ah ha!, I thought on the way to pick up Richard and Eva, I'm going to show them something tonight. Did I? You know the answer to that. Eva made her entrance in a gown of all gold lame, banded at the sleeves and décolletage with deep brown mink. After that, I just gave up. But I still enjoyed being with them, the "just plain Browns."

Eddie Albert was also a doll. His wife, Margo, was a charming, warm woman who had been a really big star in the past. (You may remember that she won an Oscar for her performance in the first *Lost Horizon*.) Now she was satisfied to retire and make a home for Eddie and their children: Edward, 14, and Maria, an adopted girl from Spain. Margo was always doing work to improve the lot of Hispanic people in Los Angeles, and I believe there are some plaques around the barrio in her honor. Edward grew up to be a fine actor and extremely attractive man. I especially loved him in the role he played recently on *Beauty and the Beast*, the television series.

Eddie was a good choice to play the gentleman farmer. He actually was just that. Their home in Pacific Palisades had a large bit of property out back where he loved to grow his own vegetables. Once when we were there at a dinner party, we were told that all the salad ingredients had come from his garden.

"Which makes that the most expensive salad you'll ever eat," Margo said wryly.

When it was time for the second course, Eddie excused himself, and there was a longish wait for the entrée. Eddie had gone out to pick the corn, shuck it, pop it into boiling water, and cook it. We really got it FRESH!

"It starts turning starchy as soon as it's picked. That's the reason for the hurry," he explained.

I didn't know much about Pat Buttram at the beginning of *Green Acres* – just as Gene Autry's sidekick – and not being a western fan, that wasn't much. I'm told he built quite a reputation as a funny after-dinner speaker – and now we look forward to hearing him as the resident wit at Pacific Pioneer Broadcasters luncheons.

Tommy Lester was just right for his part as Eb Dawson – young, hayseed, and naïve. He's a very religious young man and spends a lot of time now traveling with Christian groups. Alvy Moore, also just right as the country agent, completed the main character roster. Oh, I mustn't forget Doris and Fred Ziffel and Alph and Ralph, the carpenters, and a host of other rural characters.

Looking over other activities for that spring and summer of 1965 makes me dizzy. Tony took his second college semester at the Stanford campus in Beutelsbach, Germany. Buddy Ebsen starred in *Paint Your Wagon* at the Valley Music Theatre.

Linda worked on *Carousel* with Peter Palmer and Margot Moser at Salt Lake City's new Valley Music Hall. She played the part of the daughter, Louise, who dances the seventeen-minute ballet toward the end. Paul and I planned to go up for the opening, and when Art Linkletter found that out, he invited us to go in his private plane with a group of stars who had invested in the theatre. They included Ann Rutherford and Bill Dozier, the Robert Taylors, the Edgar Bergens, Hedda Hopper, Rhonda Fleming, and naturally, the Art Linkletters.

Even more exciting than that, when it seemed that part of the run of the play would interfere with *Petticoat Junction* shooting, Paul, the doting father, arranged for the rental of Frank Sinatra's Lear jet to take Linda back and forth. Frank's personal pilot just happened to live across the street from us. It was so handy. I went up with them once. What a sweet little plane!

Paul and I bought a radio station, KCEY, in Turlock, California, in the middle of the state where the principal crops are asparagus and turkeys. In fact, the branch of Cal State there is called "Turkey Tech." It's a nice town; we felt sentimental about radio, and we hoped it would be profitable.

Donna Douglas made a movie, *Frankie and Johnny*, that summer, starring opposite Elvis Presley, and came out of it feeling very depressed and distressed. Some people said she fell in love with Elvis. Others said he "came on" to all his leading ladies, and when Donna found out it was just a game, that's what distressed her. She said she had some personal problems.

Whatever it was, Paul was worried about her, and asked my permission to have her stay with us for a while. We had the room. Tony was touring Europe after his semester in Germany, and Carol was preparing to go back up to Berkeley to resume her college education. So Donna came. We tried our best to give her love and support. It really broke my heart to sit across the kitchen table from her as I often did, both of us with our coffee cups, and look into those big blue eyes as they filled with tears. I tried to say comforting, consoling things to her just like a mother would, and our whole family loved her.

Sometimes in the evenings, Paul and I liked to go for a walk down by Toluca Lake. Most times, Donna would come with us. One Saturday night, I couldn't help thinking what a darn shame it was for this lovely young girl to be spending her evening like that with an old married couple. It made me want to cry.

When we saw the film, *Frankie and Johnny*, we didn't think it was very good. And as for Elvis, I never could see what all the swooning was about. Forgive my generation gap!

In the fall, all three shows went on the air in living color, and they all did well in the ratings. I went back to school and became immersed in the French subjunctive – which really didn't bother me. After so many years of languages, you do know all about the subjunctive.

18

The Coziest Studio in Hollywood

General Service Studios, the last of the intimate studios, was a favorite with everybody. Small enough – only eight stages – so you could walk all around it with ease. Yet, it was big and busy enough that you could run into a lot of interesting people: *The Beverly Hillbillies*;, the *Petticoat Junction* family; the *Green Acres* gang; Ozzie, Harriet, David, and Ricky Nelson;, Juliet Prowse; *The Addams Family*; even *Mister Ed*, Arnold the Pig, darling dog Higgins, and a whole zoo of other animals.

The studio was owned by the Nasser Brothers: George, James (Jim), and Henry. Their family had been big in the picture business for years, and now George, (a bachelor) lived in his own little bungalow built right on the studio lot. Jim had offices there, but lived just blocks from us in Toluca Lake with his wife, Dorothy, a good friend of mine. And Henry, (also a bachelor) lived in San Francisco and managed some movie houses the brothers owned there.

Paul had a spacious suite of offices – his second home. Besides his own large office, there were three secretaries' offices and Paul's own adjoining private bath and shower with room for a daybed in case of overnight stays. At one end of the big office was a bar, which doubled as a kitchenette. It was furnished with electrical appliances like a coffee maker, a juicer, a toaster oven, and of course, a refrigerator. This was before microwaves.

Besides bar supplies, Gloria kept it stocked with Paul's favorite luncheon items like V8 juice, canned salmon, cheese and crackers, soups, and fruit. He often invited visitors to have lunch – and some of them were surprised at the Spartan menu. On the other hand, Buddy Ebsen, who had a large, attractive dressing room, employed a manservant who brought in tacos from The Farmers' Market, and if you were a guest there, you got tacos and champagne.

All the stars had nice big dressing rooms, not all of them with private baths, but cozy and comfortable. Bea Benaderet liked to play hostess to her makeup and wardrobe women at the end of the day when they'd all have a drink and a cigarette together in her dressing room and discuss the day's events. Linda raised one of her many kittens in her dressing room. Her fuzzy slipper was its bed, and she fed it every two hours with a doll's nursing bottle. George Burns had an office there, which he kept for years until just recently. Eva Gabor's dressing room – so they tell me – was elegant. I never saw it, but they said it was mirrors all over. If I looked like Eva, I'd want a lot of mirrors, too. Toni Haezart, the studio nurse, had an office where she dispensed vitamin shots and medications for mild ailments with the assistance of a big, fluffy calico cat named Marmalade. Besides Marmalade, Toni fed all the stray cats in Hollywood. Lots of folks on the lot contributed cat food.

All the sets and most of the offices were equipped with coffee urns going non-stop and usually doughnuts and honey cakes for those who cared to indulge. These refreshments were furnished courtesy of Filmways, and I remember hearing an actor who was working at the studio for the first time express his surprise that the goodies were free. "They charge you most places," he said.

There wasn't a commissary, but catering trucks made the rounds daily, and just out the back gate was a little café where you could go to eat and chat. The one thing they lacked, due to their small size, was enough parking space. If you were a regular executive or star, you got an assigned place on the lot, but some of the others had to park and walk and risk tickets. If you were on the lot though, you were home free. There was always a guard on duty at the gate and at night, the whole place was locked up tight.

George Nasser, a teddy bear of a man, employed an expert chef who cooked up special lunches every day and if you were invited to his bungalow, it was a great privilege. The Nassers were Lebanese, and so was the food – homemade yogurt every day and all sorts of delicacies featuring lamb, rice, cracked wheat, lentils, mint, and pine nuts. For dessert, there was often baklawa, a Middle Eastern cake made with paper-thin pastry, honey, and ground pistachio nuts. The kids used to call it grasshopper cake because the pistachios on it were green.

George was a very generous man who invited a host of friends to his bungalow and also to the Nasser retreat in Ben Lomond, California. That was a big, rangy frame house where he employed Maria, an Italian cook, who had learned to cook Lebanese part time. We never tried to diet when we went to either place.

And the parties! One year on Paul and Linda's birthdays (the same day), there was a big celebration with a cake as big as Ohio. For entertainment, they showed an episode of *The Beverly Hillbillies* dubbed in Japanese. It was really strange to hear those hillbillies speaking Japanese.

The Christmas parties at General Service were the talk of the town. Everybody who worked there and all their families were invited. One whole stage, the biggest one, would be cleared, and the professional set decorators would go to work on it. One year they painted a gigantic snow scene that covered one entire wall. There was always an enormous Christmas tree decorated as only professionals could do it, round tables with red and green tablecloths, catered food, music, and dancing. It truly was the time to be jolly! The bill was shared between Filmways and the Nassers. No wonder everybody loved to work there.

Once a year, Donna Douglas and Nancy Kulp teamed up to give a children's party with refreshments and gifts for all the kids. The children loved it but no more than Donna and Nancy.

I asked John Nicolaides, who was comptroller for Filmways, to tell me what the overall feeling was about General Service Studios. I visited often, and it was always a joy to me, but I wanted to be sure my feeling was shared by everyone. And it was. Johnny said it was because the people at the top were so generous, warm, and wonderful. Those people were Al Simon, George and Jimmy Nasser, and Paul Henning. Paul says that long before Filmways came, the Nelsons – Ozzie, Harriet, David, and Ricky – did a lot to create a warm friendly ambience.

Practically my whole family was at General Service: Paul in his suite, Carol in the Publicity Department, Linda on the stages of *Petticoat Junction*. Only Tony was far away in Palo Alto, but he usually made it home in time for the Christmas party. All during the year, I felt free to drop into General Service whenever I could. I'd pop in at Paul's office and even though he was busy and I was interrupting, his face never failed to light up when he saw me. Sometimes, I'd have lunch with him and Mark or Dick or Debbie or Buddy Atkinson or whichever writer was working with him.

It was a home away from home for everybody who worked there. They spent so much of their lives at the studio – they were lucky it was so comfortable and cozy.

Paul spent a lot of happy years at General Service: a few with *Burns and Allen*, five with *Bob Cummings*, ten with *The Beverly Hillbillies*, *Petticoat Junction*, and *Green Acres*. A lot of workers there and – some famous, some not – became lifelong friends. They all loved Paul. On the *HillbilliesHillbilly* set, they used to call the script, "The gospel according to Saint Paul."

When the shows were canceled, and it came time to leave, it was painful. Most men miss their work when they retire, but when your work is as pleasant and interesting as Paul's, you miss it even more. For a time, it was Paul's little kingdom. Nowhere else could he feel so fulfilled, so important, so successful, so catered to as he could there.

I miss it as a small pocket of glamour in a busy, workday world; a place I was always welcome to visit, to bring friends or out-of-town visitors, to be treated as special (the Queen Consort) to touch hands and hearts with my husband and my two daughters, all doing their thing, doing it well, and enjoying it.

General Service Studios has changed hands several times since the Nasser Brothers sold it. For a while, it belonged to a famous producer – and for him, it became a very different place, full of glitter, gayety, and from what we heard, excess – excess of spending, of riotous parties, maximum publicity, and expression of ego. When that went bust, businessmen owned it – absentee ownership, which can never replace the personal management, the care, the attention to detail, the love of the Nassers, and everyone who enjoyed their hospitality.

If I had a glass in hand, I would raise it now to General Service Studios, the coziest studio in Hollywood!

19

For Better, For Worse, For Goodness Sakes!

People used to ask me how Paul's success affected our marriage. My thoughtful answer is – it didn't. Not much anyway – and not for long. The good news is that we were swept up in a world full of excitement, glamour, interesting people, interesting places, and a touch of fame and fortune. The bad news is that Paul worked much too hard and began to develop high blood pressure. I didn't see nearly enough of him, neither did our children, and sometimes our lives seemed to be moving in totally different directions.

Paul was at the studio many more hours than he was at home. While he was there, he had three beautiful handmaidens to minister to his comfort: the ever present, Gloria, Janet, and Candy. They answered his phone, screened his calls, restricted his visitors, prepared his food, rubbed his back, and spoke to him in soothing tones. There were at least a hundred others to do his bidding. He had merely to pick up the phone and give an order, and it was as good as done. Whatever he needed, there was someone to see that he got it – and fast. That has to have an effect on the most modest of men.

One night Paul came home rather late for dinner. I was keeping his dinner on the hot tray in the kitchen. He came in the back way and made a beeline for the bar. Along the way – and in that house, it was a long way – he issued orders.

"Have Tony clean the garage!"

"Tell the gardener to prune those trees by the guest house."

"God – those windows are dirty. Can't you get a window washer?"

"Don't forget to have the piano tuned."

"Did you order club soda?"

"We're going to need more firewood."

I'd been following along behind him. I didn't have a pad and pencil to take down the orders like any good secretary would. By the time he reached the bar, I'd had it.

"Just a darn minute!" I said, interrupting him mid-order. "Try to remember where you are! You're not at the studio, not with three secretaries and umpteen flunkies to do your bidding. You're home. And there's nobody here but little old me."

Paul had the grace to laugh. "Forgive me," he said. "It's been a rough day. I'm all wound up."

The next day, Gloria called me. "Ruth," she said in her usual dulcet tones, "Paul says he's going to buy you a plow but he wanted to know what color you'd like."

"Tell him purple," I answered then hung up. Then I had a good laugh. You can't stay mad when you're laughing.

Of course, people pampered him. Their jobs depended on him. I'm not blaming them. Hollywood is like that. Life is like that. There are only a few prizes, and not everybody can win them – so for the sake of self-preservation, anything is permissible. I doubt whether Paul even realized all that was going on around him. He was working very hard, he had his mind on the big picture, and he was so modest. He honestly never thought he was special. No, I'm not blaming him or them.

I *am* blaming some of the girls. Not only the starlets who swarmed the studio seeking jobs, but also the secretaries, the switchboard operators, the hairdressers, the makeup women, all the dozens of workers who crossed his path. Some of them were gorgeous, plenty sexy – and young. Some of them came on pretty strong. Paul was, to all intents and purposes, the king of the studio, he had money and power (both effective aphrodisiacs) and besides, he was sweet and kind, cute and funny, and very sexy himself. Didn't I

186

fall in love with him practically at first sight when I was eighteen? Those same people used to ask me – and they still do – if I didn't worry about all those girls, the long hours he kept, and the natural attraction of working together. My answer is a resounding YES – I did worry. I trusted Paul, though. I knew he loved me. He is an honorable man. Besides, he was so busy, there wasn't time for hanky-panky.

"You've got to be kidding!" these people would say. "There's always time for hanky-panky."

Of course there is and thanks a lot, I wanted to answer, but I usually didn't. I've always had a certain philosophy – and I had plenty of chances to test it out. I did the best I could to be loving, attractive, interesting, well-informed, patient, understanding – and if that wasn't enough, whatever happened, happened.

There was one girl who pushed things a little far. Like inviting my husband to come by her apartment for cocktails on his way home. (He was always late on those nights.) Like following us to New York and spending hours with him at the Algonquin while I was out seeing editors and agents during my writing career. Like borrowing his car so he'd have to borrow mine and leave me without wheels. Like hanging around our pool in her teeny bikini. Like being blonde and built.

I came close to playing a scene from one of the old movies with her. You know, the wife, played by Norma Shearer or Ann Harding, would go to see the home wrecker and say tremulously, "Give me back my husband!" I was thinking more in terms of "Knock it off, babe!" Fortunately, I didn't have to. She suddenly reconciled with her husband, they had a baby, and that was that.

I had my own little duties. I took his clothes to the cleaner's, did his laundry, packed for his many little trips, often took his electric razor to be fixed, had his shoes shined, and cooked dinner every night.

I looked after the children when they were sick, wrote to them when they were away from home, and took the dog and the cats to the vet. I went to college and took some hard courses, some interesting, and others boring. I looked after my aging mother, taught a Sunday school class, managed our radio station with the help of our accountant, paid the bills, and saved the money. Most of all, I loved Paul. Can you hear the harps playing? Can you see the golden halo forming over my head – the wings sprouting from my shoulder blades?

The main thing was that I didn't feel close to him. Just reading over one period in my diary, I began to have a bad feeling, and I realized it was because that's the way I really felt back then. Some of the entries: Paul to Palm Springs. (He had leased a little house without much input from me.) The day he returned, it was "Paul to Ben Lomond with George Nasser." The day he returned from there, it was "Paul with Al Simon to Asilomar Conference." That affair was sponsored by TV Guide and the University of Texas. The subject was "Where is television going? Where has it been? Where is it now? Who cares?"

Are any of those things wicked? I asked myself. Of course not. The season had ended. Paul was tired, he was relaxing, doing some male bonding, having his jollies. No condemnation. It was just that I was doing this highly commendable thing – going to college – and I wasn't free to go along, even if I'd been asked. Once when I did join him for a weekend in Ben Lomond, lots of others were there too, and I still felt that distance. I couldn't wait for the cocktail hour. With a drink or two, the distance began to dissolve. Aha! I said to myself. Now I understand alcoholics better. It was the first time I'd ever used alcohol as an escape. Luckily, I'm such an easy drunk I could never get the habit. Two drinks, and I'm under the table.

Okay, that's some of the bad news. Now for the good! The good things outnumbered the bad things by about ten to one. Let me tell you about some of them.

One year we had a birthday party for Eva. It was a small select group at one of my favorite places, the Monseigneur Room at the Beverly Hilton. This was an intimate room named after the one of the same name in Paris. While you ate your dinner, you were surrounded by violins playing Viennese waltzes, gypsy music, everything florid and schmaltzy and romantic – just what I love! In the party were Eva and Richard, Zsa Zsa and her husband (forgive me if I can't remember his name), Jolie (their mother) and her husband, a dashing Polish count many years her junior, Eddie Albert, Jay and Audrey Sommers, Al and Judy Simon, and Paul and me.

We drank champagne, we wallowed in the sentimental music, we danced, we sang, we laughed, we entertained the whole room. Eva and the Count did a rousing Czarda (an exciting Hungarian dance). Jolie favored us with her specialty, "Never on Sunday," sitting on men's laps, running her fingers through their hair, chucking them under the chin. Eddie Albert sang a solo in his quite acceptable baritone. I danced with the Count who managed to teach me how to say "I love you" in both Polish and Hungarian. There was a lot of laughter and merrymaking and through it, Jolie kept nudging Paul and saying, "Look at my other daughter!" and pointing to Zsa Zsa. "Do you think she's ugly?" When Paul assured her he didn't think anything of the kind, she came back with, "Well, why don't you write a show for her, too?" When the musicians took a break, the count picked up one of the violins and played it quite expertly. Everyone in the room applauded. The Beverly Hilton should never have presented us with a bill. They should have paid us.

Another really good thing. The Advertising Round Table of Kansas City gave Paul their "Hometown Boy Makes Good" award.

We flew back and they put us up in the Muehlebach Hotel – old, classy, expensive, the crème de la crème of the city. When we lived in Kansas City, we couldn't even afford to go in to use the restroom. Radio and television units were sent to our suite to interview us, there was a brunch, a luncheon, cocktails, and dinner – the whole enchilada. During the cocktail hour, lovely soft music played in the background. It was Paul Henning, tenor, singing. Holy ego boost, Batman!

Paul and I went to New York every year, usually in the spring. We loved New York, we loved the Algonquin Hotel, we loved the plays. We'd been going regularly for years only now it was a little different. A CBS car and chauffeur always met our plane; there were flowers, candy, booze, and fruit in our suite. The CBS president urged me to use the car and chauffeur any time I wanted to.

"Should I?" I asked Paul.

"Why not?" Paul told me. "This won't last, you know. As soon as the shows go off the air, or if the ratings slip, the perks will disappear, so enjoy it while you can, honey."

I did. I had a cousin living in New Jersey. My chauffeur took me over to visit her, waited, and took me back. Boy, were they all impressed! No more than I was.

When we went to Europe, we were entertained at a luncheon in Paris by the editor of L'Illustration, a high-class French magazine. He knew about Paul and *The Beverly Hillbillies* and introduced us to the author of a play currently running in Paris, called *Croque Monsieur*. A Croque Monsieur was a popular sandwich, made of ham and cheese and as well-known as a Big Mac. There was a double meaning too. "Croque" could be translated as "peasant" – Monsieur as "gentleman." City and country, simple and sophisticated. *The Beverly Hillbillies*, right?

In Germany, we had dinner with Max Kimental, a CBS representative in Europe. He told us they were crazy about *The*

Beverly Hillbillies in Holland. Gee, it was a kick to know the right people, to be treated as special and not just another tourist.

California governor Edmond Brown called on Paul to participate in meetings, dinners, and conferences for the coming election campaign. Other guests were the movers and shakers of the state. It was between seasons and Paul had the time. He liked Governor Brown and enjoyed being with the "in" crown. Through no fault of Paul's, Governor Brown was defeated by Ronald Reagan.

We were on the fast track for a while, but we never attended the parties with the A guest list. It wasn't our style. We were busy all the time, and though our lives sometimes went in different directions, they always led back home. We were a family. We loved each other – for better or for worse, for richer or poorer. And as they say, rich was certainly better.

20

Love Comes to Hooterville

You've got a lovely setting in a pretty green valley, a quaint little hotel just right for romance, and what's more you've got three young, beautiful single girls with no steady boyfriends. What could be more natural than to introduce a member of the opposite sex? Why not have him be handsome, about six feet tall, a daring young aviator flying his own plane, who makes a crash landing in the front yard of the Shady Rest Hotel? And wouldn't it be a good idea to have Kate Bradley and her three daughters take him in, make him comfortable in one of the hotel rooms, and nurse him back to health? And what could be more appropriate than to have the role played by Bea Benaderet's own good looking son, Jack Bannon?

That was the whole idea as Paul and Bea hatched it up, with the approval of the producer, writer, and director of the series. Everybody loved the idea and the writers got to work happily writing the script. One thing didn't go according to the plan. Jack Bannon said thank you very much, but he didn't want to be on his mother's show because everyone would think he just got the part because of her. He wanted to do it all by himself – please, mother! A very noble sentiment, to be sure, but not very practical. Bea and Paul were both disappointed, but Bea said she understood. Only now, they were all really sold on the new plot and had to start looking for another hero.

This happened early in the 1966 season. By this time, although there were still three girls, they were different girls – all but one. Jeannine Riley and Pat Woodell had left after the second year to pursue their careers in other directions. Linda Henning stayed on, partly because she loved working for her father, but mostly because she knew this was the chance of a lifetime, and there was no way she was going to give it up. The blonde, Billie Jo, was now a beautiful Swedish girl named Gunilla Hutton, who, it was said, was related to Barbara Hutton. The brunette, Bobbie Jo, was a cute little pixie named Lori Saunders whom Paul had discovered on a television commercial for hair curlers. Gradually and subtly, their characters changed, too. Whereas Pat Woodell had been rather quiet and serene and fitted right in with Paul's original idea that Bobbie Jo was the bookish one, Lori Saunders was pert and peppy and did "dumb" jokes so charmingly that she became the screwball of the group. Linda, who played Betty Jo, the redhead, was still the young tomboy who drove the Hooterville Cannonball, pitched horseshoes, and played football with the boys.

Billie Jo, the blonde, had always been visualized as ambitious for a singing career and also boy crazy – and just as they were getting Gunilla Hutton comfortable in the character, she up and left after one season. She accepted a job on the show *Hee Haw*, and although it might not have been everybody's cup of tea (not mine), it was certainly successful, and she had a good long run on it.

Then began the hunt for another blonde. Paul, Al Simon, and Dick Wesson all came out to our house one Sunday, and there was a steady stream of beautiful blondes who came to audition for the part. I don't know what the neighbors thought if they were watching. And you know neighbors, they probably were.

Since it was our house, I got to sit in on the auditions and interviews, and being as outspoken as I usually am, I think I may have had some influence on the final choice. Meredith MacRae appealed to me right away because along with being beautiful, she was so intelligent, friendly, and enthusiastic, and it seemed to me she was just what was needed to round out the threesome. Luckily, the men agreed with me, and we now had a new, permanent Billie Jo. Meredith also had inherited the good singing voice of her father, Gordon MacRae, and that was a plus.

193

So now – fast forward to 1966 and the beginning of the big romance! The new guy, Steve Elliot, was earmarked for Billie Jo right from the start. After looking over a lot of actors, the one they chose (I had nothing to do with it), was Mike Minor. When I saw his screen test, I had to agree that he surely was handsome and had a sexy baritone voice – and what's more, he could sing up a storm, already had recordings. And here's a real coincidence. His father was Don Fedderson, the television producer of *The Lawrence Welk Show*, *The Liberace Show*, *The Millionaire*, *My Three Sons*, and *A Family Affair*. Besides, I'd gone to high school with Don in Kansas City but hadn't seen him since. Mike's mother, Helen Minor, known as "Tido," had been a schoolmate at the same time at dear old Central High. In case it seems like too many coincidences, you have to realize that Hollywood is really a small town, and you're always running into people you know or have known.

And so the romance began. Something strange happened, though. You think you have it all worked out and so many times people just don't follow the script. All the young people got along like a house afire, but Mike seemed to be attracted to Linda, the youngest sister, and she was simply flabbergasted at the turn of events. Linda is so much like her father. They're both so modest they never think anybody's going to notice them or be interested in them. She was born on his birthday, you remember, so maybe there is something to astrology after all. Well, she and Mike began to date.

The first time he came to our house to pick her up, I was really eager to see him in person to see if he resembled his father who had been very handsome and popular and quite the big man on campus in high school. Well, when I went to the door, it was a shock – like turning back the clock. There stood Don Fedderson looking just like he did in high school when we acted in the school plays together and went to the same dances and parties.

The plot proceeded as planned. The publicity people even sent Mike and Meredith off on a weekend personal appearance together. It was going to work out very well because they could both sing and he could entertain as well as just appear. Linda and Meredith had very quickly become buddies, and Meredith knew that Linda was beginning to be very interested in Mike. It really was hard for Linda to not be a bit jealous. But Meredith reassured her. She and Mike had gotten along fine, but there was no "chemistry," she assured Linda. Meanwhile, the plot on *Petticoat Junction* began to thicken.

There was another meeting. It seemed wrong to write love scenes for Meredith and Mike when he and Linda were becoming an item. It would be an unexpected switch to have the glamorous hero fall for the young tomboy, Betty Jo. Nobody would be expecting that. So surprise them – it might be fun. And so they did it. The cast and crew were agog, waiting to watch that first kiss on the porch swing. There hadn't been anything like that in the show so far, and besides everybody thought of Linda as just a kid, and Mike seemed so much older and more sophisticated. The scene went splendidly.

Things moved right along, and eventually, Betty Jo and Steve got married in the little country church in Hooterville. Her sisters were her bridesmaids, and she had a gorgeous wedding dress. Linda and I shopped for it together. Of course, I went down to watch them film that episode and was in the audience in the church for the filming but not on camera. The publicity people got busy and had a Press party to celebrate the wedding at Lakeside Golf Club, which is only a few blocks from our house. That's a pretty famous place all by itself. It's where Bob Hope, Bing Crosby, Johnny Weissmuller, Jack Carson, and, scads of movie stars played golf. For a while there, Spiro Agnew would land on the grounds in a helicopter to play with Hope.

That year, a big bakery company asked Linda and Mike to be on their Rose Parade float as the bride and groom on a huge wedding cake (made of flowers, of course). Linda got to wear her wedding dress again, with long underwear underneath. It's cold those early mornings in Pasadena. Being on one of those floats entails a lot more than people realize. You have to stand perfectly still for several hours. They had stands to support them and keep them from losing their balance if the streets were rough and the floats jiggled. And have you ever thought what it would be like early in the morning, after coffee, to be on display without bathroom privileges?

The momentum of the television romance had its effect and soon Linda and Michael (she never called him Mike) became engaged for real. We gave them an engagement party, the biggest, most elaborate party we ever had before or since, with a tent over the garden, caterers all over the place, musicians, the works. Michael sang Linda's favorite song that night, "When I Fall in Love – it will be completely – or I'll never fall in love." It was from *Carousel*, which Linda had already done three times, once as a senior in high school, once in the theatre in the round in Anaheim, and once in Salt Lake City. Paul and Don got acquainted and often sent memos back and forth from their respective studios: "Dear Producer-in-law."

The real wedding took place September 7, 1968. It was held at St. David's Episcopal Church in North Hollywood with its minister, Reverend Alex Campbell, the dean and founder of Campbell Hall School, where all our children attended the elementary grades. Linda wore her same wedding gown with a somewhat more elaborate veil. She had four bridesmaids in her favorite color, aquamarine. They were her sister, Carol; Tony's new wife, another Carol; also Virginia Hammond, Linda's best friend from school days; and Laura Lamb, Linda's stand-in and ballet buddy. Michael's best man was Bill Hayward, son of the famous agent, Leland Hayward, and actress, Margaret Sullavan. The ushers were Tony Henning, Greg Fedderson (Mike's brother), and Val Clenard, Mike's sister's husband.

No members of the press were allowed in the church, but outside, they were waiting in droves, particularly the Australian Press. The show was so popular there. Inside, I was wearing my mother-of-the-bride dress, pink satin with a matching hat, but as usual, when it was really important, I didn't like the dress much, and the pink satin shoes were killing me. Paul was nervous and very tense when he walked down the aisle with Linda. He told me he could hardly do it. He had to fight to keep the tears from his eyes. You know how fathers are about daughters. He just didn't want to give her to another man.

The wedding reception was at Lakeside Golf Club. We weren't members since we'd never played golf, but Curt Massey was and arranged for permission. Everybody was there! It was a wonderful occasion. I had never worked so hard in my life to plan anything, and I was almost too tired and nervous to enjoy it as I should have. I managed to stop by home on my way there from the church and slip into some more comfortable shoes.

I've just been looking at the wedding scrapbook. They were such a beautiful couple, and we had such high hopes for them. It's heartbreaking when it doesn't last. They were married just five years, and long before they parted, they knew it had been a mistake. They were carried along by the television romance. That happens to a lot of actors. Things aren't like they were when Paul and I were young. Marriage just isn't always forever.

21

Up Close and Personal

I suppose you know I stole my chapter heading from the Olympics' telecasts. I always loved those little vignettes about the competitors. People who excel in their chosen fields are usually interesting in a lot of other ways, too. I felt that way about the actors I came to know – some of them well, others merely brief encounters.

Buddy Ebsen was always number one on *The Beverly Hillbillies* set, and *The Beverly Hillbillies* was number one in the Filmways galaxy, as well as in Paul Henning's. Buddy is a gentle man, like Paul, but also strong and sure of what he knows and what he believes. They got along, and still do, very, very well.

There was an ambivalence in my relationship with Buddy at one time. First of all, I admired him tremendously. He was a fine looking man with a lot of charm and personal magnetism, and his portrayal of the true-blue Jed Clampett was right on the button. The fact that he was a dancer made me an instant fan. I could remember him in *Captain January* when he was a very young man, dancing with Shirley Temple. Then when *The Beverly Hillbillies* was in production, we had a lot of parties where there was music and sometimes dancing, and I was in heaven when I could dance with Buddy. I remember so well a gathering at Al Simon's house to honor some Canadian television tycoons; Al had hired a piano player to entertain and play background music. Buddy led me through a wonderful tango – so out of character for Jed Clampett, and even for the public Buddy Ebsen I had come to know, that it was a happy surprise. He and his wife danced together like a dream. They had had practice, of course.

Politics was our big difference. Buddy was a passionate Republican and ardent admirer of Ronald Reagan. I was the opposite.

So was Paul, but he had the good sense to keep quiet about it. As Paul used to tell me that you can never really change anyone's mind about politics or religion, so why argue about it? He was right, of course, but I couldn't seem to do that. I've always been outspoken – and yes, opinionated – but I also believed in standing up for what I believed, and my beliefs were just as passionate as Buddy's.

"Now don't talk about politics!" Paul would caution me before we went to a party.

"I won't bring up the subject, but if Buddy needles me, I can't promise," I would answer stubbornly.

What made it even more unwise on my part was that most of the rest of the cast – whether from real conviction or loyalty to their leader – followed Buddy chapter and verse. Nancy Kulp, who played the banker's secretary, Jane Hathaway, was the only one on my side. As a result, we grew to be close friends.

At that time, I was active in the Peace Movement – I was very much opposed to the Vietnam War – and that furthered my political opinions. However, I seemed to be losing a lot more than I won where national elections were concerned. I wasn't in it for the fame as some of the people I knew. I really was an idealist, and it hurt me deeply when it seemed to me that the whole world was against me. It was too difficult for me, so I retired from an active role in politics. My mind hadn't changed, but I was quiet about it. After that, Buddy and I got along fine. We all had some good times together.

Once, Paul and I went down to Balboa where the Ebsens had a beautiful home and where his catamaran, The Polynesian Concept, was docked. We had a sort of community brunch with a lot of the boat people and then went out on Buddy's boat. I tried to bow out of the trip, explaining that I might get seasick, but Buddy assured me we'd just go around the bay, never get out to the open sea, and it would be smooth as glass. Hah! Get a seaman out on the water, and there's no stopping him.

We didn't stay in the bay, and it wasn't smooth. What's more, if you're familiar with the construction of a catamaran, you know there's no solid deck to stand or walk on. It's all just beams and empty spaces between, and unless you're very sure footed, it's far too hazardous for a landlubber like me. So I was confined to the cabin where the air was close and the movement nauseating. I begged to be put ashore. Finally, they did just that, and I made my way back to the house in disgrace. Buddy won some races with the Polynesian Concept. He was never so happy as when he was out on the ocean.

Then there's the story about the Noland Road Bank in Paul's hometown of Independence, Missouri. Jessie Schulenberg, an old friend of Paul's and an officer of the bank, had suggested to the president, Allen Lefko, that she might prevail on her friend, Paul Henning, to bring a guest star back to help them celebrate the bank's fifth anniversary. There were two such occasions but for now, it's the one that involved Buddy that I want to tell you about. The three of us flew back to Kansas City and checked in at a brand-new, very fancy hotel, The Crown Center. We noted that the lobby was teeming with middle-aged ladies who were there for a beauticians' convention. As we hurried in, there were glad cries of "Jed Clampett!" and "Barnaby Jones!" Buddy smiled and waved but managed to avoid being surrounded. The bank that day was literally mobbed with fans who'd come to get Buddy's autograph. One woman who went through the line was fat and toothless and looked older than God, but she said loudly that she had been in third grade with Paul Henning. We really teased him about that.

Toward evening, Paul found me in the crowd and whispered that he was going to sneak Buddy out the back door. We were both exhausted, and we hadn't even been "on" as he had, so Paul was sure

200

he'd had quite enough for one day. We made our getaway and drove back to our fancy hotel. Paul let Buddy and me out at the front door while he went to park the car. Right away, we saw we were in for it. The beauticians had just come out of a big meeting and were flooding the lobby.

"Oh no!" Buddy said helplessly, "I don't think I can sign my name one more time, and the smile is frozen on my face."

I had such sympathy for the poor guy that I just had to think of something.

"I have an idea!" I said. "I'll hang onto your arm, and we'll look at each other as though we just can't wait to get to the room." It was a silly idea, but it was all I could think of. "Maybe they'll be polite enough not to bother us."

"Let's give it a try," Buddy said, and he proceeded to act his part like the performer he is. And it did seem to be working. All the ladies looked at Buddy as we passed, but nobody was tactless enough to invade our privacy. It was hard for me to keep from giggling, but finally we managed to reach the elevators and push the "UP" button. At that moment, we were accosted by a stern looking man.

"Are you registered at this hotel?" he asked Buddy suspiciously.

Buddy showed him his room key, and apparently, someone from management gave him the high sign because he begged our pardon and walked away. He was the house detective, we learned. Then we both exploded.

"What's so funny?" Paul asked as he joined us.

We tried to explain, but it's never as funny in the telling. A short time later, as Paul and I were relaxing in our room, the phone rang. It was Buddy.

"We've got the name. Might as well have the game," he said. "How about coming down to my room for a nightcap?" We did get together – the three of us – for some room service, and I felt as though I might be nominated for an Oscar for my acting.

After *The Beverly Hillbillies* was canceled, we didn't see as much of Buddy, but we have remained friends. Whenever he sees me or we talk on the phone, he always asks me how my tap dancing is going.

"Can you do trenches yet?" he'll ask.

"Of course!" I say cockily. (I don't even know what trenches are.)

"How about 'Over the top?'" he'll challenge.

"I can do anything you can do!" I tell him. Of course, I can't begin to do "over the top." I seriously doubt whether he can either – not now anyway. That's when one foot is off the ground and you hop over it with the other foot. Is that clear? You've seen it, I know. It's hard.

Last year, Paul and I were invited to a big party at the Beverly Wilshire Hotel to celebrate Buddy's birthday. I'm not sure which one it was but well over eighty. Simply everybody was there and the program was outstanding. I had a special dress for the occasion, and this time it *was* special, but it didn't matter because the fans gathered at the entrance with their autograph books were still looking us over and whispering, "They're nobody!" But it was fun, just like the good old days when we attended parties like that all the time.

As for the actor who played Jethro, I did had a few chances to get to know Max Baer. We had a plane ride together from New York once after we'd been there for the CBS Affiliates meeting. Max was carrying an enormous pink teddy bear for his girl of the moment. That's when he told me about how he won the audition for the part of Jethro. I always liked Max. He made a point of introducing us to his mother when she was in town. We all went to dinner together, and we found her to be a lovely woman, typically concerned about the welfare of her son. She wished he'd "settle down."

There was one incident I can laugh about now, but at the time, it was scary. After Richard Whorf, the director, left the show because of failing health, Paul moved Joe Depew up from assistant director to director. Joe was very experienced, had a terrific sense of humor, and was such a nice guy that everybody loved him. However, Max sometimes picked on him. The crew was watchful. When Max would get into a temper and start toward Joe to have it out, the big husky crew members all stopped whatever they were doing and surrounded Joe. Probably nothing would have happened, but they made sure it didn't. After all, Max had once punched his fist through a piece of scenery when everything didn't go his way.

And then there was this one day, toward the end of the afternoon, when I happened to be at the studio waiting for Paul to get through and come home with me. Gloria told me that Max was coming in to see Paul and that he seemed to be fighting mad about something. She was worried, and so was I. As I've indicated, Paul is a small man, and Max is a giant. If he ever decided to take a swing at Paul, it would be goodbye, St. Paul. Gloria and I got busy and rounded up some young, large guys around the studio to stand by. At the first sign of trouble, they were to rush in and save the day. We were all outside Paul's door listening. Not a sound – just the quiet murmur of voices, and occasionally, a laugh. Pretty soon, Max came out grinning from ear to ear.

"What happened?" I asked Paul as soon as Max was gone. "What did you do?"

"What do you mean – what happened?" Paul asked mildly. "Max had a problem, and we discussed it. I reasoned with him. He listened to reason. Everything is okay." Paul is very good at handling people. I know that. He's handled me for a lot of years. On the other hand, I'm just about his size. And I love him.

Nancy Kulp, who played, Jane Hathaway, the banker's secretary on the show, was really a good friend. We'd known her for a long time – ever since she played Pamela Livingstone, the bird watcher, on *The Bob Cummings Show*. We were kindred spirits politically, but more than that, we all loved animals. Nancy raised dogs and traveled from coast to coast entering her dogs in shows. A favorite was a large, homely dog name Hector Sweetmouth.

Another major interest she shared with Paul was football. During the season, I was the typical football widow. Every New Year's Day, we could count on Nancy showing up at our house if she were anywhere nearby, and we'd all watch the bowl games together and have our traditional bean soup for dinner. You know, of course, that it's good luck to cook beans on the first day of the New Year. Besides, it's so timely to use the bone from the Christmas ham.

I never knew anyone who moved as often as Nancy. During the time we knew her, she had had at least five or six homes in North Hollywood, one in Santa Barbara, Palm Desert, Palm Springs, Pennsylvania, Connecticut, Kentucky, or one of the Carolinas – I forget which – and of course, Florida, where she went to college. (We always had to watch the Orange Bowl with Nancy.) She taught a class at a southern college for a while and ran for Congress in her native Pennsylvania.

The very first time we helped the Noland Road Bank in Independence, Missouri, to celebrate an anniversary, we took Raymond Bailey (Milburn Drysdale, the Clampett's banker) and Nancy Kulp (his secretary, Jane Hathaway) with us for a personal appearance. What could be more appropriate, Paul thought. He had a lot of fake "Drysdale Dollars" printed up to look fairly real except that instead of George Washington's picture, it was Milburn Drysdale's.

It was a big day at the bank with thousands of people coming in to get their Drysdale dollars autographed by the stars.

The twist to the story was in the beginning. The four of us flew back to Kansas City together, and as we drew nearer to Missouri, Raymond grew tipsier and tipsier. Paul worried about it, but he didn't feel he could do anything. This was a grown man, supposedly a responsible performer. When we got to Independence, we all checked into our motel and went over to Paul's sister's for dinner. Drusilla and her husband, Petey Childers, live in a charming old Victorian house, which they cherish and have furnished authentically in period pieces. It's the kind of house with towers and turrets and gingerbread that always makes me want to say as I'm going up the front walk, "Little did I realize as I made my way for the first time up the winding walk toward Childers' House, what drama awaited me during my stay there." Very gothic, you know. This story is anything but gothic.

All of us were exclaiming over the beauty and character of the house. Paul rang the doorbell and his sister, Drusilla, tiny, white-haired, with those big brown eyes, greeted us at the door graciously.

"Are you the madame?" Raymond asked drunkenly.

Everybody started talking at once to cover up Raymond's gaucherie, and somehow we got through the evening. Next morning, Raymond was sober, brisk, and ready to do his thing. Sigh of relief!

Nancy had most of her scenes with Raymond, and a grudging respect had grown up between the two. Personality wise, they were miles apart, but professionally, they worked without a hitch.

Once, after Raymond's death, someone was discussing with Joe Depew where Raymond might be now – heaven or hell.

"I don't know," Joe mused, "but wherever he is I can guarantee one thing – he doesn't like it."

I didn't get to know Irene Ryan intimately. Once we took her to Turlock to be Grand Marshall of the Rodeo Day Parade. We all rode in a fancy white convertible with the top down. It said KCEY in big letters on the side. Paul and I sat in the back waving to the crowd, and Irene did her thing sitting on the back of the seat. Being so tiny, she had to sit up there to be seen. Sometime during the festivities, she judged a beard contest. She made it a requisite that each contestant had to kiss her, so she could test his beard. As always, everybody loved Granny.

Irene's best girlfriend was Viola Dana, a silent picture star. Still young enough to be quite attractive, the two gals had a lot of fun together. Irene got an act together and played Las Vegas. She appeared as Granny and then as herself – quite a contrast. Paul and I hated to see her wearing sequins and singing jazzy songs. To us, she was Granny and should STAY Granny. That's what happens to series stars – they get stuck in a mold, and it's hard to get out. Once when the three of us were in Missouri together, Irene consented to make a trip with us to Eldon where my relatives lived. My Aunt Oma had a reception and invited practically everyone in town to meet Granny. Everybody was thrilled. Irene was her usual wonderful self, and Aunt Oma's reputation as a social leader was made.

Just before Irene went to New York to star in the Broadway musical, *Pippin*, she was at our house for Sunday brunch. She was elated.

"All my life I was small time," she told us. "Always trying to get that big break and play the Palace. And then, because of you, Paul Henning, I've been a television star and now – to be on Broadway! I never would have believed it!"

We were so happy for her. She was a hit and got good reviews. We were planning to go back to New York and see the show, but we never made it. People who'd been there said she was great but that personally, there seemed to be a change in her. She seemed fearful living in New York, her usual joie de vivre was gone – she just wasn't

206

her old happy, enthusiastic self. On stage, she began to be vague and forgetful, stood in the way of other actors, and forgot to get out of the way of the curtain. She had to do her big number sitting down. Young people from the show told us these things. Finally, her agent, Kingsley Colton, who was about as near to a family member as she had, went to New York and brought her back to California to put her in the hospital. It was discovered she had a brain tumor, which was causing all these changes. In a short time, it killed her. Paul delivered the eulogy at her funeral. We were all sad that she had to die in the midst of her triumph. Still, she had died with her boots on – on stage – a hit! She left a legacy to help young people in the theatre – a scholarship for promising performers.

Eva Gabor went to Turlock with us one year for the rodeo. You can bet she was a hit. She always knew how to work the crowd. Paul hired a small plane to fly us to Turlock, just Paul and me, and Eva and her hairdresser. We had a lot of time to talk, and as usual, I expounded my theories on life, love, marriage, cabbage, and kings. After that, Eva had a new name for me – Super Vife! It wasn't that it was necessarily so – just that I'd talked a good philosophy.

Eva and Richard Brown had a home in Palm Springs. She opened up an interior decorating shop. She also painted in her backyard in the sun. "I don't vear anything, Roosie, dahling," she confessed, giggling. "Not even my false eyelashes."

When we bought our house there, we went down one weekend with a truckload of furniture to get settled. We worked very hard all weekend, and when Paul called Eva to say hello, she invited us to a party at her home that very night.

"We can't go," I whispered to Paul. "We didn't bring any party clothes."

"All right – we'll come for a little while," Paul was saying. Then he turned to me apologetically. "At least, we'll get a good meal. I'm tired of hamburgers and canned soup."

So we went. I was wearing a cheap little polyester knit that Eva wouldn't have been caught dead in. Neither would I – but alive and moving day – it was just right for that occasion.

We arrived after the party was in full swing. It was really an "A" guest list. Some of the girls were wearing white pants slung low on the hips, chiffon tops tied under their breasts and gold chains dangling on their bare midriffs. The men were casually dressed in desert chic – moccasins and no socks, of course. We felt like the help who'd slipped in the front door by mistake.

"Paul, go into the bathroom and take off your socks," I told him. "We've got to do something!" Still, he didn't have on the right kinds of shoes for that, so we just stayed in the corner with a big plate of wonderful food and hoped nobody would notice us. Not very likely anyone would since the guests included names and faces like Frank Sinatra and Robert Wagner.

One time, I met a very wealthy lady at a health spa in Mexico. We became friendly, and she was fascinated with some of the names I dropped. So when she was in L.A., she called and asked me to have lunch with her at the Polo Lounge of the Beverly Hills Hotel. The Polo Lounge is where all the stars and agents go to see and be seen, and to make deals. It's just alive with star power.

"Oh Lord," I thought as I drove across the canyon, "she'll expect me to be one of them. Nobody will know me; they may not even let me in." Of course, I had gotten all tarted up just in case some agent wanted to sign me up. I met my new friend, and we were ushered to a table – at least she had some clout – and no sooner did we sit down than a pair of fragrant, silk clad arms were about my neck.

"Roosie, Dahling!" It was my girlfriend, Eva, of course. She said she was so glad to see me, and we must get together soon. Bless her heart. She never let me down.

When you live in Hollywood and ,you're in show business, you do come into contact often with big names. One of my favorite anecdotes is about Mae West. Paul and I went to a party for a charity where a friend of ours, Herman Saunders, musician and director, was to be honored. We were given a choice table right up front, and at the same table were Mae West and two tall hunks, bodyguards, boyfriends, whatever – she always had more than one good-looking man with her. The thing that surprises you about Mae West is that she is so tiny. Because she is busty and curvy, you tend to think she's going to be a big woman. Busty and curvy she is – but tiny. All through the evening I tried not to stare. I never heard her say a word – she just murmured to her escorts. But when we got ready to go, I decided it would be incredibly rude not even to say goodnight.

"Miss West," I said politely, "I just want you to know it's been a pleasure seeing you tonight."

"Thanks a lot, honey," she said in that voice everybody in the world recognizes and imitates. "The pleasure is all mine!"

Once in a Beverly Hills elevator, I rode up several floors with one other occupant, Liz Taylor. I had time to check her out thoroughly and this was my conclusion: we were built exactly the same way. Same height, about five-two, nice legs, big bust, small waist, a bit wide in the hips.

"Too bad," I thought to myself. "If I were lucky enough to resemble Liz Taylor, why couldn't it have been her face instead of her figure?"

Another time, I was standing at a counter in the lingerie department of Saks Fifth Avenue. I was looking at the merchandise, paying very little attention to the other customers. Then the rather tall, well-dressed lady beside me spoke. A bell rang. There was no mistaking that voice.

"I'll take a dozen pairs of these panties," said Marlene Dietrich.

I bought a couple pairs of the same panties after she left, and I used to put them on sometimes, stand in front of the mirror, and sing, "Falling in love again – never vanted to," in a throaty voice.

Paul had an experience with Zsa Zsa Gabor when he was doing *The Bob Cummings Show*. He had hired her as a guest star and wrote a scene pulling out all the stops to make it as glamorous as possible. Zsa Zsa in is the bathtub of a gorgeous bathroom when the phone rings. As she steps out of the tub, she wraps herself in mink bath towel. What could be more glamorous than that? But Zsa Zsa came to Paul's office after the first reading.

"Dahling," she told him, "I just can't put a mink towel around myself. It's so heavy."

"What do you mean?" Paul asked, puzzled. He thought she'd like that touch of mink.

"You see, dahling," Zsa Zsa said without embarrassment, "I have a very wide butt." The towel was changed.

You already know about my continuing relationship with Cary Grant. When he and Barbara Hutton came to the nursery at Cedars of Lebanon Hospital and admired my beautiful baby. And when he visited the control room of *The Rudy Vallee Show*. And w. hen I wrote a script for *Mr. Blandings Builds His Dream House*. But you haven't heard the end of it yet.

This happened when Paul was sharing a bungalow office on the Universal lot with Stanley Shapiro. They had a bar and people dropped in sometimes at the end of the day to do a little sipping and unwinding. One of those who visited was Cary Grant. And on one of those occasions, he called me up. I was at home in my kitchen getting dinner ready when the phone rang.

"Hello, Ruth," said Cary. "This is Cary Grant."

"Oh sure," I said. He's very easy to imitate.

"Yes, it is," he insisted. "Your husband and I are having an argument, and we want you to settle it. Your husband doesn't agree with me, but I say that looks aren't important in a man."

"How would you know?" I came back like a flash. What a great answer! Usually, I think of those things at night in bed when I'm remembering my conversation.

Alas! I'm sorry to tell you that was the last time I spoke to Cary. Our affair was ended.

While I'm on a roll, telling you about the thrill of living in Hollywood and seeing stars, I might as well tell you that when our son, Tony, was small, he played with a boy across the street named Jonathon Ritter. His father was Tex Ritter, the cowboy star. Tony once used to tell us that they had two television sets side by side in their living room. On one, the sound didn't work and on the other, the picture tube was burned out, but by turning the two of them on, you had both, sound and picture. That little boy, of course, grew up to be the famous and popular John Ritter, star of stage, screen, and television. Recently, when Tony was in town, he and his wife encountered John in a restaurant. Tony hesitated even to speak to him since he's now a star. Well, he didn't have to. John came over to him and greeted him warmly, and they had a little chat about old times.

Also, across the street from us lived, for a time, George Shearing, the famous blind pianist. He had a lovely seeing-eye dog and a Braille map, so he roamed the neighborhood, going out to restaurants, stores, everywhere. Once in a while, his itinerary led him to our house. He knew our daughter, Carol, was studying the piano, and he always insisted on playing for her. His dog would lead him to the piano where he'd sit and play "Lullaby of Birdland" and other numbers he'd made famous. After that, we tried to be sure our piano was always tuned just in case George came by. Whenever, I'd see him in the drugstore or somewhere I'd always say, "Hello, George. It's Ruth Henning."

"You don't have to tell me. I knew it was you," he'd say. I don't know if he knew my walk, heard my voice preceding me, or if maybe it was the "scent of a woman."

Now we come to "close encounters of the third kind." That is – just barely touching. We were at a SHARE party at the ballroom of the Century Plaza Hotel. The girls of SHARE give one of these parties every year, and since they're all stars or wives of stars, they get the crème de la crème to be in their show. Ginnie Mancini is very active in the group, so there is always Henry Mancini's orchestra to begin with. As well as Frank Sinatra. Johnny Carson. Bob Hope. Really biggies. The girls are – many of them – dancers, so they have a chorus line, usually, and the husbands, not to be outdone, make up their own high kicking chorus line. It's really a hot ticket, the SHARE party, and they make a lot of money for their favorite charity.

One year, we were invited by Bette Lou (Mrs. Ken) Murray to sit at their table. The place was packed. The tables were very close together. To make your way through the crowd, you had to be very skinny or very agile. Suddenly, somebody passing through really hit my head with a clop. Before I could react, two gentle masculine hands took hold of my head, one on either side, and bent it back so that I was looking up into the twinkling eyes of Michael Caine.

"Sorry, Luv," he said in the English, slightly cockney, voice I've always found extremely attractive. I didn't mind the clop on the head. Not at all.

Does all this sound like I'm bragging? I hope not. None of these meetings are to my credit. It's just that if you live around here – well, so do they – and sooner or later, the twain are going to meet.

22
Travelin'

The Clampetts had been in Beverly Hills for five years, and Paul Henning wondered if they needed a change, a shot in the arm, so to speak. CBS, ever eager to preserve its biggest hit, graciously offered to foot the bill if they wanted to travel anywhere – New York, Paris, Rome, Hawaii – anywhere in the world. Paul gave it a little thought and decided on England. It was very popular there. Malcolm Muggeridge wrote: "Strolling by night as I often do about the lanes of southern England, it is by no means uncommon to hear through cottage windows the unmistakable accents of *The Beverly Hillbillies* … Week by week, they demonstrate that though possessed of great wealth, they can still just get through the needle's eye into the Kingdom of Heaven. It is tempting to seek to devise a moral equivalent to *The Beverly Hillbillies* in English terms. What would be their anglicized version? The Beatles already fill the bill. If one tries to probe the fabulous success of these four moronic and unpleasing youths with long hair and little talent, one realizes it is due precisely to the fact that, like *The Beverly Hillbillies*, they remain unspoiled."

That's an interesting analogy I'd never have thought of, and I can't entirely agree with. It isn't true, obviously, that The Beatles are unpleasing, moronic, or without talent – just as it isn't true about *The Beverly Hillbillies*. To have the talent that makes millions of people love them and tune in to them is no small accomplishment. Time has proven the special greatness of the Beatles and also of *The Beverly Hillbillies*, who, after thirty years, are still living in reruns and in the hearts of their fans.

All analysis aside, it was decided that the Hillibillies would go to England. Paul and Buddy Atkinson devised a plot in which Jed

Clampett inherits a castle, which is deep in debt. He feels it is his duty to save it, which eventually costs him about ten million dollars. Jed is always generous when it's for a worthy cause. Everyone is excited, especially Jethro who studies up on Elizabethan England and proceeds to costume everyone in the proper wardrobe. There is a hilarious scene with Paul Lynde as a harried passport clerk who is just sure the Clampetts are a plant for a scene on Candid Camera.

George King, the production manager, had gone over ahead of the cast to find the castle – and the one he found, Penshurst, stately home of the Viscount De L'isle, was just perfect. Everywhere they went, hundreds of fans besieged them; the quiet village of Penshurst was transformed overnight. The settings they used at the castle were the six hundred year old Baron's Hall, the Armoury, and the Italian Gardens. Jethro and Elly May also had an amusing scene in front of Buckingham Palace, where Jethro pours a bucket of water on the street, puts his coat over it and invites Elly May to walk on it. He'd been reading about Sir Walter Raleigh.

It's a fact that King Henry VIII once dined at Penshurst. They used an English crew and a few English actors. We still exchange Christmas cards with one, Richard Caldicott. One journalist commented that instead of riding up in their old car, *The Beverly Hillbillies* arrived in a shiny Rolls Royce.

They stayed only a week but they made a lasting impression and for the length of its run, the show out pointed all others in its time slot in England. The trades said of that first episode: "*The Beverly Hillbillies*, long may they wave, are in solid for another year." Judith Crist, in the New Yorker Magazine, said, "There are still those among us with a taste for possum and the Clampetts certainly know how to dish it out in suitable style."

While they were away, something momentous happened to me. I had a lot of quiet time to myself, and I received an insight I've never quite lost. With Paul in England, Carol in New York working for CBS News, Tony taking summer classes in Berkeley, and Linda playing in *Generation* and *High Button Shoes* in San Diego, I spent most of the daylight hours lying in the sun by the pool, and at night cuddling up in bed with my big orange cat, Michèle, watching television and sharing goodies with my feline companion. It was August – no school, no real responsibilities – so that left me free to worry a lot about my family. I didn't worry much about Paul. He was doing his thing and enjoying it, and I didn't even want to change that. Carol, though, was living alone in Manhattan, had already been mugged once, and was involved with a man I considered unsuitable. Linda was in love with Michael, but I had a lot of doubts about that. Tony was young, and I was sure he had time to find himself. But the girls – I kept thinking of them and what they ought to do, how they could avoid mistakes, what I ought to tell them, how I ought to fix things. I wanted everything to be perfect and somehow I felt it was up to me to make it that way. Suddenly, lying there in the sun, it came to me. I can't do anything. I can't say anything. I'm not even supposed to. It's their lives. They have to make their own decisions, their own mistakes. All I have to do is love them and maybe pick up the pieces, if necessary. It was like the weight of the world rolling off my shoulders!

Of course, I should have known all that from the beginning, but if you're a parent, I'm sure you can put yourself in my place. We all want to make things better for our children, to keep them from making some of the mistakes we made. I remembered reading once, "Never give your grown children advice unless they ask for it and they'll never ask for it – so that's that."

I was a happier, more relaxed person when they all came home. When the show opened in the fall, it got good reviews, and everyone seemed to think it would go on forever.

The Beverly Hillbillies went back to England once more, but Paul didn't go. He put Buddy Atkinson in charge and stayed home to mind the store. They stayed in Beverly Hills for the next two years. That's where I liked them best – and when I see the reruns, I still do. But they made one more major location trip two years later to Silver Dollar City, Missouri.

Branson, Missouri has always been a resort area. Nestled in the Ozark Mountains near the Arkansas border, it is surrounded by two of the prettiest lakes in the world – Lake Taneycomo and Table Rock Lake. The fishing is prime and the land is beautiful. A long time ago, Hugo Herschend, a Chicago Businessman, took his wife Mary, and their two young sons there for a vacation. They all fell in love with the place. Up the highway a few miles from Branson is Marvel Cave, one of the biggest caves in this country. With amazing foresight, Hugo tried to buy the property over the cave. He had some idea of retiring there and opening a park. He was disappointed when he found that the two elderly sisters who owned the land were not interested in selling, but they finally agreed to lease the property. Jubilant, Hugo took his family back to Chicago and began to make plans. At the end of the school year, he asked his wife, Mary to take the boys back to Branson and supervise the work on the park. It wasn't easy for her. She'd never been in business before, but she would try. Then, totally unexpectedly, Hugo died. There was Mary, a widow, left alone with two boys to raise, and a cave.

Mary was an amazing woman. She saw that her sons were educated and presided over the beginning of Marvel Cave Park. Son Peter studied business and helped his mother run the park. Son Jack became a spelunker (cave expert) and made improvements on the cave so that tourists could view it more easily. Eventually, to shorten this saga, the park became known as Silver Dollar City. They organized the National Crafts Foundation and attracted artisans from

217

all over the country to create and display their handiwork. All of it was pioneer stuff, skills that had almost disappeared from the American scene. They made Conestoga wagons, barrels, baskets, musical instruments, lye soap, candy, quilts, woodcarvings, candles, and had resident glassblowers. It began to attract a lot of visitors.

When *The Beverly Hillbillies* made their debut in 1962, Don Richardson, in charge of Public Relations for the park, got a brilliant idea. He found some genuine hillbillies in the hills round about – not hard to do in that area – and invited them to see some films of *The Beverly Hillbillies*. They were Junior Cobb and his wife, Helen, from the town of Three Brothers, Arkansas. The shack they lived in made the original *Beverly Hillbillies* Cabin look like a mansion. They'd never seen the television show – the nearest TV set was four hours from their cabin. Junior hadn't read anything about it either – he couldn't read.

"They's got a goo funny pergr'm," he said. "That granny – she's zackly like my Gran'ma."

Helen liked the show too. She commented, "When I used to do housework for Mrs. Mertie Lewis, I seen Red Skelton and Danny Thomas. But them *Hillbillies* is all the time in more funny scrapes."

Don wrote an article about Junior and Helen Cobb and sent it to TV Guide. Paul got a real kick out of it when he read it.

"Didn't I tell you?" he said. "Those are the same people I used to see on Boy Scout camping trips." So, a few years after that, when Paul got a letter from Don inviting him to come and visit Silver Dollar City, Paul was prepared. As soon as filming was over for the season, he took Ronnie Pearlman, a young writer he was interested in, with him to Silver Dollar City. They stayed a little over a week and when Paul came back, he couldn't stop talking about the park, the crafts, the Herschends, and everything about the whole operation. As I've mentioned a few times, when Paul likes somebody or something, he goes all out. This was one of his major enthusiasms.

The Herschends apparently were equally impressed with Paul, and it became a mutual admiration society. They asked him to be on the board of directors of the Craft Foundation. That was right up Paul's alley. He loved all those skills, especially the woodcarving. He went back a couple more times to see it all again.

When he finally took me along, I was already a little sick of the subject. I'm not proud of it, but you can understand my feeling, I'm sure. When somebody, especially your husband, is so out of his mind about something that you're not a part of, already you don't like it. The days we spent there weren't easy for me. Of course, I liked the park (though not as much as Paul did) – and of course, I liked the people – but with moderation. My problem was stepping right into that mutual admiration society all by myself.

"Wait till you meet Mary Herschend!" Paul told me on the way. "You'll be crazy about her!"

"I'm sure I will," I said, my smile a little forced.

And then when that great moment came, Paul turned to me, face beaming. "Didn't I tell you that they were wonderful?"

I smiled. "Yes, you did. And they are… wonderful!" I added.

Mary Herschend looked at Paul adoringly. "And we think Paul Henning is just the salt of the earth. I'm sure you know that, Mrs. Henning."

My smile stiffened. "Oh yes, indeed I do – salt of the earth!"

And so it went – for hours and hours. My smile was frozen to my face, and when we finally got back to our motel room, my face actually hurt from smiling. Somehow, I managed to relax a bit and enjoy the visit. There were still compliments flying every direction but not toward me. I tried not to notice.

On the way home, Paul told me that Mary had pointed out a beautiful, unspoiled section of the Ozarks practically adjacent to Silver Dollar City. She certainly hoped it wouldn't be spoiled by all the schlock shops creeping up the highway from Branson.

"I'd really like to buy that land," Paul said, still in a dream.

An alarm bell rang. Do you suppose? I wondered. Surely not! "Uh – what would you want to buy it for?" I finally asked.

"To save it!" Paul cried.

"Oh," I said. "No other reason – you're sure?"

"Of course not," he said. "But I'd hate to see that lovely mountain ruined with all those touristy souvenir shops along the highway."

The next time we went back to visit, Paul was able to buy a portion of the mountain, called Dewey Bald. That night, at dinner, everybody was drinking toasts and congratulating us because we were going to be their new neighbors. Paul didn't deny it. I felt sick.

Back at the motel, I turned to him as soon as the door was closed. "You said you wanted to buy it only to save it!" I accused.

"That's right," he said.

"Well, what's all this 'neighbor' stuff then? You didn't deny it."

Paul chuckled. "Why should I do that and spoil the moment? They'll forget all about it."

As time went on, we acquired more and more land until we owned the whole darn mountain. People in Hollywood were saying, "What about that Henning? Now he owns a mountain."

When Paul decided to film several episodes of *The Beverly Hillbillies* in Silver Dollar City, it was the biggest thing that had happened to the folks of that area. That was before country and western singers decided to move their theatres from Nashville to Branson – long before. First Paul took director Joe Depew, production

220

manager, George King, and other key people back to show them the lay of the land, so they could decide what would be needed. It's no small task to take a show on location. There have to be wardrobe people, make-up experts, hairdressers, trucks full of lighting equipment – I don't know what else – but it isn't easy, that much is certain.

The cast were all delighted. It was like a vacation. Even though they had to work, when they did have time off, they could explore the park, visit the cave, fish, boat, buy souvenirs and antiques. Every evening, at the end of the day's filming, Irene Ryan had somebody take her out on the lake in a boat to relax. She took along a shaker for martinis, and a good time was had by all.

The local Press went bonkers with headlines and praise! "IT'S SHOWTIME IN THE OZARKS" – "MISSOURI SALUTED PAUL HENNING" – "OZARK NEIGHBORS OUT FOR BEVERLY HILLBILLIES." They were impressed by the graciousness of the cast, the hard work everybody did without complaining, how they all posed for pictures and gave autographs. Betty Hearnes, wife of Missouri's governor, Warren Hearnes, came to town to present Paul with a "Distinguished Citizen Award." Everybody loved *The Beverly Hillbillies*, even the traditionally skeptical newsmen.

"These are the most delightful people anyone will ever meet anywhere," said a TV newsman from Peoria. "Missouri is really benefitting from all this. I only wish we had something like it in Illinois."

They were there only a week, but they made their mark. From there, they went on to New York and Washington, D.C., for some more filming.

Silver Dollar City has grown to many times its original size since we first saw it. They have added rides and other attractions. This year, they're even adding a roller coaster. We preferred it when it was

221

simpler, but that's progress. It's now one of the most popular theme parks in the country. I learned to like it as much as Paul did, and the people grew on me. What happened to me on my first visit wasn't their fault. Please understand, I never expected to be belle of the ball. I never have been. It was just awfully hard to step cold into a situation like that. I've confessed it all to the Herschends since then, and we've all had a good laugh about it.

The payoff to the story about Henning's Mountain, Dewey Bald, is that now it's the Ruth and Paul Henning State Forest and we're very proud of it. Over the years, we had many offers from developers, but Paul held out. Finally, he donated part of the land to the state conservation department and felt he had really saved it.

"I think it should be the Paul Henning State Forest," I told him ruefully when the time came. "After all, I never wanted to buy it in the first place. You deserve all the credit."

As usual, Paul was generous and gracious. "Of course, your name will be on it," he said. "I wouldn't have it any other way."

We don't get back there as often as we used to. Mary Herschend has passed on and so has Don Richardson. They all came out to California to visit us, and when I graduated from college, Mary sent me an exquisite box, with a French inscription, carved for me by their woodcarvers. Paul also has a life-sized hillbilly in his study carved from a single log. And over our mantelpiece, are three wooden carved letters – "P-A-X." You'd be surprised how many people ask me what that means.

23
Trial and Tragedy

Into every life a little rain must fall, the saying goes. Sometimes it's a real storm. The trial comes under the heading of rain. A cameraman for CBS in New York sued the network, Filmways, Al Simon, and anybody else who had a part in *The Beverly Hillbillies* for fifteen million dollars. He said they stole his idea. He was a man who liked to turn in ideas to his superiors at the network – usually just half page, roughly constructed ideas, most of them worthless. Still, you had to give him credit – that he wasn't just doing his job and watching the clock. He was trying to better himself. One of his ideas concerned country people who came into contact with city people. I read it, but now I can't remember exactly how it was worded. It was highly forgettable.

Of course, Paul never stole his idea. He never saw that piece of paper until after the trial started. The cameraman was in New York. Paul was in Hollywood. However, the man said he could prove the idea had been sent to someone in California, and you know how things get around out there. He had some lawyers I considered sleazy and opportunistic. I guess they were smart. I guess all lawyers have to be opportunistic. The sleazy is purely a subjective evaluation on my part. It's interesting to note that the show had been on the air eight years before he brought his suit in 1970. The spur that started the whole thing was money. The whole enterprise smelled like money – and that attracts a lot of mischief.

At any rate, a trial was held in the New York Superior Court, and Paul and I, along with a lot of others, spent some unhappy weeks there.

Among the witnesses were CBS executives, Dan Melnick and Jim Aubrey; Filmways executives, Al Simon and Marty Ransahoff; former President of the Writers' Guild, Nate Monaster; R.J. Reynolds account executive, Sam Northcross; writers, Mark Tuttle and Dick Wesson; early associates of Paul's, Ted Malone and Vick Knight; and Jed Clampett himself, Buddy Ebsen.

Since none of the witnesses knew the plaintiff, nor had they seen his idea, most of the testimony was for Paul Henning's character. Without exception, they all swore that Paul was known for his honesty and integrity and that there was no more highly regarded or respected writer in the industry than Paul Henning.

I sat in the courtroom every day and watched the jurors, trying to get some idea how they were taking it all. Our lawyers were from Lloyds of London, an impressive name – to me, anyway. What I couldn't understand was how the lawyers could be such adversaries during the trial, and as soon as the court was adjourned for the day, they were all buddy-buddy. I guess I took it too personally, but after all, the whole case hinged on my husband's honesty, and I was ready to fight anyone who inferred that he had plagiarized another man's idea.

Each evening, everybody gathered in our suite at the Algonquin – lawyers, witnesses, friends, all the interested parties. We relaxed, ordered up drinks, and discussed how things had gone that day and made plans for the next day's strategy. Then we'd go out to dinner. Sometimes Paul was so tired we'd just have a quiet room service meal, and he'd go right to sleep. I was usually too wound up to sleep, and it became a regular occurrence for Marty Ransahoff to call. We'd talk it all over endlessly, me sitting on the toilet seat in the bathroom where the Algonquin had always provided a convenient extension. Up to that time, I hadn't really known Marty, and he had seemed to me one of Hollywood's typical wheeler dealers, but after that, I thought I knew the real man and felt a warm friendship for him.

Our attorneys, in their defense strategy, spoke about how there were really no "new" ideas in the world, that it's all a question of how the ideas are handled. Especially, the plot of country people and city people in juxtaposition with each other was as old as history. Aesop used it in the fable of "The City Mouse and the Country Mouse." Molière used it in almost all of his plays. Chateaubriand wrote about the noble savage. And to cinch the argument, they showed a short piece of film on "Ma and Pa Kettle," in which they go the city.

At last, inevitably, Paul was called to the stand. There was a long questioning by our own lawyers, in which Paul explained how he had always had the idea of writing about hillbillies and had never seen or known of the existence of the infamous half sheet of paper. That much wasn't too difficult. Then the other attorneys took over and cross-examined Paul for several hours. They asked questions which really couldn't be answered with "yes" or "no," and yet, that's what they insisted on. I sat in the audience suffering for Paul because I could see that he was very nervous, angry, and hurt. He was beginning to shout his answers. There was a recess, and I took him aside and tried to calm him down, suggesting that he make his answers thoughtful, calm, and quiet. He did better after that, but it still took its toll.

There was never any possibility that we personally would have to pay any of the fifteen million dollars in the lawsuit if we lost, but there was a question of honor and that meant a lot to Paul. After that vicious cross-examination that left Paul shaken and pale, one of the opposing lawyers came up to me and put out his hand.

"It's all in the day's work, little lady," he said, chuckling.

"Not to me," I snapped, and refused to shake his hand.

The case went to the jury on a Friday afternoon. Paul's first impulse was to get on the first available plane and go home. The lawyers begged him to stay. They said there was a real psychological advantage in being there to face the jury as they announced their decision.

A long weekend stretched out before us. We decided that escape would be the best medicine. We didn't want to see any of the participants. We didn't want to talk to any of them on the phone. We got a newspaper and made a schedule of movies we'd like to see. We saw three on Saturday, leaving very little time in between for brooding. On Sunday, we saw two, had a quiet dinner, and went to bed early.

Monday morning, we appeared in court to face the jurors and guess what? It was a hung jury. They polled the jurors. Sure enough, they hadn't been able to agree. Paul was excused to go home, which we did. Nobody wanted to go through the travail of another trial, so I'm told the network made some settlement with the New York cameraman. It was everyone's opinion that the jurors never really thought that Paul had stolen the idea, but there was this little guy against the powerful network and TV company, and they wanted him to get something. I hope he enjoyed it.

Well, that's the rain.

Now for the storm.

Early in 1967, Bea Benaderet found out she had lung cancer. Kate Bradley was written out of *Petticoat Junction*, supposedly to go to a beloved cousin who was ill and needed her. Bea had cobalt treatment, among other things, and rallied some. In May, the CBS Affiliates had their annual meeting in Los Angeles. Paul and I went with Bea and her husband, Gene Twombley. Bea was honored at the meeting and looked very beautiful, all in white, almost ethereal, you might say. That spring and summer, she and Gene rented a condo in

226

Palm Springs, and since Paul and I still had our rental house, we saw quite a bit of them, going out to dinner together, even having a home cooked meal – cooked by Bea – at their place.

Always one to ask questions, to jump in where angels fear to tread, I remember asking Bea, "Does it hurt? Are you in pain?"

"No," she smiled. "Sometimes it's hard to breathe."

Meanwhile, that year on the show was difficult for the writers of *Petticoat Junction*. While Kate Bradley prolonged her stay at her ailing cousin's side, various female relatives were brought in to mother the girls, help run the Shady Rest Hotel, and provide some kind of substitute for the missing star. Rosemary DeCamp paid a visit as Aunt Helen. Joan Blondell made a very brief appearance. Shirley Mitchell was Cousin May, and finally, June Lockhart came to Shady Rest as Dr. Janet Craig, opened an office there, mothered the girls, and kept an eye on Uncle Joe and the hotel.

Filming always began in midsummer for the new season. It was summer of 1968 when Bea made her triumphal return. There was a big celebration. Everyone welcomed her gladly and she was able to do a few episodes. Not many, though. Her health was rapidly failing, and Kate's ailing cousin needed her again so she had to leave. Betty Jo, who had married Steve Elliot the year before, was expecting a baby, and Bea really hated not being there to see her through it and to be the typical doting grandmother. She was able to record some messages, and they became "letters" to her daughter in her own voice.

Early in October, Bea died. Everyone was devastated, even though it was not unexpected. Paul felt her loss keenly. He'd known her for so many years, had watched her performing brilliantly so many times, as second banana, and now that she was finally starring in her own show, it really didn't seem fair to have such a tragedy end it all. Her funeral was October 16. Her son, Jack Bannon, conducted the services lovingly with the help of his sister, Maggie. On October 17,

Bea's husband, Gene Twombley, died of a heart attack. Or perhaps a broken heart. Jack Bannon was too broken up to conduct the service. It was just too much to expect of one little family.

Life went on, as it always does, both in the Hooterville Valley and in North Hollywood. It wasn't very joyful in either place. My mother who was in her eighties had to have major surgery in December, and at Christmas, most of us came down with the flu. Linda and Michael bought their own little home in the hills of Sherman Oaks. Tony and Carol moved to New Haven, where he attended Yale Law School, and our daughter, Carol, was hired by CBS News full-time and moved to New York. Our perfect world seemed to be changing daily. I realized the only thing that remains the same is change itself.

Television shows come and television shows go – but families are forever! Not a very original observation maybe, but nonetheless true. Never – not even during Paul's busiest years – did he ever lose sight of his family's interests, nor did he fail to feel our loving support for him. Sometimes we didn't see much of him, but he was always, whether present or not, the linchpin that held the turning wheels.

Our extended family includes our children, their significant others, my sister and her family, and whatever other relatives, close or distant, happen to enter our orbit. We celebrate everybody's birthdays and every holiday. Paul and I almost never go out and party on New Year's Eve because to him, New Year's Day is the big one! Football! He is passionate about football. It doesn't have to be the home team or the Super Bowl, just football – any football. At kickoff time of the Rose Bowl game, company starts drifting in, and we sit at two different sets with munchies and beer or cokes. Somehow, between the Rose Bowl and the Orange Bowl, I manage to serve my traditional bean soup and corn bread, and we go right on watching.

Easter is a highly creative Easter egg hunt organized by Linda like a treasure hunt with rhyming clues. Then brunch. Then the jellybean guessing contest. There is always some kind of pretty glass container full of jellybeans, and everybody gets a guess. The one who comes closest gets to take the jellybeans home.

July Fourth our patio is decorated within an inch of its life – everything red, white, and blue – a picnic dinner, and later on, we can sit beside our pool and watch the fireworks' display from Lakeside Golf Club. Sometimes, in the morning, there's a boat parade on Toluca Lake. The boat people decorate their boats and bring their children and dogs and sometimes patriotic music, and the rest of us stand on the bank with our coffee mugs waving flags or hands as the case may be.

Christmas at our house has become a tradition not only for our family but also for friends we never see any other time. Carol's college roommate, a few actors Linda has worked with in theatres around the country, a Rabbi and his family who are good friends of Tony and Carol, our beloved retired family doctor, Josephus Reynolds, and all the widows and orphans we can gather up.

The order of the day is Santa Claus, presents, brunch, and in the evening, a big crowd for a buffet. After that comes carol singing. All of us have had some experience with choral singing, and we love that. Carol and her ex-roommate even go to Idylwild, a quaint mountain village above Palm Springs every year to sing the Messiah at a special event. Finally, we all settle ourselves comfortably and see a movie, which is Linda's gift to the crowd. It's always a comedy or musical, and it's a perfect way to wind down after the busy days that went before. We have a movie screen that comes down from a beam in our living room and a hidden projection room.

"It's just like *Brigadoon*," said one actress, as she was taking her leave. "We'll see you next Christmas." You remember that Brigadoon was the magic Scottish village which appeared only one day a year, but life went on continuously from year to year just the same.

You can't know Paul Henning without knowing something about our children. Our first born, Carol Alice, of whom we are very proud, graduated from the University of California at Berkeley with a degree in Political Science, and after some years in between of travel and working at the studio, gravitated to CBS News in New York. During the '60's, the Vietnam War, she was a peace activist, and no doubt, influenced me to follow suit. She was able to explain the

230

history of that conflict, so that I understood it better than I ever could have otherwise.

Paul was not really the activist type. In the first place, he was too busy, but beyond that, no matter how strong his convictions, he never wanted to make waves and upset the equilibrium of his working family. Once, during the McGovern campaign, when I became terribly discouraged – I'd just found out that one of our favorite writers had been writing speeches for Spiro Agnew – after a sleepless night, I called Paul at the office and literally made an appointment to see him that day.

"Am I wrong?" I asked him. "I feel so strongly about this and I've worked so hard and now it seems everyone is against me or they just don't care."

"No, you're not wrong," he said. "I think you're right, and I'm proud of you for all you've done."

That was all I needed to hear. The day after the election, when McGovern was defeated in a landslide, I received a beautiful flower arrangement from Paul. The card read: "We are not bound to win, but we are bound to do our best. You did and I love you for it."

Paul worried about Carol a lot, living alone in New York, traveling the world alone, eating native food, and having her flings with European suitors.

"What if she marries one of them and lives halfway round the world?" he worried.

When she came home to live again, we were both relieved. I think she was lonely in New York, and she had a burning desire to do some more traveling.

During the meteoric popularity of the book *Jonathan Livingston Seagull*, Carol and Joe Benti, a local anchorman on the news, collaborated on a satirical book, *J. Power Buzzard*, which one could interpret only as a comment on the Nixon years. During that period, she and Joe both invested in a restaurant on Ventura Boulevard called "The Times," which they hoped would become a hangout for news people. I believe it did for a while. It was there one night where she casually met a musician named Jackie Kelso.

Several months later, he called her up. "I don't know if you'll remember me," he began.

She did, vaguely, but wasn't sure she'd even recognize him if she saw him again. With typical Carolian originality, she suggested they meet in North Hollywood Park. They were each to begin walking toward the center of the park from different directions, and if they recognized each other when they met, well, they could take it from there.

We all had a good laugh about that. Nobody but Carol would think of something like it. We all recognized the fact that Carol was a true intellectual, but as a lot of them are, she was – well – different.

The meeting in the park happened over twenty years ago. They met, they did know each other, they got to know each other better, and they are still together. Jack plays saxophone, clarinet, flute, piccolo – all the single reed instruments – in recording studios, theatres, movies, television, concerts – wherever they want good jazz music. Every year, he tours Japan with an orchestra, and Carol goes with him sometimes.

"In Japan, I walk two paces behind him," she laughed, "and I always say, 'Yes, master,' to all his commands. He loves it."

Meanwhile, Carol went back to school, to UCLA this time, and got a Master's Degree and her credential as a teacher of what is popularly known as ESL, or English as a Second Language. She has taught for years at Cal State L.A. and is a superb creative teacher. She also loves it. All her students are foreigners.

Every time Carol gets a day or two off, she has a trip planned, many times with the Sierra Club, camping out or doing something

232

primitive. She is a tireless worker for the environment and inspires all the rest of the family to do likewise. She was appalled that, in all the time Paul and I have lived here, we'd never seen some of California's natural wonders, so she and Jack have started a program to remedy that. They've taken us as their guests to Yosemite and Death Valley. We don't know what's next on the agenda, but whatever it is, Carol is the best travel guide we've ever had.

Paul takes Carol with him every summer to Estes Park, Colorado, where his sister, Drusilla, and her husband have a cabin. Carol and her cousin, Mary, love to look after the animals and climb the mountain trails. I'm not much good at that sort of thing, and besides, I think it's nice for them to have some father-daughter bonding, so I stay home.

If you saw Carol with her students, you'd think she was the youngest of the bunch. She's tiny with long blonde hair, which she most often wears down, and unless you examine her very closely, she looks like a teenager.

"Living with Carol is like living with the Encyclopedia Britannica with a monthly supplement," Jack says. It's true.

Both she and Jack are originals. They march to a different drummer, but they're happy and that's all that matters.

I've already written quite a bit about Linda because she comes naturally into the narrative about Paul's career, but I would like to mention that after *Petticoat Junction*, she did regional theatre all over the country and was much in demand. The plays and musicals she did, the stars she worked with, the cities where she worked would fill a page at least. She loved it, but it was a lonely life living in hotels and leaving your family and friends for weeks at a time. Alas, she was in that box that most series regulars find themselves in when they leave their shows. Nobody can see them in any other character. I never go out with Linda without someone recognizing her and getting very excited about seeing "Betty Jo" from *Petticoat Junction*.

Linda has always loved animals, and now she's found a real interest in being a docent at the L.A. Zoo. She conducts tours, puts on shows, gives talks, sometimes with a boa constrictor wrapped around her body, and I just can't stand to think of that. I've never seen it and don't want to.

Tony, our youngest, named after the character Paul played all those years ago on *Happy Hollow*, married his Carol the day after they both graduated from Stanford. It was a lovely wedding in Palo Alto, and we all went up for the festivities. Carol and Linda were bridesmaids. I shopped all over to find a special dress for "mother of the groom," and as usual, I hated it. How could I continue to do that?

We gave them their honeymoon trip. Tony had gone to Hong Kong one summer on a Stanford program to teach English to children. He wanted very much to take Carol to the Orient on their honeymoon. When they returned, they were in Linda's wedding and then went straight to New Haven where Tony entered Yale Law School. He really wasn't sure what he wanted to do with his future, but he knew his dad would be pleased if he studied law. He had been accepted by every university to which he applied since he graduated "With Great Distinction" – the honor Stanford gives instead of any of the Cum Laudes.

As his first semester was ending, we received a long, long letter from him. He wanted us to understand that he hated the study of law. He had hated every minute of the past semester, and if he thought he would have to do that for the rest of his life, he didn't see how he could stand it. He wasn't sure what he wanted to do, but he knew it would have to be something in the arts. They returned to California and settled in San Francisco. That much they were sure of – they loved the Bay Area. Tony became a professional photographer.

He was good at it, and he liked it well enough, but we all knew he wasn't using the brains and talents God had given him.

They had two sons, Alex Joseph and Jesse Matthew. They moved to Berkeley and bought a home. Tony had his dark room and a studio at home, as well as one in the city. He was around a lot to do good parenting. He remembered how he had missed seeing more of his dad as he was growing up and wanted to be there for his boys.

Tony's Carol is also artistic and brilliant. She has tried many things, all successful. She weaves. She makes jewelry. Her consuming interest has become gourmet cooking, and nobody is more gourmet-ish. Now she is employed as the regular chef of a big winery in the Napa Valley. She cooks multiple course meals for their prospective customers, a different wine with each course, naturally, and always receives a standing ovation. The job is only now and then – but that works out perfectly with the running of a home and raising two sons.

A few years ago, Tony became part of a new company started by a friend of his. It concerns computer programming and also fine art. Don't ask me to explain exactly what, how, and why. I'm not of the computer generation. All I know is that Tony has, at last, found his niche. He travels a lot – all over the world – selling, demonstrating, making speeches. In Paris, he was able to conduct business with the Louvre in French. He is a charismatic speaker; I've always known that, ever since he became president of the student body of North Hollywood High School. The boys are growing up, and in June, our whole family will go to Berkeley to see Jesse play the lead in his school play. He will be Joseph in *Joseph and His Amazing Technicolor Dream Coat*. That pleases me to no end. I've always been stage struck, but I'm glad to see the genes are going on.

You know a lot about me already. I must tell you about my graduation though. Yes, I finally graduated in 1968 and got my BA degree in French. Bobby Kennedy had been shot only a few days before, and many of us wore armbands to show our grief and respect. I had my own little fan section made up of my extended family and close friends. They announced the Cum Laudes, not very many. Next were the Magna Cum Laudes, even less. Then the Summa Cum Laude. Only one – me. My cheering section stood up and raised hail Columbia.

Paul gave a party for me afterward in a small private room at Sportsman's Lodge. It was decorated with a huge sign that said, "Summa Mama." I wore my cap and gown to the party. It had been a lot of work and a lot of fun, and I was very proud. I didn't fool myself. I was far from being the smartest graduate. I had taken a long time to do it. I had cared a lot and done my best. I didn't have the distracting interests of young people who have to earn a living, plan their futures, and worry about their love life. I was more mature. You may not memorize as easily, but maturity has a lot of advantages. You understand your teachers. You know they're human just like you, and you know a little more about how to please them. However, I make no apologies. I was Summa Mama, and I loved every moment of it.

Now that I could free myself from the tyranny of the books, I found myself thinking about a new project. The children had all left home, Linda and Tony married, Carol the same as, living with Jack in their own house. Here we were, Paul and I, rattling around in our big house with five bedroom and a guesthouse. It needed some major redecorating and perhaps even remodeling. But instead of spending a lot of money on that house, why couldn't we sell it and maybe – just maybe – finally, I could build my dream house.

We had tried to do that once before, even bought a lot in Beverly Hills where I always thought I wanted to live. But World War II came along, you couldn't get materials, and besides, we began to realize we could never afford to build it the way we wanted to. So we sold the lot and bought the house in Toluca Lake. Now things were different. *The Beverly Hillbillies* had made a lot of things possible.

A realtor in the area solved our problem of where to build it. We really didn't want to move, so he suggested we subdivide our present extensive property and use a third of it for the new house. Perfect! We didn't need a big yard for children to play in. We didn't need such a big house. We just needed a special house – my dream house.

Paul, still very busy at the studio, said it sounded like a good idea to him and encouraged me to move full speed ahead. After interviewing several architects who all proceeded to tell me what was wrong with my ideas, I found one who not only liked my ideas but improved on them. He was Robert Byrd, well-known in our area. A Byrd house is to be cherished. We cherish ours.

We started right in. Every day we met together with an interior designer and a landscape architect. We talked for hours. Every night, I made lists of things I'd forgotten to mention. This went on for six months. Finally, we had the completed plans ready to show to Paul. He looked at them, his eyes somewhat glazed over, and said, "Fine!" He signed the contract, and we were in business.

The next thing we had to do was get the approval of our financial advisors, our lawyer, Norman Tyre, and our accountant, Allan Landman. The meeting was to be in Paul's office at the studio. I was scared. I could just hear them saying, "You can't do that!" "The cost is exorbitant!" "Why do you need such a fancy house at your time of life?" I was late to the meeting. It was probably Freudian. I didn't want to hear any discouraging words.

When I got there, everybody looked happy. They all smiled at me and said the house sounded just great, and they wished us every happiness in it. I couldn't believe my ears. Later, I heard that Paul had said, "This girl has never wanted anything expensive before – not designer clothes, not jewels, not furs – only this house. And I want her to have it." Is that a darling husband or what?

It took about a year and a half to build. Sometimes it was frustrating. Mostly, it was thrilling. Living next door, I could really keep an eye on things, and I loved each new addition. As the framing went up, I took Paul through it, and he kept exclaiming, "Ohhh – so that's the way it's going to be!"

"You saw the plans!" I said.

"Yes, but I didn't understand them."

We moved into our house September 2, 1971. It was far from finished. We lived there while the finishing touches were made – a sort of shakedown cruise. We were still trying to sell the house next door. Real estate had been booming, so we thought, but now that we had something to sell, it seemed the bottom had dropped out.

I won't try to describe our house. I don't want to bore you. I'll just say it's as wonderful as I always dreamed it would be. To this day, more than twenty years later, I never take it for granted. Every time I walk in the door, I love it more. I discover new things about it all the time.

People used to ask me, "Now that it's finished, be honest. Isn't there something you wish you could change?"

"No," I said – and that was the truth.

The contractor said, "You're a rare customer. You never asked us to change anything midstream."

That's because I knew what I wanted. I'd known it almost all my life, it seemed. And I had a good architect who knew how to give it to me.

When it was pretty much complete, we had a little party and invited our lawyer, our accountant, and other key people. I wrote a parody for the occasion. I have a file full of parodies I've written for just about every important event of my life. I'd really like you to hear this one. It's to the tune of "September Song." I sang it to them that night.

When a man and his wife – they build a house
They play a waiting game –
They make their plans with an architect
They'll be in by Christmas they expect
But December comes and no halls are decked
By New Year's it's still the waiting game
Any by April it's all the same –

And it's a long, long time – from May to December –
That was May '69 – as I remember –
And Paul has lost some hair –
And my back's a little lame –
And we haven't got time for the waiting game.
And the days hurry by
And the work is slow
September – November –
And when it all will end – we still don't know –
When it will end – we still don't know.

We have four strong men who work with stone
And others who work with brick
The master carpenter works alone
Each one has a union of his own
Their hourly wages make us groan
And the total makes us sick.

For it's a long time from May to December
And the problems mount, as we reach September –

The cabinetmakers goof
And the pool won't drain
And we have no roof
If it should rain.
And we can't get the tile
Cause it's out of stock –
September – November –
But still we smile – as we go in hock –
We try to smile – in a state of shock.

It really isn't a simple thing
To make a dream come true
You watch and wait and worry and weep
Sometimes you really don't get much sleep
Wondering how you got in so deep
And you'd like to fire the whole darn crew
You'd like to fire the crew.

And it's a long, long time from May to December
And the cash grows short – as we reach September
And Allan Landman sighs – as the costs go higher
And we hear anguished cries – from Norman Tyre
And the funds dwindle down – to a precious few
A bank loan – a mortgage –
And these few borrowed funds –
We'll spend them too
These borrowed funds – we'll spend – them too!

Paul loves the house as much as I do. Sometimes when we consider taking a trip, we sit side by side in our kitchen rockers, brochures on our laps, and talk about it.

240

"I sure hate to leave my television programs and the *Los Angeles Times*," I say.

"And I hate to leave our comfortable bed and our wonderful shower," Paul says.

"Oh yes, I'd really miss my electric bed. And my study – and my electric typewriter."

"And my bar. I love my bar," Paul adds.

"And the children and all our friends," I go on.

Finally, we look at each other and grin and say almost together, "Let's stay home!"

25

The Real Paul Henning

People have called Paul Henning the writer nobody knows. I can go along with that. Sometimes I wonder if I really know him. He isn't easy to know. He thinks a lot but doesn't say much. He doesn't like to talk about himself, especially his innermost feelings. If you try to have a heart-to-heart talk with him, you get only so far and then a door clangs shut, and you might as well give up. Ask him a serious question and you're likely to get a funny answer. Like many comedians, the jokes cover things that are too personal to reveal.

Paul will try to tell you he's not a witty man in person, that writing humor is a serious business, hard work, and that there's nothing funny about him. This is not true. Ask our children. They can tell you time after time when he's made them laugh. Ask me. I can tell you he's kept me laughing for nearly 60 years. I started to write some of the funny things he's said, but Paul said not to do it.

"They don't translate to the page," he said. "They were ad lib and when you write them down, they're not funny."

He's the family expert on humor, so I have to accept his judgment on that. Maybe he's right. Maybe they just seem funny to us because we remember how we felt when he said them.

Paul has a way of looking at things that's just a little different, a little offbeat. When he says something, it seems like the most natural thing in the world, only none of the rest of us would have thought to say it. That's why it's funny.

Like most creative people, he's moody. In our earlier years, the moods were much more pronounced and I suffered because I often thought it was my fault, that I'd done something to displease him.

Once when he had been in an absolutely black mood for several days, I demanded an explanation.

"It's just the script," he said, looking down at his plate, and sounding as though he'd lost his last friend. "It just isn't going right."

"Well, for goodness sakes, if writing makes you this miserable, if it brings on all this suffering, I suggest you get into another line of work. Don't do it for me! I don't want to be the cause of so much self-sacrifice!"

He remained silent, still looking down at his plate.

By this time, I was really worked up to my subject. "Quit!" I shouted. "Quit today!" I slammed a few dishes around. "I can't stand another day of this."

Paul seemed stunned at my tirade. I don't think he realized what he was putting me through. "I don't hate my work," he said, "I love it!" For the first time in days, he began to look like a normal human being. "I can't think of anything else I'd rather do than what I'm doing."

"If that's true," I said, my voice softening, "why can't you enjoy it? Why can't you realize this little problem with the script is only temporary and it'll all work out? Why can't you smile and talk to us and make us believe you love us?"

You know, it worked. I don't lose my temper often, but when I do, it usually helps. He's never been in one of those black, black moods since. Little ones, sure. The leopard can't completely change his spots, but I'm sure he always remembers that little tirade of mine.

I've dedicated this chapter to the real Paul Henning. I hope I can do him justice. As I've been writing this memoir, a thought has constantly been bubbling up to the surface of my mind, until at last, it's ready to come out. When I was studying French literature for all those years in college, there was an expression we often used: porte parole. If a character in a book was the author's porte parole, that

243

meant he was speaking for the author, that he was the spokesperson, the alter ego, the writer himself in disguise. I really don't think there's an exact translation. But here's what I've come up with. Jed Clampett is Paul Henning's porte parole.

Jed Clampett is a simple man. So is Paul. He never wants to show off, to try to be something he isn't, to do anything that could be considered pretentious.

Jed Clampett is generous. So is Paul – generous to a fault. By that, I mean that Paul wants to help the whole world. Just let him hear about somebody who's having a hard time, and right away he wants to give them something – a little money, or more likely, a lot of money. He is an incurable check picker-upper. Hardly a month goes by that Paul doesn't come to me looking a little sheepish and pleading, "I'd like to give so-and-so some money." I look after our finances because, as Paul knows, if it were left to him, we'd always be broke.

He's not only generous with his money, but with his time and with himself. He's always willing to see a new writer and give advice, encouragement, a pat on the back. He's always ready to take all the dogs and cats of the family to the vet's. He used to invite people we hardly knew to come and stay at our house. He probably didn't realize how much trouble that was for me.

Finally, I said, "If we have one more house guest this summer, I'm running away from home."

Paul always got to the studio early and roamed around checking out everything in his little domain. He noticed that Bea Benaderet's dressing room could use a good vacuuming, so later in the day, he went by there, armed with the vacuum, to clean it up. While he was there, Bea came in with a reporter who wanted to interview her.

"Oh, hello, Paul," she greeted him and introduced him to the reporter.

Paul finished with his chore and was ready to take his leave.

"You're really the producer, Paul Henning?" the reporter asked, aghast. "Do you do this kind of janitor service for all your people?"

He smiled at Bea. "Only for those I love," he said.

Jed Clampett loves his family. So does Paul. Even when the things we do are exasperating, he still loves us and tries to make life easier for us. If I'm sick, he's a wonderful nurse. He shows such TLC, it's almost worth being sick. When Tony and his family come to visit, it's Paul who checks the guest suite over and over to see that they have everything they need, that the temperature is adjusted just right, that the rooms are aired and the sheets clean. It's Paul who orders their favorite wines and soft drinks. It's Paul who's always ready to slip them a little something extra to spend on a day out.

And, of course, he adores his daughters. He thinks they're smart, and beautiful, and talented, and when one of them comes over to see us, or just drops by, it makes his day.

Jed Clampett is loyal. So is Paul. Jed is loyal to his family and to Cousin Pearl back home even though she sometimes behaves foolishly. He's even loyal to Mr. Drysdale, the banker, who is so money hungry, he does outrageous things. It's a given that Paul is loyal to his family – and that includes his sisters and his cousins and his aunts – and mine, too. As for the people he has worked with over the years, he is loyal and will probably be to the end of time. What if somebody disappoints him? Never mind. What if they goof off, or get a few little scams going, or take him for granted, or impose on him? Never mind. Whatever it is, if he likes you, he likes you a lot, and usually, for life. Lucky for me.

Jed is not a bigot. Neither is Paul. Most of us, even if we don't think so, have some deeply ingrained little prejudice, so I asked Paul to search his mind and tell me if he did.

245

"Aren't you prejudiced against anybody?" I asked.

"Only tall people," he said.

While I had him in a rare talkative mood, I asked a few other questions.

"What would you say is your best quality in your writing?"

"Persistence, I guess. I always keep on trying till I get it right."

"What do you enjoy most about your work?"

"I enjoy the reaction of the artists, the audience, the crew. I like to hear them laugh."

"But don't you know – you must know – when you've written something really good?"

"I can't be sure till I get the reaction."

"Of all the shows you've done, what are your favorites? Of course, I can guess *The Beverly Hillbillies* is number one," I said.

"Of course," he admitted. "And second would be *Burns and Allen*."

That rather surprised me. Even though he loved George and Gracie and had ten wonderful years with them, he'd had bigger personal successes in other projects.

"I know this isn't exactly fair," I said apologetically, "and I wouldn't ask you to evaluate the writers who've worked with you, but is there any one that comes to mind instantly which was a happy, productive partnership?"

"Mark Tuttle," he said, without hesitation. That surprised me, too, because I knew Mark had been a secretary at the studio and had had little or no actual writing experience. The way Paul explained it, it was that Mark was young and bright and had no preconceived notions of how to write a show, didn't know all the old jokes to keep re-working, had a young, contemporary outlook that perhaps Paul himself lacked. He liked taking this promising young man under his wing and "molding" him so to speak. He had a great sense of humor and they worked together joyfully and profitably.

Paul is not really a churchgoer. When he was a small boy, he'd had to sit still for a two-hour sermon in German, and that's enough to discourage any child. I'd always enjoyed church and Sunday School and had taught a Sunday School class for over twenty years. If someone commented on why my husband rarely accompanied me to church, I always replied, "He's a better Christian than I am with all my church going." What does the Bible say? "Love one another. Love thy neighbor." That's Paul – absolutely.

One time, when I was too sick to teach my Sunday School class of third graders, Paul offered to go in my place. I was amazed. So was the minister, who was delighted, and took a snapshot of Paul with the children.

Music is an important part of Paul's life. He would have loved to be a singer all his life. He has a sweet, crooning voice, but he realized that wasn't his way to fame and fortune. Like most people of our generation, he loved the show tunes, the music of Irving Berlin, Cole Porter, Vernon Duke, Rogers and Hammerstein, etc. Among his favorites are "Tenderly" and "Fly Me to the Moon." Thank goodness we have some recordings of his singing. Otherwise, the children could hardly have believed it. About the only time he sings now is on the occasions when we call people, local or long distance, and sing Happy Birthday in harmony. We call it the Mormon Tabernacle Choir greeting.

Hal Kanter said, "I predict Paul Henning will go down in history as the greatest folklore comedy writer that ever was." Maybe so.

Carl Reiner wrote to him in a letter, "You see, it is possible to be a gentleman and still have the biggest hit on TV." Definitely.

I'd like to close this chapter with an inspiring quote by journalist Royce Brier: "Jed Clampett is one of the most admirable men you ever came across. He is devoid of meanness in a mean world, the epitome of unpretentiousness in a world gorged with pretense. He is a man of eminent common sense in a world where common sense is not esteemed, a low-pressure man in a high-pressure world soggy with neuroses. These traits alone could be raised to the rank of a virtue if anybody cared. He is patient, invariably ruminative, seeing the other fellow's point of view, rational in the face of Granny's prejudice. You wonder what would happen if forty million viewers were to disregard Jed's drolleries and start emulating his character in their everyday lives. Well – forget it – it's only a thought."

Substitute Paul Henning for Jed Clampett in the paragraph and you have a pretty good picture of Paul, the man.

26

Is the Magic Gone?

In the spring of 1971, CBS canceled every show that had a tree in it. I don't know who said that first. It was attributed to Pat Buttram – it sounds like him. Unfortunately, it was true. That meant curtains for the Hooterville Trilogy, as some people called *The Beverly Hillbillies, Petticoat Junction*, and *Green Acres*. Paul was sorry – tired – but sorry. The shows were still successful, and Paul felt they were good for a few more years.

The reason for the wholesale cancellation was a new and popular term, "demographics." According to the dictionary, that means "population statistics." In other words, forty million country people, small town people, older people, younger people might be crazy about the show, but they didn't have as much money to spend as the thirty-something, upwardly mobile, educated city people, and it was assumed the latter preferred more sophisticated programming.

I'm not at all sure that was right. A lot of city people were fans of *The Beverly Hillbillies*, and a lot of country people had money to spend. Who knows? Money makes the world go round, and money makes the sponsor's products move off the shelf. Nobody wanted to take the chance.

It had been a long, hard ten years for Paul and he was utterly exhausted. He welcomed a rest. He was still under contract to Filmways, but any new projects would have to wait. He kept his office at General Service Studios, he kept his secretary, Gloria, but spent most of his time in Palm Springs. He loved the desert. Now, at last, he was free to indulge in his sun worshiping as much as he wanted to. I went with him sometimes, but my life hadn't changed drastically as his had. I still had my regular commitments. Besides, I wasn't a sun worshiper. I didn't even try anymore. My dermatologist had finally convinced me to go for the shade.

I liked having Paul around more. We were putting the finishing touches to our new house, though Paul left that almost entirely up to me. We had a more active social life, went out to restaurants, the theatre, movies, and as soon as we felt the house was ready, we began to have a lot of company. Paul always managed to be at home for any important occasion. He loved to drive and thought nothing of driving the 120 miles to and from our Palm Springs pad every few days.

I was still somewhat involved in politics and had taken on a lot of volunteer work for the American Cancer Society. I organized support groups all over the valley and helped with fundraisers. The peace movement was still important to me. I attended a conference, Pacem in Terris, in Washington, D.C., and had a long letter published in the *Los Angeles Times* about the mining of Haiphong Harbor. Political liberalist, John Kenneth Galbraith, spoke at a meeting at our house. Around the holiday season, after Paul and I had been named on President Nixon's White House Enemy List, CBS sent a mobile unit to our house to film an interview for the eleven o'clock news. Paul applauded all my actions but declined to take part.

He did go down to the office sometimes and have meetings with Filmways executives. They discussed ideas for new television series. He and Stanley Shapiro talked about doing another film together. Both USC and UCLA approached Paul about possibly teaching a class in their film departments. He enjoyed the talks and certainly intended to do another series when they hit the right one. Somehow, that never happened.

In just a short time, the network picture had changed a lot. Jim Aubrey and the other CBS executives who had been Paul's champions were no longer around. In their place were brisk young men who, if they remembered Paul's show at all, discounted it as cornpone trash. Many of them treated Paul like a pitiful old has-been. In show business, memories are short. Now they wanted sex and violence and social significance! Paul would come home shaking his head.

He actually wrote a pilot, at Al Simon's request, a charming, funny, sweet, and warm story about endearing people, but after "they" read it, they suggested that he put in some "jiggle." That term was being used a lot those days meaning shaking of female body parts. Pretty girls without girdles or bras. He tried to re-write his script, but it made him sick.

He began to doubt himself. That's easy for a writer to do, especially one like Paul. Where was the famous Henning Magic everyone had talked about? Was it gone?

We traveled around a lot – not big trips – just around the country: to Missouri to see family; to New York to check up on the Algonquin, Broadway shows, and old friends; to Dallas, Hartford, San Diego, Milwaukee, and lots of other places to see Linda in plays. We took our whole family to Silver Dollar City and happened to be there when the astronauts walked on the moon. Linda and Michael had been appearing in Little Rock in the play, *The Paisley Convertible*.

There was no pressing reason for Paul to keep hustling, trying to get another show on the air. *The Beverly Hillbillies* had left us comfortable in the lifestyle to which we had grown accustomed.

I started a dance class in our garage, taught by a fabulous teacher, Lassie Ahern. There were about eight women, friends and neighbors, and we learned regular dances and gave shows now and then. It wasn't just aerobics. We fixed up the garage with a new surface, compatible for both cars and dancing, hung the walls with a collection of cat posters, and Paul volunteered to mop the garage every Tuesday and Thursday morning before our class. It was the best-looking garage in the neighborhood.

And then, after a few easy years, it was decided to do a *Beverly Hillbillies* reunion; a two-hour television film, which was called *The Beverly Hillbillies Solve the Energy Crisis* but which most of us thought of as *The Return of The Beverly Hillbillies*. From the beginning, the project was fraught with difficulties. Irene Ryan was dead. No Granny. Raymond Bailey was dead. No banker. Max Baer declined. No Jethro. On top of all that, just as they were going into production and Paul saw the need for some major re-writes, the Writer's Guild called a strike. He didn't dare change anything. Imogene Coca was hired to play Granny's mother. A reasonable facsimile actor was hired to play Jethro. They made the best of the script they had. But it wasn't the same. Paul enjoyed being back in the harness, going to the studio every day. We all did. But we could see the handwriting on the wall. This was not going to repeat the meteoric success of the original.

Maybe the magic was gone.

We talked about it just the other day. I kept trying to find excuses for why it wasn't very good. Paul would have none of that. He took all the responsibility.

"If it isn't on the page, it isn't on the stage," he said.

Okay. I guess so. Still, the breaks were against him. And if that weren't enough, the night in October when they put it on the air just happened to be the day Yasser Arafat was assassinated. It was also opposite the World Series. We didn't know that back in June, of course, but they did have a screening, and I was afraid it would be very depressing for Paul. So I planned a trip. We hadn't had a big trip for a long time, so I worked with a travel agent and we got out of town the last day of June. We flew to London, then directly to Oslo to visit our Norwegian family, then back to London and a bus tour of the

252

British Isles. It was totally delightful. Paul was happy. He seemed to be taking the TV film and its shortcomings in stride.

"You put on a good trip, ma'am," Paul told me. "Let's do another one."

So we did. And another. And another, and so on. Paul says he isn't sure when he decided that he was through with television or vice versa, but I really believe it was after that disastrous reunion film.

In January 1982, we went on a nine-week cruise on the Queen Elizabeth II, or QEII. We went everywhere and fell in love with that ship. In June of the same year, we took a Black Sea Cruise on the Golden Odyssey with Curt and Edythe Massey to celebrate their golden wedding anniversary. From then on, there was no stopping us. We cruised the South Seas, the Orient, Australia and New Zealand, Mexico, Alaska, the Mediterranean, the Holy Land, through the Panama Canal, the Scandinavian Countries. You name it. If a ship can get to it, we've been there. We got more or less cruised out.

So we started on bus trips. Two tours of the Deep South including New Orleans, Savannah, Charleston, Hilton Head, all those places I'd never been. We went on a New England fall foliage tour with Ted Malone and his wife. Paul and I flew to Florida and drove all over the state seeing old friends who had retired there. We drove up the Pacific Coast to Victoria and had high tea in the famed Empress Hotel.

To celebrate our golden anniversary, we took all three of our children and their significant others to New Orleans and then up the Mississippi River on a steamboat. We visited Antebellum plantations and Civil War battlefields, we ate like there was no tomorrow, and we sat out on our balconies – all connecting – watching the river ripple by while sipping mint juleps. It was out there on the balcony that the kids put on a special show for our anniversary. I don't know when I've ever been so happy.

"Look at all those wonderful adults!" I said to Paul. "Can you believe we started this whole thing?"

The last big trip we took was a bus tour through France and down to the Riviera and Monaco. I love France, and I loved that trip – except for one thing. In Monte Carlo, Paul began to get a strange pain in his back. He'd had that same symptom before and was afraid he knew what it was. Kidney stone! He managed to endure for a few days with pain pills, and I hoped maybe our visit to Lourdes and the famous Grotto of Bernadette might give him a miraculous cure. It didn't. Jennifer Jones, were you just kidding? Finally, we had to leave the tour in Blois and put Paul in the hospital.

It was a lovely, modern hospital, but not one soul spoke a word of English. Doctors, nurses, office employees, NOBODY. My education finally paid off. They rolled in a cot for me and I translated for Paul and the doctors and nurses. I took him by ambulance to the American Hospital in Paris and after a few days, we flew home. Rather an anticlimax.

That was five years ago. Every year, we talk about going somewhere really big. We sit in our rocking chairs and look at the brochures, and it always ends the same way. We decided to stay home. We like it here. A lot. Paul echoes Jed Clampett's statement. "A fellow would be a danged fool to leave all this."

Has the magic gone? No. There's more than one kind of magic. There's another kind that we have every day of our lives. We start every day with a walk – about two miles – around our beautiful neighborhood. Then we sit in our rocking chairs, side by side, in our kitchen and drink our coffee and read the paper. On chilly days, Paul puts a fire in the kitchen fireplace. Our much loved cat, Billy White Shoes, joins us and purrs in our laps. Most times then, we go our separate ways, each with our own little agenda. We always come together again around five o'clock for a glass of wine and a simple

254

dinner. We're closer than we've ever been. I don't get tired of having my husband around. I've never felt like repeating that old cliché, "For better or worse but not for lunch!" We each fix our own lunch anyway.

They say couples who live together a long time grow to be alike. There's a lot to that. Paul always liked the early to bed, early to rise habit. That was hard for me when we were young, but now I like it too. I don't get carsick any more. I love to take motor trips. He doesn't sunbathe now – he's had his own warning from the dermatologist. We both love to read. We both love movies. We both love the theatre. He still doesn't dance. Oh well, you can't have everything.

"What would you think if I hired a gigolo to take me dancing?" I asked him once.

"It's okay with me," he said.

I never did it. Maybe I wouldn't be able to do the new dances anyway.

We were just about to hold hands and walk off into the sunset when things began happening. Last September was the thirtieth anniversary of the night *The Beverly Hillbillies* first went on the air. There was an impromptu party at our house. Buddy and Donna and Max all came. Steve Cox, who had just written a book about *The Beverly Hillbillies*, came and brought a birthday cake. Linda came and helped cut the cake. *Los Angeles Times* photographers came. A cable news network came. Buddy and I did a little tap dance. We had a ball!

Then Twentieth Century Fox decided to make a big budget movie of *The Beverly Hillbillies*. All new cast, of course. Paul has nothing to do with it, except that they're his characters, of course. The director, Penelope Spheeris, invited us to visit the set. They were filming in the ballroom of an incredible mansion high in Benedict

Canyon – a birthday party for Jed Clampett. All the new cast was there plus Dolly Parton to sing "Happy Birthday." The producer, Ian Bryce, saw to our comfort and treated us royally. We had lunch out under a tent with the cast. Before we left, they presented Paul with his own director's chair with his name and "The Beverly Hillbillies" printed on it. Penelope Spheeris assured us we would be invited to the "Wrap" party and the premiere.

And that's not all! CBS decided to do an hour special about *The Beverly Hillbillies* this month. This is a nostalgia show, with film clips, the original hillbillies, Earl Scruggs and the bluegrass musicians, and even a little scene for Paul. The director, Jay Levey, invited us to visit their set, far out in Topanga Canyon at a log cabin they were using for Jed Clampett's home. All the gang was there. We had lunch with them, too, and especially loved listening to the musicians play that popular song, "The Ballad of Jed Clampett."

For a while, reruns of the show were not shown locally, but now every morning on our Channel 11, we get two episodes back-to-back. We watch whenever we can. They seem even funnier to me now than they did thirty years ago.

With all this renewed activity, the press is waking up again. I really like an article by *Associated Press* reporter Frazier Moore. He writes: "From the first twangs of its bluegrass title ballad, *The Beverly Hillbillies* sent critics into orbit like John Glenn….Meanwhile, the show, like the Clampetts' flatbed truck, will run forever in reruns. Some 274 half-hours worth are syndicated in 55 cities and the series is parked on the TBS schedule at 6:05 p.m. Monday through Friday. Now on its 30th anniversary, *The Beverly Hillbillies* remains among the funniest, most inspired of all TV comedies – and yet one that even its fans still watch down their noses… Smirk, if you must, but the Clampetts look smarter with every passing season. More than ever, the joke is on the rest of us."

Right on, Frazier!

Right on, *Hillbillies*!

Right on, Paul Henning!

Epilogue

As mother tap danced into her '80s, she decided she'd rather not drive her car if she didn't have to. This was a wise decision but, for a Los Angeles resident, a drastic one. Often Linda or I would drive her wherever she wanted to go. On Sundays I often drove her to church. Mother felt comfortable at the Church of Religious Science in North Hollywood. One Sunday she confided to me, "If anything happened to Paul, I would get even more active in this church." She and all of us expected that daddy would pass away first. Men so often go before their wives do, and she was two years younger than he. It didn't happen that way.

On January 15, 2002, mother died unexpectedly of a heart attack. It was one day after their 63rd wedding anniversary. She and daddy had drunk their morning coffee in the kitchen and, as she walked through the house, she felt a sudden chest pain and collapsed on the bedroom carpet. It was over.

It was a good way to go. Mother was 88 years old. Having survived Hodgkin's disease, she was enjoying her life until the moment it ended. She and daddy had lived for 30 years in the dream house she helped design. They spent important holidays with children, grandchildren, nephews, nieces—all the family they could gather. Mother got together with her extended family once a year for a Cousins' Reunion in Missouri.

She always loved the theater. A week before she died, I had taken her to see a revival of "Flower Drum Song." She wrote me a thank you note. That was our way. Mother was a wonderful letter-writer. She seemed to see her life as an endless series of excellent adventures, and her letters were full of details: of a film she'd seen, a meal she'd cooked or eaten, a person she'd met. She not only loved to watch performances; she loved to perform. One of her earliest memories was when the Armistice was signed at the end of World War I. Her mother, who was "always fiercely patriotic, organized a neighborhood parade. It featured, in the lead, who else but little Ruthie dressed like the statue of liberty holding aloft a gilded cardboard torch and wearing a paper crown."

This probably marked the opening event in a career that included leading roles in school plays, acting in radio soap operas and later in Little Theater and as the star of plays put on by students in the Spanish class on board the QE 2. Finally, she directed and all but wrote the script for her memorial service—specifying the venue, the celebrants, and the music to be performed.

In her own words: "I've had a wonderful, full, interesting life....They say you can't have it all—and I guess you can't—but I've had a lot of it. And for that, I have to thank the good Lord and Paul Henning." He (Paul, not the good Lord) died three years later.

Carol Henning

About Woodneath Press, the Woodneath Story Center, and Libraries as Publishers

Despite how they are sometimes perceived by the public, modern libraries are exciting and dynamic. While some changes are dramatic and paradigm shifting others are subtle and gradual. Regardless of the rate of change, what Heraclitus suggested over 2,500 years ago remains true: The only constant is change.

Libraries have enjoyed a symbiotic relationship with publishers for a very long time. Whether one of the large publishers from New York or a local small press, libraries could count on publishers to discover great authors, develop and improve a storyteller's ideas, provide both a check on the quality and the content and produce a finished product any library would want to put on its shelves. Publishers created good works. Libraries bought those works and helped sustain markets for the publishers and authors.

Technology created a new relationship between authors, libraries and publishers. Authors started publishing their own work, using small presses, vanity presses, and online options. Meanwhile, publishing houses started to consolidate and smaller independent publishers went out of business making the entry point for first time authors more challenging. Access to independent printing and publishing was liberating, but it also resulted in many manuscripts that would not have been published a few short years ago finding their way to vanity presses. There were scores of people itching to tell their stories, but they weren't always ready to tell that story.

Due to the new and changing environment, libraries started to see more and more unsolicited titles being donated by authors. These authors did not have access to the distribution channels associated with traditional publishing. Sending books directly to libraries seemed to be a rational and cost-effective distribution method for authors trying to do it all. Unfortunately, many of these authors had not gone through a quality assurance process and many of the books were full of both technical and content errors.

One day, we realized something. With publishing changing so dramatically, why must the library's role remain at the end of the story production process? What if a library could help the storyteller throughout the creative process up to and including publishing? If a library could do that, then the final product would be something a library would want to add to the collection because it would have a lower likelihood of the kinds of problems sometimes present in self-published works. The end product would be something others would want to read even buy. This was the core idea behind the concept known as "libraries as publishers." Many libraries had a similar idea around the same time. Mid-Continent Public Library's Woodneath Story Center is a unique application of this model.

The Woodneath Story Center helps storytellers create, refine, and share stories in written, oral, and visual formats. There are classes and courses to help people improve the needed skills to share an idea or story. Focusing on multiple storytelling methods and providing the classes and the skills to tell stories is part of what sets the Story Center apart from other institutions employing "library as publisher." We have a community of authors and storytellers that help with the peer editing and review process. We bring established authors to share about their latest projects, but also how they employ their craft and how they learned their skills. Aspiring storytellers can earn certification from the Woodneath Story Center. Knowing that an author has been through this certification process helps to increase the chances that the end result will be of sufficient quality that our library will want to add it to the collection. Consequently, a *Woodneath*

Certified Storyteller will have the option of being published by Woodneath Press.

Why is any of this important? Honestly, the initial motivation was self-preservation. The library could engage the local community of independent authors and could build a community relationship (as opposed to a transactional relationship). Such a relationship would become a win-win, like libraries used to have with traditional publishers. However, we also learned that people need help with effective communication. The ability to disseminate a brief idea all over the world via social media has rendered the skill of effective complex communication in short supply. These skills are necessary for people to effectively participate in the workforce and in business. Libraries could help people learn these skills.

I am a baseball fan. I always liken the Woodneath Story Center to be like the Arizona Instructional League. This special minor baseball league is filled with teams that bring new high school and college aged players together for their first taste of professional baseball. Players come to the league with different skills but all come with a desire to learn more about the game. Some will learn a lot through the drills and training and will find themselves moving up the ladder to the next level of minor league baseball. Other players will have their baseball career end in Arizona. However, those players will have learned more about baseball that they can use to coach a high school team back home, or they will have learned leadership and "followership" skills that they can apply in everyday life. We do the same thing with aspiring authors. A few storytellers may move on and sign a contract with a big publisher. But everyone else will learn skills that will improve their storytelling translating into better opportunities throughout their lives.

The Woodneath Story Center also fills another important role through our collaboration with the Jackson County Historical Society.

As publishing consolidated, storytellers found less avenues for their content as traditional publishing outlets interested in local stories or local arts slowly went away. But collecting stories, information, and work from local artists has always been a role for the local public library. *The First Beverly Hillbilly* and *Cowtown: Cattle Trails and West Bottoms Tales* are both examples of this role. The Jackson County Historical Society brought these projects to Woodneath Press to help collect and to share stories that are very meaningful to the people of our region. This is an important part of what a library can do to help create a stronger community. Nearly any library can take on parts of this model and nearly every library should!

A letter was found with the manuscript for *The First Beverly Hillbilly*. The letter was written in 1994 by Ruth Henning to her friend and journalist, Sue Gentry. The final paragraph read as follows:

"Thank you for being on my side about this book. I really believe one day it will find a publisher."

Ruth Henning was right. The book did find a publisher. But it took a major disruption in the publishing industry, a collaboration between a local library and historical society, a program with the goal to improve the relationship between authors and libraries, and the desire to create a stronger community through helping people be better storytellers. Our hope is this model, as serendipitous as its birth may have been, will be around quite some time. At the very least, the Woodneath Story Center intends to be around long enough for you to visit us and for us to help you tell your story.

Steven V. Potter
Library Director and C.E.O, Mid-Continent Public Library
Director, Woodneath Story Center

H

Haezart, Toni, 181
Haglund, Norma, 80
Haiphong Harbor, 250
Hallmark Hall of Fame, 80
Hamlet, 49
Happy Hollow, 22, 234
Happy Time, The, 173
Harding, Ann, 187
Hartford, CT, 251
Hawaii, 93, 106, 214
Haymes, Dick, 51
Hayward, Bill, 196
Hayward, Leland, 196
Hearnes, Betty, 221
Hearnes, Warren, 221
Hearst Syndicate, 63
Hee Haw, 193
Hellman, Jack, 149
Helm, Harvey, 60
Henning, Cotton, 36, 54, 83, 114
Henning, Sophia, 17
Herschend, Hugo, 217
Herschend, Mary, 217, 219, 220, 222
Hickman, Dwayne, 87
Higgins, 163, 164, 171
High Button Shoes, 216
High Noon, 93
Hillcrest Golf Club, 62
Hilton Head, 253
Hold Back the Dawn, 51
Holden, William, 37
Holland, 191
Hollywood, 209
Hollywood Boulevard, 15, 32, 35, 39, 51
Hollywood High School, 103, 105, 117
Hollywood Hills, 56
Hollywood Palladium, 170
Hollywood Plaza Hotel, 58
Hollywood Ranch Market, 33, 34
Hollywood Reporter, 79, 89, 149
Hollywood, CA, 16, 21, 22, 29, 30, 31, 33, 35, 37, 49, 54, 64, 73, 75, 92, 95, 97, 115, 128, 129, 134, 150, 169, 172, 181, 184, 186, 194, 196, 204, 209, 211, 220, 223, 225, 228
Hollywoodland Sign, 35
Holy Land, 253

Hometown Boy Makes Good Award, 189
Hong Kong, 49, 234
Hope, Bob, 13, 53, 195, 212
Hopper, Hedda, 167, 168, 171, 177
Horace Heidt Show, 34
Horace Heidt Show, The, 34
Horn, 160
How to Succeed in Business Without Really Trying, 56, 135
Hudson, Rochelle, 22
Hudson, Rock, 112, 114, 115, 116
Hughes, Howard, 16
Humane Society, The, 170
Hutton, Barbara, 51, 193, 210
Hutton, Gunilla, 193
Hyde Park, 109

I

I Love Lucy, 79
IATSE, 170
Idylwild, CA, 230
If You Were the Only Girl in the World, 41
Illinois, 221
Independence, MO, 17, 19, 134, 135, 159, 200, 204, 205
Indianapolis, IN, 36
Indy 500, 36
Inge, William, 117
Inglewood, 115
Inn, Frank, 152, 163, 164, 169, 170
Isaacs, Charlie, 34, 35, 36, 37, 41, 42, 43, 48, 51, 53
It Happened One Night, 116
Italian Gardens, 215
Ito, Eileen, 53
Iturbi, Jose, 68
Ivar Street, 37

J

J. Power Buzzard, 231
Jack Benny Show, The, 77
James, Jeri Lou, 78
James, Sheila, 165
James, Sheilah, 78
Jamieson, Martha, 133
Japan, 15, 159, 232

271

Acknowledgments

This project would have never happened without the help and assistance of so many people.

The Family of Paul and Ruth Henning:
Mary Childers, Carol Henning, Linda Henning, Tony Henning

The Jackson County Historical Society:
Caitlin Eckard, Steve Noll, Brent Schondelmeyer
www.jchs.org

Creative Center of America:
Robin Blakely
www.creativecenterofamerica.com

Writing Help KC:
Valerie Abbott
www.writinghelpkc.com

Our Colleagues at Mid-Continent Public Library:
Mary Altman, Emily Brown, David Burns, Cody Croan, Dylan Little, Andie Paloutzian, David Reynolds, Gail Schmitt, Jim Staley, Melissa Stan

Special Publishing Assistance:
Gretchen McCord, Digital Information Law
www.digitalinfolaw.com
Josh Floyd, Ingram
Vivien Jennings, Rainy Day Books

Special Thanks for Help with Photographic Images:
Karin Grant, Stuart Hinds

Additional Resources

Access information on Paul Henning and his family not listed within the contents of this book through *The First Beverly Hillbilly* website.
www.beverlyhillbilly.org

Learn more about the importance of preserving and promoting local history through the Jackson County Historical Society website.
www.jchs.org

Learn more about the Story Center, the Woodneath Press, and Mid-Continent Public Library by visiting these websites.
www.mystorycenter.org
www.mymcpl.org

Cover Photo Credits and Permissions

Back Flap

Photo of Ruth and Paul Henning: Used with permission from Mary Childers of the Henning Family.

Back Cover

Photo of Paul Henning: Photo by Allan Grant (Allan Grant Estate). Used with permission.

Photo of Paul Henning: Used by permission of the University of Missouri-Kansas City Libraries, Dr. Kenneth J. LaBudde Department of Special Collections.

Photo of the Henning Family: Photo of Ruth and Paul Henning: Used with permission from Mary Childers of the Henning Family.

Photo of *The Beverly Hillbillies* cast: Photo by Allan Grant (Allan Grant Estate). Used with permission.

CPSIA information can be obtained
at www.ICGtesting.com
Printed in the USA
LVOW12*1303171117
556693LV00003B/19/P